3 Weeks to STARTUP

A **HIGH-SPEED** GUIDE TO STARTING A BUSINESS

➤ Streamline the startup steps with online tools and resources

➤ Follow weekly checklists to stay on track

➤ Easily find and access industry specifics, experts, red-tape alerts and more

Tim Berry and Sabrina Parsons

PRINCIPALS OF PALO ALTO SOFTWARE, THE PROVIDER OF BUSINESS PLAN PRO

Jere L. Calmes, Publisher
Cover Design: Desktop Miracles
Composition and Production: MillerWorks

© 2008 by Entrepreneur Press
All rights reserved.

This publication is designed to provide accurate and authoritative information
in regard to the subject matter covered. It is sold with the understanding that the
publisher is not engaged in rendering legal, accounting or other professional services.
If legal advice or other expert assistance is required, the services of a
competent professional person should be sought.

Library of Congress Cataloging-in-Publication Data

Berry, Timothy.
3 weeks to startup / by Tim Berry and Sabrina Parsons.
    p. cm.
   ISBN 978-1-59918-196-7 (alk. paper)
    1. New business enterprises. 2. Entrepreneurship. 3. Business planning.
    I. Parsons, Sabrina. II. Title. III. Title: Three weeks to startup.
HD62.5.B4845 2008   658.1'1—dc22
2008023176

Printed in Canada

11 10 09 08   10 9 8 7 6 5 4 3 2 1

CONTENTS

Introduction 1

WEEK 1: GET GOING!

CHAPTER 1: Concept Kick Start. 9
Identify Yourself and Your Business 10
    Know What You Do Best 11
    Know What You Like or What You're Good At 11
    Define Your Success 12
What You're Selling, and to Whom 13
    What Are You Really Selling? 13
    Who Is Your Customer? 14
    Finding the Ideal Target 14
Strategy Is Focus. 15
    Know What You Aren't Doing 16
    Missions, Mantras, Visions, and All That 16
And In the Meantime, Get Going 16
Online Tools 17

CHAPTER 2: Need to Know 19
Establishing Your Business Location. 21
How Much Money Will It Take? 23
Your Business Plan. 26
If You Dread Planning Your Startup, Get a Clue 30
Online Tools 31

CHAPTER 3: About Your Market 33

Other Reasons for Market Research 35
Market Analysis 35
    Market Demographics 35
    Market Characteristics 36
Industry Analysis 37
    Industry Participants 37
    Industry Growth, Trends, Etc. 37
Distribution 38
Gathering Information 39
    Get on the Web 39
    Go Shopping 40
    Give Something Away 41
    Specific Research 42
    Talk to People 42
    Get On the Telephone 42
    Talk to Customers 43
    Make Some Sales 43
More Formal Research 44
    Government Information and Statistics 45
    General Web Search and Literature Search 47
    Associations 49
    Colleges and Universities 50
    Community Organizations 50
    D&B 50
    Other Sources 51
Doing Your Own Research 51
    Focus Groups 52
    Telephone Interviews 52
    Direct-mail Interviews 53
    E-mail Interviews 53
Making a List 53
Online Tools 55

CHAPTER 4: Make It Legal 59

About Your Business Name 60
Above All, Get It In Writing 61

3 WEEKS TO STARTUP

Choosing a Business Structure 64
   Sole Proprietorship 65
   Partnership 66
   Corporation 67
   Limited Liability Corporation 72
   The Nonprofit Option 73
Online Tools 75

CHAPTER 5: Getting Financed 79
Set the Right Scale 80
   A Few Thousand Dollars or Less 81
   Tens of Thousands of Dollars 81
   Hundreds of Thousands 82
   Millions 82
Bootstrapping vs. Getting Financed 82
Friends and Family 84
   Loan or Investment 85
   The Right Source 86
   Putting It On Paper 87
   Taxing Matters 88
   Keep 'Em Happy 90
Debt Financing 90
   How To Get Government Loans 90
   7(a) Guaranty Loan Program 92
   SBAExpress Program 92
   CAPLines 93
   Pre-Qualification Program 94
   MicroLoan Program 94
   504 Loan Program 94
   Empowerment Zones/Enterprise Communities 95
   8(a) Program 96
   Export Working Capital Program 97
   Special Purpose Loans 97
   Making the Most of the SBA 98
Government Grants 99
Finding Outside Investors 100
   Venture Capital vs. Angel Investment 101

What You Need 102
How It Works 103
The Summary Memo 103
The Pitch Presentation 104
The Business Plan 104
The Deal 105
Choose an Investor As You Would a Spouse 106
Online Tools 106

WEEK 1 CHECKLIST **109**

WEEK 2: KEEP MOVING!

CHAPTER 6: Getting Paid **113**
Establishing a Credit Policy 114
Give 'Em Credit 116
Payment Due 117
Accepting Checks 120
Electronic Help 122
Follow Policy 123
Accepting Credit Cards 124
Merchant Status 124
Money Matters 129
Getting Equipped 129
Online Payments 130
Accepting Debit Cards 131
Online Tools 133

CHAPTER 7: Cover Your Assets **135**
Basic Insurance Needs 136
Workers' Compensation 136
General Liability 138
Auto Insurance 139
Property/Casualty Coverage 140
Beyond the Basics 141
Umbrella Coverage 141
Business Interruption Coverage 141

3 WEEKS TO STARTUP

Life Insurance 141

Disability Insurance 143

Choosing an Insurance Agent 143

Insurance Costs 146

Package Deal 147

The Name's Bond 148

Staking Your Claim 148

Online Tools 149

CHAPTER 8: Build Your Team 151

Defining Your Staffing Needs 152

Job Analysis 152

Job Description 153

Writing the Ad 153

Recruiting Employees 155

Pre-Screening Candidates 156

Interviewing Applicants 159

Off Limits 162

Checking References 163

After the Hire 165

Alternatives to Full-Time Employees 166

Leased Employees 166

Look Before You Lease 168

Temporary Employees 169

Part-Time Personnel 171

Outsourcing Options 173

A Family Affair 174

Online Tools 175

CHAPTER 9: Manage Your Team 177

Create a Culture 178

Benefit Basics 178

Legally Speaking 180

Expensive Errors 181

Health Insurance 183

Cost Containment 184

Retirement Plans 186

Individual Retirement Account (IRA) 187
Savings Incentive Match Plan for Employees (SIMPLE) 188
Simplified Employee Pension (SEP) Plan 189
Where to Go 189
Low-Cost Benefits 190
Employee Policies 193
Paying Employees 193
Nonexempt and Exempt Employees 194
Tip Credits 195
Overtime Requirements 195
Workplace Safety 196
OSHA Regulations 196
Compliance With OSHA 197
Put It In Writing 198
Discriminatory Treatment? 199
Online Tools 201

CHAPTER 10: Brand Aid 203
What Is Branding, Exactly? 204
Building a Branding Strategy 206
Step One: Set Yourself Apart 207
Step Two: Know Your Target Customer 207
Step Three: Develop a Personality 208
Bringing It All Together 209
Online Tools 209

CHAPTER 11: Spin the Web 211
Get Started: Build Your Site 212
A Marketing Tool 214
Attracting Visitors to Your Site 216
Search Engines 216
Paid Search Services 219
Keeping Visitors at Your Site 220
Online Tools 222

CHAPTER 12: Spread the Word 225
Getting Publicity 226

3 WEEKS TO STARTUP

Talking to the Media 228
Meet the Press 230
Image Power 231
Special Events 232
  Grand Openings 233
  Entertainment and Novelty Attractions 234
  Holidays and Seasonal Events 234
  Co-sponsoring 234
  Games and Contests 235
Networking 235
You're the Expert 239
Social Media 240
Online Tools 241

WEEK 2 CHECKLIST 243

WEEK 3: LAUNCH IT!

CHAPTER 13: Sell It!

Understanding Your Unique Selling Proposition .248
  Uncover Your USP 249
Cold-Calling 251
Following Up 256
Making Sales Presentations 257
  Before the Presentation 258
  In the Customer's Office 259
  After the Sale 263
Speaking Effectively 264
Online Tools 265

CHAPTER 14: Superior Customer Service 269

Building Customer Relationships 270
Customer Service 272
Interacting with Customers 274
Going Above and Beyond 276
Online Tools 278

CONTENTS

CHAPTER 15: Keeping Track 283
Bookkeeping Basics 285
Choosing Your Software or Online Application 287
    Do You Have a Choice? 287
    Check Out Your Bank 287
    Data Management Made Easy 287
    Online or Not 288
    Some Other Factors to Consider 289
Basic Accounting Principles 290
Know Your Accounting 291
    Chart of Accounts 291
    General Ledger 292
    Source Documents 292
    Accounts Receivable 292
    Inventory 293
    Fixed Assets 294
    Accounts Payable 294
Payroll 295
Cost Accounting 295
Under Control 296
Financial Statements 298
Online Tools 299

WEEK 3 CHECKLIST 301

BEYOND 3 WEEKS

CHAPTER 16: Managing the Money .305
Fundamentals 306
    Seven Useful Definitions 306
The Three Main Financial Statements 307
    The Profit & Loss 308
    The Balance Sheet 309
    The Cash Flow 311
Profitability 311
    Beware of False Profits 311
    Timing Matters 314

3 WEEKS TO STARTUP

Timing of Sales 314
Timing of Costs 315
Timing of Expenses 316
Your Gross Margin 316
Understanding Costs 317
Cost of Sales 317
Fixed vs. Variable Costs 319
Your Burn Rate 320
Managing Gross Margin 321
Computing Markup 322
Managing Cash Flow 324
Every Dollar of Receivables is a Dollar Less Cash 324
Every Dollar of Inventory is a Dollar Less Cash 326
Every Dollar of Payables is a Dollar More Cash 326
Waiting for Payment 326
Inventory: What a Difference Two Months Make 328
Ten Rules for Managing Cash 328
Cash and Working Capital 330
Planning, Forecasting, Budgeting 332
Managing a Sales Forecast 332
Managing and Budgeting Expenses 333
Manage Payroll as Part of Expenses 335
Stocking Up 336
How Do You Rate? 337
Profitability Ratios 338
Liquidity Ratios 338
Activity Ratios 338
Leverage Ratios 338
Where Credit Is Due 338
For the Record 339
Online Tools 341

CHAPTER 17: Paying Taxes 343
First Things First 344
Ins and Outs of Payroll Taxes 345
Declaration of Independents 348
Selecting Your Tax Year 350

Filing Your Tax Return 351
    Sole Proprietorships 351
    Partnerships and Limited Liability Companies (LLCs) 352
    Corporations 352
Sales Taxes 352
Tax-Deductible Business Expenses 354
    Equipment Purchases 354
    Business Expenses 354
    Auto Expenses 355
    Meals and Entertainment Expenses 356
    Travel Expenses 357
    Home Office 357
Tax Planning 357
Online Tools 358

About the Authors 359

Glossary 361

Index 373

ACKNOWLEDGMENTS

W e'd like to thank several people who helped us with some of the specifics. Freelance author J. Tol Broome Jr. contributed to the *Keeping Track* and *Managing the Money* chapters. Tax expert Joan Zsabo wrote the chapter *Paying Taxes*. A team at Palo Alto Software pitched in as well: A lot of additional information was provided by Vie Radeka for the *Make It Legal* chapter; by Steve Lange for several chapters; by Teri Epperly for several chapters and the glossary; by Jake Weatherly for *Superior Customer Service* and *Sell It*; by Beth Anne Whalen on *Sell It*; by Chelle Parmele for *Spread the Word*; by Nicole Poole and Josh Cochrane for *Spin the Web*; and by Kristen Langham on *Build Your Team*.

INTRODUCTION

Three weeks?

Can you really start a business in three weeks? What about all those people saying you need to build a business plan first? What about all those obstacles—the right name, the right legal entity, the right location, and so forth?

Yes, you can. You can do this. And you can do it in three weeks. Here are the two most important reasons why that's so:

1. The world has changed dramatically in the last few years and we all know it. In today's new world, we can use online tools, information, contacts, and services to do things much faster than was possible just five years ago.

INTRODUCTION

2. When you look at the core elements of a new business, the actual tasks involved—just the real tasks, not the thinking and studying and researching and long time deciding—don't take that much time. Technically, it takes about an hour to register a name for your business and become a legal entity. And setting up a location can take a couple of hours if it's in your home, and as little as a day or two if it's an office somewhere near where you live. Delaying decisions doesn't make them better.

It is true that not all businesses can go straight from the first spark of an idea to the full and complete execution in just three weeks. You can't start a new steel manufacturing business and expect to have trucks rolling out to the customers in three weeks. Most people can't raise millions of dollars in three weeks.

However, it is also true that most businesses are not manufacturing steel or raising millions of dollars. Most businesses don't even have employees. Here's an interesting fact: SBA (the federal Small Business Administration) statistics indicate that of the 26 million businesses in the United States, 21 million have no employees. And most businesses don't require raising millions of dollars. Here's another interesting fact: A Wells Fargo Bank study showed that the average startup cost of a new business in the United States is about $10,000.

We put those two facts here because they show that the vast majority of new businesses are like the one you want to start, meaning they aren't the multi-million-dollar new manufacturing business, but rather they are your business—manageable, focused, and ready for you to get going.

So, with that in mind, here's how it works! The following timetables show you how you go from where you are to up and running in just three weeks.

TIMETABLE: WEEK 1

THE ABSOLUTE ESSENTIALS: What you really have to do, no matter what	... and where you'll find it in this book
The main idea. Is there a *there* there? Does anybody need (or want) what you intend to sell? Is there a market? How big is it? How will you focus? Do you have a strategy, or are you just going to do everything for everybody?	**Chapter 1 Concept Kick Start**, and a bit of **Chapter 2, Need to Know**. For startups requiring substantial investment and more risk, or startups by people unsure of the market, you'll also need the market research discussed in **Chapter 3, About Your Market**.
Talk to your co-founders. If you have co-founders, talk with them about the tough topics: who owns how much of the company and why, who does what, and why. If you don't have co-founders, then things are even easier.	**Chapter 2, Need to Know**, with additional detail in **Chapter 4, Make It Legal**
Get it in writing. If you have co-founders, then you should have basic ownership and responsibilities agreed on and written before you take the formal legal step.	**Chapter 4, Make It Legal**
Name it. If you're not just selling under your own name, then you have to check possible names for availability, and start taking the legal steps required to establish your ownership rights.	**Chapter 4, Make It Legal**
Initial sales forecast. Some people dread the forecasting, but don't worry; we'll show you how to do the simple forecasts you need. It's not that hard to do the startup sales forecast and it helps a lot. You use it to help estimate expenses, and also to estimate your initial cash needs, as part of your starting costs.	**Chapter 2, Need to Know**
Initial expense budget. Like the sales forecast, the expense budget is very useful and easier to do than most people think.	**Chapter 2, Need to Know**
Estimate starting costs. We start helping you estimate the starting costs, and to refine that estimate	**Chapter 2, Need to Know** **Chapter 5, Getting Financed**.
Make the sale. Though this is a Week 3 item, we also list it for Week 1 because for some businesses, the first sale is what really gets the rest of the startup process started.	**Chapter 13, Sell It!**

TIMETABLE: WEEK 2	
THE ABSOLUTE ESSENTIALS: What you really have to do, no matter what	... and where you'll find it in this book
Plan your marketing strategy. We'll go over your marketing strategy and implementation details; your plan should be ready by the end of the second week.	Chapter 12: Spread the Word
Develop look and feel: logos, signs, letterhead, graphic standards. We go over the branding essentials you'll need to know as you start up.	Chapter 10: Brand Aid
Start your website. Not all businesses need websites, but websites are the core of the business for many new web businesses, absolutely essential for other startups, and good to have for most. If your business is the exception and you don't need and don't want a website, this chapter will reassure you.	Chapter 11: Spin the Web
Set up your merchant account to be able to accept credit cards. Taking credit cars is vital for some businesses, irrelevant for others. If you do need to accept credit cards, you'll want to get started with the process now. We'll explain how to get set up to take credit cards.	Chapter 6: Getting Paid
Get insurance. Insurance is one of those necessary tasks that doesn't take much time, and is easy to skip over, but should be done.	Chapter 7: Cover Your Assets
Start recruiting startup employees. We'll help you start the hunt during Week 2; the hiring step follows in Week 3.	Chapter 8: Build Your Team

TIMETABLE: WEEK 3

THE ABSOLUTE ESSENTIALS: What you really have to do, no matter what	... and where you'll find it in this book
Establish your location. This task depends on the specifics of your business. It can be fairly easy for the home office startup. If you have to rent offices or establish a retail location, or manufacturing and distribution, it can take more time. Realistically, not all startups can establish a new location and fix and furnish it in three weeks, but most can. We'll help you plan your location so it matches your startup needs.	Chapter 2: Need to Know.
Set up your bookkeeping. We'll go over the selection of the right system for you. It's not that hard to do and you really have to do it.	Chapter 15: Keeping Track
Make it legal. Take the legal steps, depending on specific needs, to start your business on the right legal foundations.	We go over the decisions you have to make, tradeoffs involved, and actual legal steps to take in **Chapter 4: Make It Legal.**
Hire startup employees. You started recruiting in Week 2. By Week 3, you've found them and you're actually hiring.	**Chapter 8: Build the Team,** helps you recruit the right people.
Settle the financing. This is another one that depends on the details. It can be as easy as deciding you're going to spend a few thousand dollars that you already have, or as hard as raising millions from professional investors. Your simple startup consisting of a home office and a computer might need nothing more than what you can get in Office Depot in an afternoon. If you have to raise more money than you have, then you've got to do a more detailed business plan, find potential investors, and do a lot more work. You should revise your goals by setting the three weeks startup to be the beginning of serious investor meetings.	Chapter 5: Getting Financed
Make the Sale. Make the sale today, tomorrow, in Week 1, 2 and 3. We made this point in the Week 1 list; it reflects the importance of making the sale.	Chapter 13: Sell It!

BEYOND 3 WEEKS	
THE ABSOLUTE ESSENTIALS: What you really have to do, no matter what	... and where you'll find it in this book
Make the Sale. Make the sale today, tomorrow, and every day!	Chapter 13: Sell It!
Pay your taxes	Chapter 17: Pay Your Taxes
Customer service	Chapter 14: Superior Customer Service
Do your marketing.	Chapter 12: Spread the Word
Develop employer policies, benefits, systems, and management decisions.	Chapter 9: Manage Your Team

WEEK 1:
GET GOING!

CHAPTER 1

CONCEPT KICK START

Here is an interesting fact: of the 28 million businesses in the United States, 21 million have no employees. And here's another: The average investment in a new business in the United States, according to a recent study by Wells Fargo Bank, is $10,000. And the average time to start? Who knows. But it might as well be three weeks as three months, or three years. True, some businesses need long ramp-ups, millions of dollars of investment, prototypes, carefully planned and painstaking marketing launches; some need new locations, or construction, or rigorous cleanup and setup. But most need you, your resolve, your understanding of what you sell to whom, and why.

We don't mean you can start all businesses from conception to initial sales in three weeks. But you can start most of them that quickly. And for those that take longer, you can set the initial concept, define the business, gather together the team, and at least get going inside of three weeks. And what does it really take to start a business? It takes going out and getting customers.

That's what we're all about with this book: Getting going.

Identify Yourself and Your Business

Your business is about you, what you want, what you do well, how you're different. We like to call it business identity.

Determining your business identity is like looking into a mirror and examining what you see. It might be you, or it might be (note the sidebar) a group of you, which we'll call a team.

What works best is you trying to build something you want to build, in an area where you like to operate, doing something you want to do. And also we'd hope it's something you do better than others, or want to do more than others. We hope it's something that reflects your strengths, weaknesses, and goals. We hope you're looking to do something that you believe needs to be done and ought to be done.

Yes, there are exceptions to every rule, and a lot of things we say in this book will have exceptions. But the generalities often do apply. Very few busi-

---

WEEK 1

TAKE NOTES!

One of the biggest misunderstandings in starting a business is the idea that you always have to do it all yourself. **You don't.** You don't have to build it alone. You can build a team or join a team to start a business. Not all of us want to do the selling, delivering, building, managing, or administering all by ourselves.

As we go through all the various pieces in this book, we'll take you through just about everything. But the fact that we explain market research and bookkeeping and taxes doesn't mean you have to do these things all yourself. For example, many people hire a part-time bookkeeper for a few hours a week to record checks and deposits, especially when they are just starting. Most people have their taxes done by a tax service or accountant.

We're going to be dealing with the whole process in this book, but keep teamwork in mind. **You don't have to do it all.**

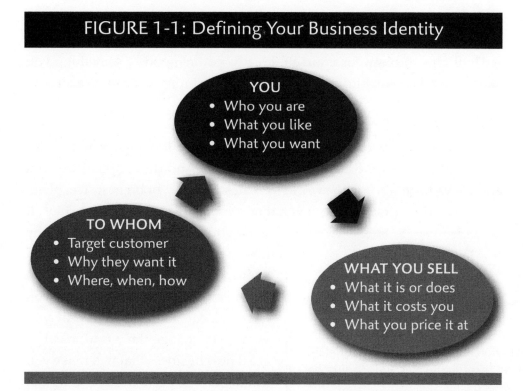

FIGURE 1-1: Defining Your Business Identity

nesses don't start because somebody looks at a list of good businesses to start. They start because somebody wants to do something that needs doing.

Know What You Do Best

If you like buzzwords, call what you do best your "core competence." It's good to keep in mind. Think of it as your whole team, if you have a team, or just yourself. The new world of today has lots more opportunities for small and different and exclusive than for big and dominant. Seth Godin's wise little book, *The Dip*, talks about finding what you can be the best at.

Know What You Like or What You're Good At

Last year, there was an interesting discussion on "Planning Startups Stories," one of our blogs. In an e-mail, someone asked: "Do I do what I like or what I'm good at?" We thought those things were the same things, but they probably aren't—at least not for everybody.

Think this through for yourself. Ideally, you're good at something you like to do. When you build your own business, you're going to do a lot of it.

Define Your Success

Start by defining success for yourself. What are you looking for in the business you're starting? Be honest with yourself. And don't apologize. You don't have to be starting the world's greatest website, or biggest steel plant, or the world's first water-powered automobile to make it important. If what you want is to turn your hobby into a second income, or to have build a business from home, or escape from that commute you hate to a job you hate, we can help you. If what you want is to change the world, create a great new business that will make you a zillionaire 10 years from now, we can help you with that too. The point is, however, that you don't want to let us drag you down one path when what you really want is another.

What is important is that you not kid yourself. Let us help you get going without the assumption that every business is the same, or that we know what you want. You're supposed to know what you want, but in this startup world, lots of people start the race before they know which direction they're going.

Jump ahead in your mind and imagine what you want this new business to be like a year from now. Then imagine three or five years in the future. Are you on the cover of *Entrepreneur Magazine*? Cool, but be prepared to work for it. Are you able to coach the kids' soccer team two afternoons a

WEEK 1 — TAKE NOTES!

Very few businesses are all fun. Even if most of the time the business is doing what you like, there's also the administration, the management, the details. The ski instructor, the painter, and the artist has down days and other stuff to do.

If you're successful, as you grow you bring in people to help with the stuff you don't like. Hire a bookkeeper, a manager, a salesperson, an artist, a writer. Focus on what you like best.

But there will always be some hard days, some parts of it you don't like. Expect it. **It's not going to be all fun.**

week? Take a few days off every now and then to go fishing, or skiing, or whatever? Are you financially independent? Are you still doing what you love, but now for money?

What You're Selling, and to Whom

Why would people buy what you want to sell? What needs are you satisfying? What problems do you solve? What is it that people really want from you? If you don't understand the answer to that, stop. Get that right before you go on. It isn't as obvious as you might think, and it has a lot to do with successful strategy.

What Are You Really Selling?

Marketing guru and long-time Harvard professor Theodore Leavitt gets credit for pointing out that people don't buy quarter-inch drills because they want the drills: They buy them because they want quarter-inch holes.

Another long-time tale of marketing is how the railroads thought they were selling railroads, when what they were really selling was transportation. Highways and airlines took over their business.

Another example is the restaurant business. Position yourself. Is your restaurant about fine food and fine dining—white tablecloths, dressy wait staff, and flowers on each table? Or is it about driving through with half the kids' soccer team in the van, getting a fast bunch of hamburgers and fries?

Say you're a business plan consultant. Can you do detailed market research for high-budget situations, like major companies looking for information about entering new markets? Or are you aiming at the people next door trying to start a business? Do you want buyers who expect to pay tens of thousands of dollars, and can you give them what they expect to get? Or are you aiming at those people who are borderline between having somebody do it and doing it themselves, who would pay $500 to get a plan done, but not $1,000? These are huge differences.

Now you're a blog. How and why will people find your blog, and what will make them return? Imagine a conversation between your favorite customer and a friend or acquaintance, about your business. What do they say? "It's pricey, but the food is fabulous so it's worth it." Or "It's a price performer. Not bad if you're in the neighborhood."

Do you really know what benefits you're going to offer? Do you understand the essential why-to-buy for your new business?

Who Is Your Customer?

No business—particularly a small one—can be all things to all people. The more narrowly you can define your target market, the better. This process is known as creating a niche and is key to success for even the biggest companies. Wal-Mart and Tiffany & Co. are both retailers, but they have very different niches: Wal-Mart caters to bargain-minded shoppers, while Tiffany appeals to upscale jewelry consumers.

"When you properly target your clients, you will discover that you no longer have to work with jerks," writes John Jantsch in *Duct Tape Marketing*. His Chapter 1 in that groundbreaking book is titled "Identify Your Ideal Client." We'd broaden that slightly to call it customer instead of client, but John makes a very good point.

> You can choose to attract [customers] that value what you offer, view working with you as partnership, and want you to succeed, but only if you have a picture of what the ideal [customer] looks like.
>
> The primary purpose of this foundational step is to help you identify, describe, and focus on a narrow target of clients or segments that are perfectly suited for your business.

Finding the Ideal Target

That first chapter of *Duct Tape Marketing* recommends four action steps:

1. Look for common characteristics such as age and gender among your best clients. (Broaden that to customers, and if you're looking at selling to businesses, you can talk about business demographics, too: size, location, type of business, decision-making practices, related needs.)

3 WEEKS TO STARTUP

2. Uncover a common frustration among your target market.

3. Write a description of your ideal target market in terms that are easy to communicate.

4. Determine whether your ideal target market is large enough to support your business.

Strategy Is Focus

Rather than creating a niche, many entrepreneurs make the mistake of falling into the "all over the map" trap, claiming they can do many things and be good at all of them. These people quickly learn a tough lesson. Strategy is focus.

Some people make a big deal about business strategy. The Amazon.com search for books about business strategy is daunting. People do doctoral theses on it, and then they charge huge fees to help huge companies figure out strategy.

But this is the real world: It is your business, not a theory. And when you pull it back down out of the ivory tower, the good strategies are usually pretty obvious. Some would say boring.

Strategizing pulls in both identity

TAKE NOTES!

WEEK 1

The Principle of Displacement is perhaps the most misunderstood given of small business in the real world. Everything you do rules out something else that you can't do. So do the right things.

and market. On the identity side of things, you want to focus on strengths, and away from weaknesses. You want to take advantage of your core competencies. On the market side of things, you want to focus on a well-defined target market so you can tailor your message and your business offering. You don't want to be just a restaurant; you want to be a restaurant with a focus that fits a target market, with price, food, and ambience to match. You don't want to be just a market research and planning consultant, you want to be a market research and planning consultant, with a focus on personal computer markets in Latin America.

Know What You Aren't Doing

Bill Cosby says the secret to failure is trying to please everybody. Another secret to failure is trying to do everything; and, particularly, trying to do everything at once. We all want to do everything at once, and everything right, and everything that should be done. But realistically, how many of those long to-do lists really get done? How can you make sure you do what's really important if you're worried about doing everything else? You can't do everything, so do the right things.

Missions, Mantras, Visions, and All That

Thinking about some of these might help get you focused. They may be interchangeable. One might fit your business better than another. And if it doesn't seem to help, then don't bother.

- A mission statement should be your company's long-term goals stated as what it will do for three target groups: its customers, its employees, and its owners. It should never be just empty hype or high-sounding phrases that could be used by anybody. It has to reflect your own identity.

- A mantra is a simple word or phrase that encompasses your business, such as "healthy fast goods" or "authentic athletic performance" or "wholesome family entertainment."

- A vision is a view of the future, usually three or five years ahead, showing what your business will be like then.

And In the Meantime, Get Going

The great fallacy of waiting, of spending long periods planning a business, is that most businesses find themselves as they get going. Both authors have had personal experience with several startups and all of them have had to change as they went along.

One was Borland International, a major software company that went from bare-bones startup to a large, publicly traded company, selling close to $100 million annually, in less than four years. It was founded to do one thing (software called *MenuMaster*, which became unimportant) and did something quite different (its growth was fueled by two software products, *Turbo Pascal* and *Sidekick*, that became very popular in the middle 1980s). Borland had a plan when it started, but more important, it had a sense of what was good software, and the intu-

> **TAKE NOTES!**
>
> Recommended reading: Guy Kawasaki on mission vs. mantra. It's a chapter in his book *Art of the Start,* and a post on his blog.

ition to make that more important than following the plan.

Infoplan, which became Palo Alto Software (now the market leader in business plan software for Windows, with 40 employees, and 25 years of history), was started for writing computer books and ended up following client requests into market research and business planning. Lighting Out, an internet marketing consulting company that was eventually put aside for Palo Alto Software, was started in a week with some formal paperwork, an initial website, and clients who needed help.

ONLINE TOOLS

If you are really aiming to start your business in three weeks, you are going to have to get good and comfortable using the internet and accessing information, tools, and services that are available online.

For this step in getting your business started, you should rely on the great websites and small business and start-up experts that are available online. You will want to make sure that you allocate time for surfing and absorbing information. We highly recommend the following websites as you kickstart your business.

This first group includes blogs that we write or contribute to. We post often about startups in these:

- Planning Startups Stories: blog.timberry.com
- Up And Running: upandrunning.entrepreneur.com

- MommyCEO: mommyceo.wordpress.com

This next group includes other blogs and websites, some of which we contribute to, all of which we read and recommend for anybody looking to start or run a business:

- bplans.com

- entrepreneur.com

- smalllbusinesstrends.com

- ducttapemarketing.com

- smallbusiness.alltop.com

- startups.alltop.com

These are some favorite posts and articles covering material related to this chapter. Most of these have very long web addresses, so instead of typing them, go to the main page and use the search facilities.

- "You Don't Have to Be First to Start a Business:" bplans.com

- "The Right Business for You:" bplans.com

- "Planning, Startups, Stories: Business Strategy:" blog.timberry.com

- "Planning Demystified:" allbusiness.com; "Strategy is Focus" in Tim's Planning Demystified blog on allbusiness.com

- "Kick-Start Your Concept:" bplans.com

- "How to Change the World: Mantras Versus Missions:" blog.guykawasaki.com

And finally, online videos, including some that are interviews with your authors:

- Stanford's Educators Corner, *Top 20 Videos*: edcorner.stanford.edu

- How to Change the World, *The Art of the Start Video*: blog.guykawasaki.com

- Interviews with Tim Berry: sbtv.com

CHAPTER 2

NEED TO KNOW

What does it really take to start your business? Can you really do it in three weeks? That depends, of course, on what your business is. Startups are not all the same. They are about as different, one from another, as people are. And yet a lot of talk, advice, and writing about startups make this confusing, as if all startups were home offices, or all startups were high-tech, high-end, venture-capital-literate startups with experienced entrepreneurs and long, formal business plans. But what if you're starting your own business doing the professional services you already know how to do?

Your startup might be graphic design, landscape architecture, writing, consulting, and so forth. You don't necessarily need to think about renting a location, fixing it up, getting signs and fittings, or getting equipment. What you really need to start your business is customers (or clients, which is the same thing—just different terminology). You don't need much more than your know-how and your computer to get going.

RED TAPE ALERT!

Keep in mind that some businesses will require permits, inspections, applications to the city, county or state for licenses, etc. You can certainly start a business in three weeks, but for some particular businesses, you may have to plan ahead to get through the red tape.

Or perhaps you're starting a retail store or a restaurant. In this case you're going to need thousands of dollars worth of equipment, furnishings and fixtures, signs, interior decoration, and other expenses. Cleaning and fixing up a new rental location can also be a matter of thousands of dollars. So you probably have to think about raising money, unless you have enough on your own; and even if you do have your own money to spend, before you raise or commit that kind of money, you should have a pretty good idea of what's required, what the market prospects are, what your strategy is, and how much money—a reasonable estimate at least—it's going to take. You probably have partners, or you need partners. There's probably a substantial investment to be made, and that's money that becomes at risk.

And then suppose you're thinking about doing a high-end venture capital startup, using new technology, opening new markets, and requiring in many cases millions of dollars of investment. This is yet another scale entirely, involving a lot more elaborate planning, investment, and so on.

The point here is that startups are not all the same thing; each one is different. As we go through the process in this book, keep your scale in mind. Some startups take a lot more work than others.

Establishing Your Business Location

Make your business location match your strategy and your resources. Think it through before you jump. It doesn't take a long time, but it does take opening your mind and considering your options. There is no such thing as a good business location or a bad business location: It has to match your strategy, and you have to be able to afford it.

The quickest and easiest and most economical location, without question, is your home office, your computer, and your website. You already have the space, your expenses won't increase, and your commute will be the best possible.

Of course, many businesses won't work in a home office. If you are expecting customers to visit you, if you are going to start a store, or if you need to have employees, then you need to rent your business location.

There are disadvantages to the home office as well. Some people find it hard to work in the home office because of distractions. Will the dog be barking? Can you separate work life from home life? Do you have to? Will your business require a commercial space?

Here's a list of questions you should ask:

1. **Will your customers ever see your space?** Are they physically there? For example, at Palo Alto Software in Eugene, Oregon, we get maybe two or three customers at our actual location per year. If we were accountants or attorneys, every client would see our space. If we were a restaurant, every customer would sit and eat in our space. This makes a huge difference.

2. **How will customers get there?**

3. **Will they have to park a car when they come?**

4. **What kind of location matches your strategy?** For example, professionals such as attorneys and accountants are often judged by their office surroundings, but home repair and limousine services aren't. Restaurants have to match location to their strategy, too, such as putting a high-end restaurant

in a nice neighborhood. There are ways to get around these problems, but you have to start with strategic alignment. Will your location tell your customers something? Does it match what you want to tell them?

5. **How much business value is there** in renting space that offers advantages to your customers, such as easy parking or access to the subway?

6. **Are you going to be hiring employees?** Where will they live, and how will they get to their workplace every day? Will employees be required to be at the workplace (as opposed to working at home, telecommuting, etc.)?

7. **How will space affect your employment strategy?** Factors such as location, windows, views, parking and amenities cost money that you'll spend as monthly rent. How much business value is there in more expensive rent that offers advantages to employees?

8. **Are you getting carried away with ideas about your workspace?** While planning a new business, be realistic about renting retail, industrial, office space or whatever. Don't get space to build your ego unless that's part of your business objective.

You should have some idea of how much space you need to have at the beginning. A software company with five people is going to need about 1,000 square feet of space, just to give you some idea. How do you know that? Calculate about 125 square feet per person, plus logistics such as copy machine, fax, printers, hallways, etc. Rental rates vary depending on your location, but where we are located (Eugene, Oregon), second- or third-class office space—which is all that is needed for a software startup—is going to cost about $1 per square foot per month, maybe a bit more if it's less than 3,000 square feet. If you have no idea and you're planning a startup, talk to some commercial real estate brokers. They will know.

For a startup, expect to have to sign a personal guarantee. There are exceptions, but they're rare. This is unfortunately a real risk you have to take. For almost any commercial space, expect to have to lease that space for at least a year. That's not always pleasant, I know, because it turns a startup business into a real commitment. But it's necessary.

For flexibility, match the pain of committing to a steady monthly rent for a year or more to the hope that you will grow and need more space. Take up space in a building that has a lot of offices in it. By the time you need to expand, you have a greater chance that somebody else will be moving out. Palo Alto Software, for example, started with 2,000 square feet of space in an office building with a lot of other tenants and increased its space eight times in 12 years without ever moving or changing its address.

Owners of commercial space always want you to commit to a longer lease than you want to sign. Startups always want to sign a shorter lease. Expect to negotiate, and use a commercial real estate broker to help. And remember that there are two sides to this battle: You also have the possibility that you like the space you're in and want to

> **RED TAPE ALERT!**
>
> Buying a franchise? Many municipalities and states have financing programs that can underwrite the cost of a franchise. Be aware, however, that the focus of these programs is job creation. To find programs in your area, call the nearest Small Business Development Center or economic development program. It takes a bit of investigating and some time to find the programs, but the results could be well worth the effort and wait.
>
> **WEEK 1**

stay, but the building changes hands and you are forced to move. That is when you wish you had a longer-term contract. And then there's the possibility that you grow too fast and have to shrink, in which case you wish you could get out of that longer-term contract.

If you live in a major city, you may be able to find temporary offices that rent by the day, week, or month. These often have additional facilities such as an internet connection, copy machines, conferences rooms, and in some cases, secretarial assistance.

How Much Money Will It Take?

There's a lot of potential confusion about startup costs. You tend to jump right into one of those accounting vocabulary problems that often trip people up, because they want to make things mean what they ought to mean, instead of what standard accounting and financial analysis make them mean.

Startup costs include two kinds of spending. You might not care about the distinction, but standard accounting and finance do, and, more importantly, the government does, as it affects taxes. Take a couple minutes and understand the distinction.

1. **Expenses**. These will be deductible against future profits, so they will eventually reduce taxes (if you ever make a profit). Keep track of all your expenses, such as rent, payroll, travel, meals, consulting, most (but not all) legal expenses, and things like that.

2. **Assets**. Money you spend on assets isn't deductible against taxable income, so the bookkeeping is different. Like it or not, it doesn't mix well. Assets are things like signs, furniture, fixtures, cars, trucks, buildings, land, and—harder to deal with—cash on hand, and inventory on hand.

It seems like the toughest estimate to make is what you need as cash on hand when you start the business. On the one hand, you have people telling you that you need working capital, and on the other, you have to raise it somehow or take it from your own savings and invest it in the business to make it cash on hand.

For expenses, timing is very important. Expenses like rent and payroll are startup expenses until your business is up and running; after that, they are just operating expenses, that come out of your profits as deductible against income, so they reduce your taxable income. The only difference between rent paid before the company starts (which is a startup expense) and rent paid during the normal course of the business is timing. When it happens before day one, it's startup expense. Afterwards, it's a regular business expense.

If you are a startup, your basic business numbers should include startup costs. Make it a simple list, or actually two simple lists, one of expenses and the other one of assets. You'll need this information to set up initial business balances and to estimate startup expenses, such as legal fees, stationery design, brochures, and others. Don't underestimate costs.

Table 2-1 reproduces a typical startup plan for a home-based service business; in this case, a resume writing service. The assumptions used in this illustration show how even simple, service-based businesses need some startup money. You can see in the illustration how you have two simple lists, one for expenses, and one for assets.

These are estimates. Where do they come from? Part of the planning for a startup is figuring this out. Either you already have a pretty good idea, because you've worked in this area before, or somebody who does know—a partner, team member, advisor, or friend—is helping you. You

Table 2-1: Startup Requirements Worksheet	
REQUIREMENTS	
STARTUP EXPENSES	
Legal	$1,000
Stationery, etc.	$3,000
Brochures	$5,000
Consultants	$5,000
Insurance	$350
Expensed Computer Equipment	$3,000
Other	$1,000
Total Startup Expenses	**$18,350**
STARTUP ASSETS	
Cash Required	$25,000
Other Current Assets	$7,000
Long Term Assets	$0
Total Startup Assets	**$32,000**
TOTAL REQUIREMENTS	**$50,350**

can also find some industry-specific startup information on the web and in bookstores. Sometimes a carefully selected sample business plan will help, but if you try that, be careful, because sample business plans are just about one case for one business at one specific location some time in the past. They are not intended to stand for all businesses; you have to know your own case.

You might also make a list of the assets. For example, "Other Current Assets" are things that you need to buy but don't last long enough to be depreciated. That might be coffee-making equipment, packaging equipment, printing and layout materials, and maybe chairs and tables as well.

If you're looking at starting a company that has significant long-term assets, such as manufacturing equipment, vehicles, land and/or buildings, you can also make a list of those.

You don't want to start a company without having a pretty good idea of what you have to spend to get it started.

Your Business Plan

You don't necessarily need a complete and complex business plan. If you have something you can do without investing more than you have, and you have somebody who wants to buy it, you might not have to have a formal plan. However, if you're like most of the vast majority of real startup businesses, it's just plain stupid to start a business without planning it first.

Notice we say "planning," not necessarily "a plan" or "a business plan." Former president and military leader Dwight D. Eisenhower once said it: "The plan is useless; but planning is essential." That's also true with starting your business.

As you get going, we assume you're developing an appropriate plan. That doesn't mean a complete formal written business plan document, at least not necessarily, and certainly not if you don't think anybody would have to read it if you did it. We're serious about getting you started in three weeks, so we very much don't want you to take more than that much time developing a business plan as a formal document. However, we do think that from day one, from today, you want to start planning.

We definitely recommend the plan-as-you-go business plan, which means you start right away with whichever important piece appeals to you first. Not all people are alike, so there isn't necessarily a certain unbreakable series of steps. You choose where you want to start, and get going. There are, of course, some common areas you probably want to address.

1. **The heart of your plan is your core strategy**—the heart of your business. That's a matter of your identity as a business, your market, the needs and wants you satisfy, and your strategic focus. It doesn't have to be written down necessarily or spoken or put into pictures, but you have to know it. That's what we were talking about in Chapter 1, Concept Kick Start.

2. **You need to know what's supposed to happen.** What do you need to do, and when? Who's going to do it? In what order? This doesn't have to be a formal document, but you'll be better off if you write the main parts of this down so you can track results and revise and review. We call this a milestones table (see Table 2-2).

3. **You need to do some basic numbers.** Don't be put off; it doesn't have to be a big formal set of financial projections, but you need to think about:

   • **Startup costs.** That's just exactly what we did in the previous section. Write them down, estimate them, track them, and keep records of them. The expenses part of your startup costs will be tax deductible; plan it ahead and keep track of it afterwards. You should not start a business without a good estimate of what it is going to cost.

   • **A sales forecast.** Every business should have one (see Table 2-3). This doesn't have to be a big deal, but it really should exist.

   • **An expense budget** (see Table 2-4). Here too, you don't need to be a CPA or MBA, but you do need to estimate and manage your business's spending with a budget. Having that budget allows you to track expenses and plan ahead, so you'll have a better hold on your business finances.

MILESTONE	Start Date	End Date	Budget	Manager	Department
Table 2-2: Milestones Table					
Corporate Identity	1-Dec	17-Dec	$10,000	TJ	Marketing
Seminar Implementation	1-Jan	10-Jan	$1,000	IR	Sales
Business Plan Review	2-Jan	11-Jan	$0	RJ	GM
Upgrade Mailer	2-Jan	17-Jan	$5,000	IR	Sales
New Corporate Brochure	2-Jan	17-Jan	$5,000	TJ	Marketing
Delivery Vans	1-Jan	25-Jan	$12,500	SD	Service
Direct Mail	2-Feb	17-Feb	$3,500	IR	Marketing
Advertising	2-Feb	17-Feb	$115,000	RI	GM
X4 Prototype	1-Feb	25-Feb	$2,500	SG	Product
Service Revamp	1-Feb	25-Feb	$2,500	SD	Product
Six Presentations	2-Feb	26-Feb	$0	IR	Sales
X4 Testing	1-Mar	6-Mar	$1,000	SG	Product
Three Accounts	1-Mar	17-Mar	$0	SDI	Sales
L30 Prototype	1-Mar	26-Mar	2,500	PR	Product
Tech Expo	1-Apr	12-Apr	$15,000	TB	Marketing
VP S&M Hired	1-Jun	11-Jun	$1,000	JK	Sales
Mailing System	1-Jul	25-Jul	$5,000	SD	Service
TOTAL			**$181,500**		

Table 2-3: Sales Forecast

SALES	JAN	DEC	YEAR 1	YEAR 2
Retainer Consulting	$10,000	$20,000	$200,000	$350,000
Project Consulting	$0	$15,000	$270,000	$325,000
Market Research	$0	$20,000	$122,000	$150,000
Strategic Reports	$0	$0	$0	$50,000
TOTAL SALES	**$10,000**	**$55,000**	**$592,000**	**$875,000**
DIRECT COST OF SALES	**JAN**	**DEC**	**YEAR 1**	**YEAR 2**
Retainer Consulting	$2,500	$2,500	$30,000	$38,000
Project Consulting	$0	$2,500	$45,000	$56,000
Market Research	$0	$14,000	$84,000	$105,000
Strategic Reports	$0	$0	$0	$20,000
SUBTOTAL DIRECT COST OF SALES	**$2,500**	**$19,000**	**$159,000**	**$219,000**

Table 2-4: Expense Budget

Payroll	$12,000	$12,000	$27,250	$27,250	$194,750
Advertising	$13,500	$13,500	$13,500	$13,500	$162,000
Leases	$500	$500	$500	$500	$6,000
Utilities	$1,000	$1,000	$1,000	$1,000	$12,000
Insurance	$300	$300	$300	$300	$3,600
Rent	$1,500	$1,500	$1,500	$1,500	$18,000
Payroll Tax	$1,680	$1,680	$3,815	$3,815	$27,265
Other	$0	$100	$200	$300	$1,000
TOTAL	**$30,480**	**$30,580**	**$48,065**	**$48,165**	**$424,615**

If You Dread Planning Your Startup, Get a Clue

Earlier today, I had one of those light bulbs go off in my head. I'm refer-ring to those times when you're reminded of something you already knew, but had forgotten. In my case today, it was this: Planning your new busi-ness, the one you're thinking of starting, ought to be fun. Planning isn't about writing some ponderous homework assignment or dull business memo; it's about that business that you want to create. It should be fas-cinating to you. What do people want, how are you going to get it to them, how are you different, and what do you do better than anybody else?

Honestly, isn't that related to the dreaming that makes some of us want to build our own businesses? It was for me, every time, including those that made it and those that failed. Dreaming about the next thing I wanted to do was always part of it. Dreaming is related to looking forward, antic-ipating, and (in this case) business planning.

This came up this morning during my second day of video sessions for SBTV, which has been filming me on starting and managing a business, and business planning. I was answering Beth Haselhorst's question relat-ing starting a business to getting out of the cubicle, when I realized that I was in danger of forgetting that business planning is part of the dreaming and part of the fun.

I think what's important is that none of us should be intimidated by business planning because of what I've called the not-so-big business plan, or the point I made in my blog last month about starting anywhere you like. The business plan is a way to lay out your thoughts and think it through—it shouldn't be some dull ponderous task you just have to get through.

If thinking through the core elements of your business, or for that mat-ter the details of your business, isn't interesting, then get a clue. You're not really looking forward to it. Do you not want to do it?

Remember, you don't have to do the whole plan all at once. One of the most common and damaging myths about planning is that you are supposed to work only on your business plan until you finish that plan. To the contrary, you should be enjoying thinking about the market, what you do well, how you want to focus, what sales might be, what costs might be, and so forth; and you should be writing some of that down, simply and without a lot of intimidation; just write it down and save it and then do something else. You start your plan wherever you want to, and you start using it the next day, and you don't worry about exactly when it is formally done, because it never will be. Just get going, but enjoy the thinking and planning while you do.

If you dread the planning of your next vacation, stay home. If you dread the planning of your new startup, don't start it.

(Reprinted with permission from the blog "Up and Running" at upandrunning.entrepreneur.com)

ONLINE TOOLS

There's a lot of business planning in this chapter. In addition, we have a lot of online solutions for business planning, so remember to check us out online at 3weekstostart.com.

We are actively involved in several sites about business planning, including bplans.com (see below), the world's biggest resource for business planning on the internet, with more than 100 sample business plans, several hundred articles, and free online tools including a starting costs calculator, break-even analysis, and others. Also, Tim's new book, *The Plan-As-You-Go Business Plan,* has a site associated with it. Tim's previous book (the *Hurdle* book below) is also posted online in its entirety, and available for free download at bplans.com.

- BPlans: bplans.com
- The Plan-As-You-Go Business Plan: at planasyougo.com
- *Hurdle: the Book on Business Planning,* at hurdlebook.com

Although there are a lot of other online websites that are relevant, these deserve special mention:

- entrepreneur.com
- Duct Tape Marketing, at ducttapemarketing.com

And, finally, one particular article that stands out, related to this chapter:

- "Kick-Start Your Concept:" it has a long website address, so go to bplans.com and type "kick-start" into the search bar to find it

CHAPTER 3

ABOUT YOUR MARKET

The term "market research"

smacks of expensive research studies and data analysis, and is a bit off-putting. Today's startups have to move fast. Market research needs to be more than producing detailed data to prove a market; it's about getting to know a market well enough to make the right educated guesses as you develop and implement you strategy.

The best market research is sales—people buying what you're selling. Borland International launched its first successful software product in 1983, Turbo Pascal, without researching the market. It simply published great software, at a very attractive price, and after its initial advertising took hold, it was hard to make the packaged software product fast enough to supply demand.

There was no time for market research, and nobody to read it if it had been done. Those of us involved with the early launch knew it was a great product and that people would be happy to buy it.

TAKE NOTES!

What's the value of information when you are starting up a business? How much should you spend on collecting data? In our opinion, information is not worth money if you don't use it to make better decisions. Information in business is worth the decisions it causes. If it doesn't change what you do, don't bother.

Warning: That's a success story, but there are many failures. Good market research can help you avoid expensive failure. If you can afford the luxury, test your market assumptions. Are there enough people interested in what you're selling? How can you tell?

You make some real choices with research. Lots of people just put their product out there and hope people will buy. And, if people do, they've launched a business.

Is that you? Maybe you're selling greeting cards or catering services, jewelry or fine iron works, business plan consulting or resume writing, or whatever. If you're sure of what you're doing and sure that people will pay for it, then don't let market research get in the way.

However, lots of startups need to prove their market to get money, or to recruit team members. You may be sure of what your market is but the mere assertion of it isn't enough to convince the investors. A lot of market research is done to generate supporting information.

And there's also the idea of stepping back to take a good look at your market, with an open mind and clear vision. Don't assume you know—research the market. Often, you'll discover opportunities you weren't seeing before the research.

And finally, you know your business. Some businesses can let sales be the first market research, and some involve a lot more study, positioning, prototypes, and tuning features and benefits. As we say in the sidebar, information is worth the decisions it causes.

So this chapter is about market research—not because every startup needs it but because every startup ought to at least make an intelligent, informed decision about what to do and what not to do. Don't do market research just because it is a tradition or because experts say you need it. Maybe it's a good thing to do when you are deciding whether to mortgage your house for your startup and you want to be sure of the market for it. Or when wealthy backers are interested in your business idea and might want to put some money into it, but want you to prove there is a market first. Or when that one person you live with doesn't believe in your idea, is worried about you, and is urging you to keep your day job.

Other Reasons for Market Research

Perhaps you are sure enough of your market to get going anyhow—we were with our own startup—but there are reasons besides proof for startup that you might want or need more market research. These include:

- Having to prove to others the viability of a market before you can make sales. For example, you need to convince investors, and maybe commercial lenders or partners. You may be sure, but they aren't.

- Taking a fresh look. Are you wise enough to recognize that you might not know what you think you know? Often research is a way to open your mind, clear your vision, and review your assumptions.

Market Analysis

A market analysis looks at the potential market, its size, its growth, its characteristics, its trends, and so on. A classic market analysis breaks a market into subgroups, called segments. Sometimes segmentation is the most creative part of marketing. A good segmentation leads to target marketing— marketing methods that carefully define details about certain segments, leading to much more powerful and more economic marketing.

Market Demographics

Market demographics is basically counting potential customers. How many are out there? Are they individual consumers, families, institutions, businesses, or organizations? For consumers, define them as carefully as you can. Remember in Chapter 1 we quoted John Jantsch about defining your target market? Here we are again. It's important. Use variables like age, income, geography, employment, and such for consumers; and variables like size, number of employees, type of business, and decision patterns for businesses.

Market Characteristics

Aside from just counting the customers, you also want to know what they need, what they want, and what makes them buy. The more you know about them, the better. For individuals as customers, you probably want to know their average age, income levels, family size, media preferences, buying patterns, and as much else as you can find out that relates to your business. If you can, you want to divide them into groups according to useful classifications, such as income, age, buying habits, social behavior, values, or whatever other factors are important. Using a shoe store as an example, shoe size is good, but you might also want activity preferences and even psychographics.

Psychographics divides customers into cultural groups, value groups, social sets, motivator sets, or other interesting categories that might be useful. For example, in literature intended for potential retailers, First Colony Mall of Sugarland, Texas, describes its local area psychographics as including:

- 25 percent Kid and Cul-de-Sacs (upscale suburban families, affluent)

- 5.4 percent Winner's Circle (suburban executives, wealthy)

- 19.2 percent Boomers and Babies (young white-collar suburban, upper middle income)

- 7 percent Country Squires (elite ex-urban, wealthy).

Going into more detail, it calls the Kids and Cul-de-Sacs group "a noisy medley of bikes, dogs, carpools, rock music, and sports." The Winner's Circle customers are "well-educated, mobile, executives and professionals with teen-aged families. Big producers, prolific spenders, and global travelers."

The Country Squires are "where the wealthy have escaped urban stress to live in rustic luxury. No. 4 in affluence, big bucks in the boondocks."

Industry Analysis

Particularly if you're wanting to bring in outsiders of any kind, you might also have to be able to explain the general state of the industry and the nature of the business. You might be able to skip this for an internal plan because most of the target readers already know the

> **RED TAPE ALERT!**
>
> **WEEK 1**
>
> Be cautious when investigating competitors. If you are calling their company under false pretenses, you could get into some hot water. Be careful and err on the side of caution.

industry, but even in this case, taking a step away and taking a fresh look can be valuable.

Industry Participants

You can't easily describe a type of business without describing the nature of the participants. There is a huge difference, for example, between an industry like long-distance telephone services, in which there are only a few huge companies in any one country, and one like dry cleaning, in which there are tens of thousands of smaller participants.

This can make a big difference to a business and a business plan. The restaurant industry, for example, is what we call "pulverized," which, like the dry cleaning industry, is made up of many small participants. The fast-food business, on the other hand, is composed of a few national brands participating in thousands of branded outlets, many of them franchised.

Industry Growth, Trends, Etc.

Economists talk of consolidation in an industry as a time when many small participants tend to disappear and a few large players emerge. In accounting, for example, there are a few large international firms whose names are well known and tens of thousands of smaller firms. The automobile business is composed of a few national brands participating in thousands of branded dealerships. In computer manufacturing there are a few large international firms whose names are well known, and thousands of smaller firms.

Distribution

If you're dealing with physical products, you should have some idea about distribution, and channels of distribution. These days the easiest by far is distribution online, over the web, followed up by shipping via courier. If you're thinking about things to sell through stores or distributors, though, then you should know how those channels work. How do your target channels deal with new products? What are the standard margins? Do stores buy direct from producers, or only through distributors? And if you're thinking about becoming a store and selling products, you should know how you get those products in that industry. Who are the distributors?

In many product categories there are several alternatives, and distribution choices are strategic. Encyclopedias and vacuum cleaners were traditionally sold door-to-door, but are now also sold in stores and direct from manufacturer to consumer through radio, television, and Sunday newspaper print ads.

WEEK 1

TAKE NOTES!

Do you know what your competition is up to? If not, you could be headed for trouble. A study by professors at UCLA and Stanford University showed most business owners are clueless about the competition. Almost 80 percent were blind to their opponents' actions—which can lead to lost customers and market share. The answer? Role play. Put yourself in the competitors' shoes and analyze their strategies. Visit their stores. Use the internet to dig up as much information as you can about them, their tactics and their goals.

Many products are distributed through direct business-to-business sales, and in long-term contracts such as the ones between car manufacturers and their suppliers of parts, materials, and components. In some industries, companies use representatives, agents, or commissioned salespeople.

Technology can change the patterns of distribution in an industry or product category. The internet, for example, is changing the options for software, books, and music distribution, as well as other products. Cable communication is changing the options for distributing video products and video games.

Gathering Information

You don't need research companies and exhaustive studies; knowing your market is easier than that. Start your research with simple, practical methods.

Get on the Web

Don't delay. If you're going to start your business in three weeks, you're going to be using the web first and as your main source of information. It's going to give you an extremely quick and as comprehensive as you want to make it view of what's out there, what seems to be working right now, what people are buying, and what people are searching for. It's a new world. To research anything fast, you go to the web.

Make sure you understand how to do a basic web search. Start with Google at google.com. Search for a keyword that seems related to your business and watch what comes up. How many references are cited? What references are coming up? Notice the paid links along the top and along the side. What sort of companies are paying to get links to show up for people who just did the same search you did? Click on the paid links, see where that leads you. Quickly, you'll be able to get a sense of what's out there, what people are searching for, and what they are finding.

Learn to deal with search terms. Search "restaurant" and the results are almost useless. Search for "Mexican Restaurant" and it's not much better. But search for "Mexican Restaurant Peoria" and suddenly you have an idea who's in the Mexican restaurant business in Peoria, Illinois. It might not be an exhaustive, comprehensive list, but it's a good idea. Compare the results of that search with the results of "Mexican Restaurant El Paso TX" and you'll see a very different picture, many more entries in El Paso than in Peoria. Focus your search for better information.

Are you looking for statistics? Industry statistics on Mexican restaurants? Search for "Mexican restaurant industry statistics" and see what comes up.

For general statistics, see the Online Tools section for some good starting points on government statistics, economic statistics, census, and so on.

Later, in Chapter 11, we're going to help you work with Google AdWords to put your business in front of the people searching for it. In this chapter, in context of research, simply be sure you can find out what search words generate the most business, and how much buying a click on those search terms costs. Here are two examples:

1. If you're researching resume-writing software, you should be able to quickly find out what's available for that search in Google, which companies are paying to participate in the ad links, and, once you know how to use ad words, how much they are paying. What does it mean to your business that people are paying $3 per click to get good placement for that search?

2. What does it tell you if a search term is very cheap, just a few pennies? That might be a good thing if you are the first one to sell something related to that search term, but it also means nobody is making money with that.

Become familiar with Google AdWords and related tools for online marketing, such as competing facilities from other vendors. These can help you do a lot more than just signing up to advertise. They include additional information on search terms and traffic.

Do a lot of obvious web searching first. Find every conceivable business like yours, with every conceivable search term, and see who's advertising and how. Experiment as much as you can with reasonable keywords; see what kinds of businesses are advertising with those keywords.

Go Shopping

Go to the web and shop for what you're going to sell. There's no substitute for this kind of research. You search in order to know what's out there, what people might be buying now compared to what you're selling, and of course what search terms they are using, what companies they are now buying from, and what they are paying.

3 WEEKS TO STARTUP

Depending on what business you're starting, you might also do some real shopping in real stores. Or eating in restaurants, or riding in taxis, or whatever. Sometimes the use of the term "market research" makes us look past the obvious. If you're going to sell footwear, then you should go out and shop for footwear. If you're going to sell organic foods, shop for everything related. Maybe you don't buy everything related to your business, but see it, price it, touch it, and either know it or know about it.

> **TAKE NOTES!**
>
> **WEEK 1**
>
> Internet searches are something anybody can learn. Search for "how to web search" first and read through some of those to get an idea. Try it over and over again until you get used to it. You won't break the computer, the internet, or your budget. Searching is cheap, and easy enough to learn. You get the hang of it very fast. You're not going to start your business without it, so get in there and do it.

Give Something Away

At the University of Notre Dame's McCloskey Venture Competition a few years ago, one of the finalists presented a plan for creating a fish taco restaurant in Baton Rouge, LA. The team involved included somebody who was familiar with the vibrant market for fish tacos in San Diego, and somebody who knew Baton Rouge, which had no fish taco restaurants.

A question came from the panel of judges: "How do you know that people in Baton Rouge like fish tacos?"

He followed that question with the suggestion, "You should make a batch of them and go to the most popular place in town about noon on a warm Saturday, and give them away. See if people like them." And he added: "Be sure to check the garbage cans on either side, to see if they just tossed them."

This story is a reminder of the true nature of market research: Testing a market to answer the vital question of whether or not people want what you're selling. It's also a reminder that you find a lot about a market by just starting up the restaurant and offering the fish tacos for sale—but that's a lot more expensive if people don't buy them. It's better to know ahead of time.

Specific Research

If you're starting a physical "brick and mortar" business, spend some time in a business like the one you want to start—or across the street, or nearby—and do some counting. Count customers coming in, customers coming out, how many of those people have shopping bags when they exit, how long they spend in the store, and so on. Do this at different times of the day to figure out when people shop at this kind of store. Details depend on what business you're starting.

For a web business, there is also counting to be done. Are there ads on the site? If they're using Google AdWords or some other known platform or vendor, then you can find out what those ads cost. Does the site look successful? For the top few hundred thousand sites, you can find out how successful it is to use traffic comparison sites such as alexa.com and compete.com.

Talk to People

One time at our business, Palo Alto Software, we were going to explore a new market; software contiguous to what we were already doing, but to a different kind of buyer in a different kind of company.

We had one smart person find people who fit the general profile of the target customer, and talk to them. When she had ten good interviews with people in the right kind of potential buyer companies who seemed to listen and offer real opinions, she came back with results. It turned out there were problems with our idea. Real people in the market didn't seem to want what we were going to build. We didn't take it any further.

We believe that many times having a good, thorough, and real conversation with just a few carefully selected people can be much more valuable than elaborate random surveys. You do have to be careful not to sell the idea and influence the results you get. You have to listen.

Get On the Telephone

No, we don't mean become one of those obnoxious market research telephone callers who call people in their homes in the evening, but there's nothing wrong with finding a few people—particularly if they are people in business, in the case that you are going to be selling to businesses—and talking to them about what they need and don't need, or like and dislike, about your business or business idea. If you do it right, and you have perseverance, you will be able to talk to people.

Another good idea is to use the web to find businesses that are like yours but don't compete. For example, if you're going to start a fish taco restaurant in Baton Rouge, find somebody who started one in Atlanta, or Orlando, or Boulder, and talk to them about their market, what people like, and how it went for them. You can do that if you introduce it right, and find a time when a person isn't busy. Most people like to talk about their business if it isn't to a competitor. Or, if you're selling resume-writing software, find somebody who sells job listings, and then several people advertising that they write resumes, and get on the phone and talk to them.

Talk to Customers

Always talk to potential customers. In the shoe store example, talk to people coming out of the stores. Talk to your neighbors, talk to your friends, talk to your relatives. Ask them how often they buy shoes, what sizes, where, at what price, and whatever else you can think of. If you're starting a restaurant, landscape architecture business, butcher shop, bakery, or whatever, talk to people who buy these products or services.

Make Some Sales

Don't forget—the best market research is sales. If you're really going to start your business fast, make some sales.

Some businesses can take off with a single customer. For example, many consulting businesses started with one person leaving a company and making that same company his or her first big client. Many professional service businesses start with one client and go from there. Your first customer is twice as hard to get as your second, and your second twice as hard as your third, but the cycle continues and it gets easier. Investors and banks like to see market research data, like demographics and surveys, but sales are usually even more convincing.

More Formal Research

As a rule of thumb, market research should provide you with information about three critical areas: the industry, the consumer, and the competition.

1. **Industry information.** In researching the industry, look for the latest trends. Compare the statistics and growth in the industry. What areas of the industry appear to be expanding, and what areas are declining? Is the industry catering to new types of customers? What technological developments are affecting the industry? How can you use them to your advantage? A thriving, stable industry is key; you don't want to start a new business in a field that is on the decline.

2. **Consumer close-up.** On the consumer side, your market research should begin with a market survey. A thorough market survey will help you make a reasonable sales forecast for your new business. To do a market survey, you first need to determine the market limits or physical boundaries of the area to which your business sells. Next, study the spending characteristics of the population within this location.

   Estimate the location's purchasing power, based on its per-capita income, its median income level, the unemployment rate, population, and other demographic factors. Determine the current sales volume in the area for the type of product or service you will sell.

   Finally, estimate how much of the total sales volume you can reasonably obtain. (This last step is extremely important. Opening your new business in a given community won't necessarily generate additional business volume; it may simply redistribute the business that's already there.)

3. **Competition close-up.** Based on a combination of industry research and consumer research, a clearer picture of your competition will emerge. Do not underestimate the number of competitors out there. Keep an eye out for potential future competitors as well as current ones.

Examine the number of competitors on a local and, if relevant, national scale. Study their strategies and operations. Your analysis should supply a clear picture of potential threats, opportunities, and the weaknesses and strengths of the competition facing your new business.

When looking at the competition, try to see what trends have been established in the industry and whether there's an opportunity or advantage for your business. Use the library, the internet, and other secondary research sources described later in this chapter to research competitors. Read as many articles as you can on the companies with whom you will be competing. If you are researching publicly owned companies, contact them and obtain copies of their annual reports. These often show not only how successful a company is, but also what products or services it plans to emphasize in the future.

Government Information and Statistics

Most business plans contain an analysis of potential customers. As an essential first step, you should have a good idea of how many potential customers there are. The way you find that out depends on your type of business. For example, a retail shoe store needs to know about individuals living in a local area, a graphic design firm needs to know about local businesses, and a national catalog needs to know about households and companies in an entire nation. In almost all cases, you go straight to the web.

What constitutes good sources depends on what you need. It's very likely you'll get enough to go with on the web, whether that's through government and commercial statistics or other sites. In some rare cases, you may end up purchasing information from professional publishers or contract researchers.

For general demographic data about a local area, or about consumers in general, the U.S. population, or types of businesses by size or location, go first to the census bureau website at census.gov.

The U.S. Census Bureau turns out reams of inexpensive or free business information, most of which is available on the internet:

- The Census Bureau's State and Metropolitan Area Data Book offers statistics for metropolitan areas, central cities, and counties.

- The Census Product Update is a monthly listing of recently released and upcoming products from the U.S. Census Bureau. Sign up for a free e-mail subscription at census.gov.

- County Business Patterns is an excellent Census product that reports the number of a given type of business in a county by Standard Industrial Classification code (four-digit codes for all industries in the United States).

- For breakdowns by cities, look to the Economic Census, which is published every five years.

- The American Factfinder website (factfinder.census.gov) provides excellent access to census information, including a "Search Your Street" feature that displays a map.

- The Statistical Abstract of the United States (census.gov/statab/www) has statistical information from government and private sources compiled by the Census Bureau. It can be downloaded for free.

- The Census Bureau's International Database (census.gov/ipc/idbnew.html) furnishes data on foreign countries.

Just browsing the Census Bureau website while writing this book, it took me about 10 minutes to discover that my home county has 378 general contractors, of which 360 have fewer than 20 employees and the remaining 18 have between 20 and 100. There are 238 legal businesses in my county, of which only 12 have more than 20 employees. Also, following the shoe store example, there are 32 shoe stores in the county, none of them having more than 20 employees. There are 111,000 households in the county, 61 percent of them owner occupied, and an average of 2.49 people per household. Some 22 percent of adults in the county are college graduates, and the median household income is $26,000. All of this information was available for free at the U.S. Census Bureau website.

3 WEEKS TO STARTUP

The U.S. Government has an official web portal that is another good source of information. For instance, at the FirstGov's website (firstgov.gov), you'll find a section for businesses that is a one-stop link to all the information and service that the federal government provides for the business community. Tax questions? Wondering about how best to deal with all the regulations and red tape? Chances are you'll find your answers at business.gov by clicking the "Taxes" link.

The U.S. Department of Labor has statistics on jobs, including types of jobs and numbers of people performing jobs, salary levels, locations, and size of their employer companies, at bls.gov.

Or you might try the Commerce Department's Economic Indicators web page (economicindicators.gov). Curious if the world is ready to spend money on your exercise equipment for goldfish? Then the Economic Indicators site is for you. Literally every day, they're releasing key economic indicators from the Bureau of Economic Analysis and the U.S. Census Bureau.

If you're planning to get into exporting, contact the Department of Commerce's International Trade Administration (ITA). The ITA publishes several thousand reports and statistical surveys, not to mention hundreds of books on everything entrepreneurs need to know about exporting. Many of the reports and books are available for downloading immediately from the ITA's publication department (ita.doc.gov). Here, you'll also find information on how to order printed copies, including archived publications. Or if you prefer, call the Trade Information Center at (800) USA-TRADE.

Another excellent source of information is the national Small Business Development Center (SBDC) network, a collection of approximately 1,000 centers in the U.S. funded by a combination of federal and state funds, and local educational institutions. Although the services offered vary from state to state, the SBDCs are in general very professional and surprisingly economical.

General Web Search and Literature Search

Aside from the standard government sources, turn to your web searching techniques again to do the following research.

- Look for quotes from industry websites or business publications to give you information on general market statistics, growth, trends, and so on. Do the right search and you'll find quotes to help you prove that market to the skeptics. For example, *Business Week* (or *Financial Times, The New York Times,* or *The Wall Street Journal*) said your market was growing at 15 percent per year. Searching can be frustrating, very much hit or miss, but hits are well worth it.

- Look for published financial data of the larger companies operating in your industry. Go to their websites, find their annual reports, read through the information they are sharing with stockholders. See what their growth rates are and how business has been going for them.

Other websites you should be sure to visit include the following:

- knowthis.com's marketing virtual library includes a section on the site called "Market Research" that contains links to a wide variety of market research web resources.

- bizminer.com lets you choose from more than 900,000 industry reports, 30,000 financial analysis profiles, and 3,000 area-vitality profiles, all online.

- marketresearch.com has more than 95,000 research reports from hundreds of sources consolidated into one accessible collection that's updated daily. No subscription fee is required, and you pay for only the report sections you need with its "Buy by the Slice" feature. You can also save on shipping charges by opting for "Instant Online Delivery."

All the sources mentioned earlier (trade associations, government agencies) should also have websites you can visit to get information quickly. For instance, the Census Bureau offers the many helpful websites mentioned above.

One of the better websites for researching the competition is Hoover's Online (hoovers.com), which, for a fee, provides in-depth profiles of more than 18,000 public and private companies. There is also free content available on the site as well.

If you don't have time to investigate online services yourself, consider hiring an information broker to find the information you need. Information brokers gather information quickly and can act as a small company's research arm, identifying the most accurate and cost-effective information sources.

To find information brokers, look online first. If a good search doesn't turn enough up, look in the Yellow Pages or ask the research librarian at your local library. Many research librarians deal with information brokers and will be able to give you good recommendations.

Associations

Do a good web search for associations, like industry associations and chambers of industry and commerce, in your business area. Here, too, the best tool is the web, searching creatively for industry associations. There are reference lists of associations published, and these days you can find most of that in the web searchers.

Some industry trade associations can offer a wealth of information such as market statistics, lists of members, and books and reference materials. Talking to others in your association can be one of the most valuable ways of gaining informal data about a region or customer base. The quality and quantity of information varies widely from industry to industry, and from association to association.

In a pinch, look for the *Encyclopedia of Associations* (Gale Research), found in most brick-and-mortar libraries, to find associations relevant to your industry. If you sell to businesses, you may also want to investigate your customers' trade associations for information that can help you market to them. Most trade associations provide information free of charge.

If you're lucky, you can read your trade associations' publications, as well as those aimed at your target customers, to get an idea of current and future trends and buying patterns. And keep an eye out for more; new magazines and newsletters are launched every year. If you're not following all of them, you could be missing out on valuable information about new products and your competitors.

Colleges and Universities

Local colleges and universities are valuable sources of information. Many college business departments have students who are eager to work in the "real world," gathering information and doing research at little or no cost.

Finally, local business schools are a great source of experts. Many business professors do consulting on the side, and some will even be happy to offer you marketing, sales, strategic planning, or financial information for free. Call professors who specialize in these areas; if they can't help, they'll be able to put you in touch with someone who can.

Community Organizations

Your local chamber of commerce or business development agency can supply useful information. They can provide assistance with site selection, demographic reports, and directories of local businesses. They may also offer seminars on marketing and related topics that can help you do research.

D&B

Financial and business services firm D&B offers a range of reference sources that can help startups. Some of the information they offer as part of their Sales and Marketing Solutions are directories for career opportunities, consultants, service companies, and regional businesses. Visit their website at dnb.com, or call (800) 624-5669 for more information. D&B's Regional Business Directories provide detailed information to help identify new business prospects and assess market potential. Besides basic information (telephone number, address, and company description), the directories also tell when the company was started, sales volume, number of employees, parent company (if any), and, if it's a public company, on which exchange it's traded.

D&B's Million Dollar Database can help you develop a marketing campaign for B2B sales. The Million Dollar Database lists approximately 1.6

million U.S. and Canadian leading public and private companies and includes information regarding the number of employees, annual sales, and ownership type. The database also includes biographical information on owners and officers, giving insight into their backgrounds and business experiences. For more information, go to dnbmdd.com.

Other Sources

Magazines provide another good source of demographics. If you're selling to computer stores, for example, call *Computer Retail Week* and *Computer Reseller News* and ask for a media kit. Media kits are intended to sell pages of advertising to potential advertisers and are frequently full of demographics on their readers. For information on any specific type of business, get the media kits for the magazines that cater to those types of businesses as readers.

Doing Your Own Research

So far we've been discussing what is called secondary research. Primary research is information that comes directly from the source—that is, potential customers. You can compile this information yourself or hire someone else to gather it for you via surveys, focus groups, and other methods.

A market research firm can help you if you feel that primary research is too complicated to do on your own, and you have the money to hire one. These firms will charge a few thousand dollars or more, but depending on the complexity of the information you need, you may feel this is money well spent. Your local chamber of commerce can recommend firms or individuals who can conduct market research for smaller businesses on a budget.

If you need assistance but don't want to spend that kind of cash, you can go to your SBA district office for guidance; their counselors can help you figure out what types of questions you need to ask your target market. As with secondary research, the SBA, SBDCs, colleges, and universities are good sources of help with primary research.

Whether get help from the SBA, use a market research firm, or go it alone, there are simple ways you can get primary research information.

Focus Groups

A focus group consists of 5 to 12 potential customers who are asked their opinions in a group interview. Participants should fit your target market— for example, single men ages 18 to 25 or working mothers. To find participants, just go to your local mall or college campus and ask people fitting your customer profile if they would answer a few questions. Focus groups typically pay participants $75 to $100 each.

TAKE NOTES!

It's very easy to get false messages from focus groups. One vocal person can influence a group. It's hard to be cynical enough. Random opinions can suddenly seem like fact. Be very, very, careful when making decisions based on focus group feedback.

Although focus group interviews are informal, you should have a list of questions to help you direct the discussion. Start by asking whether your product or service is one the participants would buy. If so, what is the highest price they would pay? Where would they shop for such a product? Do they like or dislike the product's packaging? Your questions should center on predetermined objectives, such as figuring out how high you can price your product or service or what to name your business.

If you're going the do-it-yourself route, you will probably act as the focus group moderator. Encourage an open-ended flow of conversation and be sure to solicit comments from quieter members, or you may end up getting all your information from only the talkative participants.

Telephone Interviews

This is a fast and inexpensive way to get information from potential customers. Prepare a script before making the calls to ensure you cover all your objectives. Most people don't like to spend a lot of time on the phone, so keep your questions simple, clearly worded, and brief. If you don't have time to make the calls yourself, hire college students to do it for you.

Direct-mail Interviews

If you want to survey a wider audience, direct mail can be just the ticket. Your survey can be as simple as a postcard or as elaborate as a cover letter, questionnaire, and reply envelope. Keep questionnaires to a maximum of one page (front and back), and ask no more than 20 questions. Ideally, direct-mail surveys should be simple, structured with "yes/no" or "agree/disagree" check-off boxes so respondents can answer quickly and easily. If possible, only ask for one or two write-in answers at most.

E-mail Interviews

Many of the principles used in direct-mail interviews also apply to these surveys. For example, just as the address, envelope, and salutation matter in direct mail, so too does the subject matter in e-mail. Most people scan their e-mail boxes very quickly, so try to make the subject line inviting. Give clear instructions on how to respond, and be appreciative in advance for the data you get back. Make responding easier by using e-mail forms as much as possible; even a simple text questionnaire form will help. Be careful to avoid spamming or being mistaken for spam (unsolicited commercial e-mail). Our favorite summary is under the topic "spam" at wikipedia.org. Use the web to search for tips and techniques to avoid the spam filter problem.

Making a List

How do you get the names of potential customers to call or mail questionnaires to? You can get lists from many places, including website offerings, your suppliers, trade associations or a list-rental company. List-rental companies can give you access to a mailing list of a group of people who fit into your desired market. Refer to your local Yellow Pages for the names of list-rental companies. If none are listed, contact the Direct Marketing Association at the-dma.org, or (212) 768-7277.

A less sophisticated approach to finding potential customer names is picking them at random from the phone book. If you've developed a latex glove for the medical field, for example, you can get doctors' and dentists' names out of the Yellow Pages. Whatever method you use to gather your information, the key to market research is using what you learn. The most sophisticated survey in the world does you no good if you ignore the information and the feedback customers provide.

"A recent survey shows…" just might be the most overused, misused and abused phrase in modern life. Try hard enough, and you can find a survey that proves four out of five Americans have been aboard a UFO, think they can flap their arms and fly to the moon, or believe Elvis is alive and living in their spare bedroom. With all the half-baked surveys out there, how do you know what to believe?

First, consider the source. Many surveys are conducted by trade associations, which inevitably are biased in favor of good news. This doesn't mean trade association surveys are necessarily inaccurate; just keep in mind that they are likely to play up positive results and downplay negative ones. When looking at any survey, consider what the source has to gain from the information presented. Then you'll have a better idea of whether to take the information with a grain of salt.

Meaningful surveys generally share the following characteristics:

- **Short-term focus.** In general, respondents are more likely to be accurate when they make predictions about the next three to six months. When it comes to predicting the long term (a year or more ahead), they're usually guessing.

- **Adequate sample size.** What constitutes adequate size depends on the topic you're surveying. In general, the broader the topic, the larger the number of respondents should be. If the survey talks about broad manufacturing trends, for example, it should survey 1,000 companies or more. Also consider where the respondents come from. If you're starting a small regional business, a large national sample may not be relevant to your needs because the sample size from your area is probably too small to tell you anything about your region.

- **Knowledgeable respondents.** Asking entrepreneurs in the electronics business to forecast the future of the electronics industry obviously carries more weight than asking the same question of teachers or random people on the street.

- **Continual replication.** The best surveys are repeated regularly to different groups, using the same methods, so there is a good basis for comparison from survey to survey.

- **Specific information relevant to your business.** In a nutshell, the best surveys are those where respondents answer questions that are narrowly targeted to your region and niche.

TAKE NOTES!

When doing any type of survey, whether it is a focus group, a written questionnaire, or a phone survey, pay attention to customers who complain or give you negative feedback. You don't need to worry about the customers who love your product or service, but the ones who tell you where you're going wrong provide valuable information to help you improve.

WEEK
1

ONLINE TOOLS

These days market research lives on the web. It's the best place by far for almost any kind of secondary research. The power of text search through publications online is obvious. Also, because of e-mail surveys and the newer survey sites, it's now the best place for general surveys as well.

Information Sources

These websites offer general information, government statistics, company information, or similar data:

- The U.S. Government's official web portal: usa.gov

- U.S. Census Bureau housing topics: census.gov/hhes/www/housing.html

- U.S. Census Bureau: Longitudinal Employer-Household Dynamics: lehd.did.census.gov/led/index.html
- Hoovers Company Database: hoovers.com/free
- The 2008 Census Statistical Abstract: census.gov/compendia/statab
- Census Bureau Survey of Business Owners (SBO): census.gov/csd/sbo/index.html
- Stats: ClickZ, at clickz.com/showPage.html?page=stats S
- Sales leads and company information at D&B Sales & Marketing Solutions: zapdata.com/
- Population projections, U.S. Census Bureau: census.gov/population/www/projections/popproj.html
- Population estimates, U.S. Census Bureau: census.gov/popest/estimates.php
- Oxxford Information Technology Home Page: oxxfordinfo.com
- 2002 Economic Census: census.gov/econ/census02
- Income, U.S. Census Bureau: census.gov/hhes/www/income/income.html
- National SBDC Information Clearinghouse: sbdcnet.org
- FedStats: fedstats.gov
- E-Stats, U.S. Census Bureau: census.gov/eos/www/ebusiness614.htm
- Census Bureau Home Page: census.gov
- Census 2000 Gateway: census.gov/main/www/cen2000.html
- Bureau of Labor Statistics Home Page: bls.gov

Survey Sites

These websites offer tools and resources for developing, delivering, and digesting surveys such as customer surveys, general market surveys, etc.

3 WEEKS TO STARTUP

- Buying advice and free survey provider quotes from national vendors: buyerzone.com/marketing/market_research/index.html

- SurveyMonkey, a powerful tool for creating web surveys and online survey software made easy: surveymonkey.com

- Web survey software tools by Zoomerang: zoomerang.com

- Google Search: google.com/search?q=online+survey

Market Research for Sale

These websites sell prepared studies and consulting services or custom market studies.

- Marketing Research Association, Directing the Future of Research: mra-net.org

- JupiterResearch, market research, trends, and statistics: jupiterresearch.com/bin/item.pl/home

- Plunkett Research: plunkettresearch.com/Home/tabid/ 36/Default.aspx

- Market research reports: marketresearch.com

- JJ Hill, business information resources, research tools, online library: jjhill.org

- MindBranch, industry market research reports and business analysis: mindbranch.com

Lists

These websites offer mailing lists, address lists, e-mail address lists, company contact lists, and similar lists of sales leads.

- usadata.com

- Free marketing research resources 15/4: researchinfo.com

Additional Information

Articles about market research and sources of additional information:

- "Know Your Industry Before You Start Your Business," business plan help and small business articles: bplans.com
- "BNET Today," management, strategy, work life skills and advice for professionals: bnet.com

CHAPTER 4

MAKE IT LEGAL

A legal company in 3 weeks?

Yes, it can be done! We recommend reading what we have here, following up with additional information on the web if that helps you feel comfortable, and then finishing up with an attorney. What you ought to do during this three-week period is establish your name, ownership, and responsibilities, and then work with an attorney or an online vendor you trust, to make that all legal. It takes planning, but not a lot of time.

About Your Business Name

The business name causes so much confusion that we'll start with that topic. Legally, technically, business names are not that different from people's names. Do you know someone with the common American name John Smith? Did you ever think that only one John Smith is the real John Smith, and all the rest of them are illegal? Of course they are not. Every John Smith who was legally named that is legally able to be John Smith.

But what if one John Smith pretends to be another John Smith? A John Smith who doesn't own a house at 1211 Maple Lane claims to be the John Smith who does, and borrows money off of that house that he doesn't own, and runs off with it. That's illegal. It's fraud to pretend you're somebody you're not, particularly for commercial reasons. The first John Smith can sue the other one who preyed on his name and reputation.

It's a lot like that with companies too. We could incorporate a Berry Parsons Corporation in Oregon, and that would prevent anybody else from incorporating with that name in Oregon. It would not, however, prevent others from incorporating their own Berry Parsons Corporation in any other state. Nor would it prevent somebody from creating a sole proprietorship in any county in Oregon or in any county of any other state named Berry Parsons Company. There could also be partnerships and Limited Liability Corporations (LLCs) named Berry Parsons or Berry Parsons LLC.

WEEK 1

TAKE NOTES!

We did business with a company in Portland, Oregon, that discovered, after marketing itself under a certain name for more than a year, that a company in Texas was operating in a similar market with the same name. Upon investigation, it turned out that the Texas company had started first and could prove it. So our vendors had to change their name. It is very painful to have to change a name after you've been using it for a while.

The problems arise when the companies with similar names conflict or confuse or compete. If we were first with Berry Parsons Corporation in Oregon, and we do business and market under that name, we can then prevent anybody else from doing business with the same name somewhere else. To do that, we'd have to deal with lawyers, insisting that you not market your business under the Berry Parsons name because it would confuse people with our business. If you contested that, ultimately we'd fight over who had the name first, and the one of us who first established a business entity with that name, and could prove it, would win.

So there's the so-called rub. It might well be that no legal authority, as in Secretary of State for corporations or county registries for sole proprietorships, will tell you that Berry Parsons isn't a good name. You can own it, but you can't market it.

All of this makes naming your company harder because it's up to you to determine that your name doesn't con-

TAKE NOTES!

We don't think you should get too hung up with your website domain name while naming your company. The fact that you can't reserve bluesail.com, for example, doesn't mean you don't name your restaurant The Blue Sail. You shouldn't separate the domain name from the discussion, but the domain name doesn't necessarily determine your business name.

flict with some other company that is already in the world marketing itself under that name. You don't want to end up having to change your name like the Portland company in the sidebar did.

The quick and simple way to do a name search is to use the web and search for that name in Google, Yahoo, MSN, and whatever other search engine you like to use. Be careful, though, to make your search wide enough to catch similar names that could cause you problems. If you want to do Berry Parsons, to follow our example, recognize that lots of similar names could also cause you trouble later.

Don't rule out asking your attorney to do a name search for you. This might cost you a few hundred dollars, but imagine how much it will cost you to change your company name after you've started.

Above All, Get It In Writing

If you're doing this all by yourself, relax, don't worry so much, skip ahead. You'll have other problems, but not these problems. But if you aren't alone, believe me—it is almost comical how much easier these things are to do now, before you start, when compared to how hard they are later, when

things get all wrapped up in each other, and there is money, ego, history, and business at stake. Please—get it in writing. Even before we get into the formal legal stuff, there's a whole lot to discuss about who owns what, who does what, fairness, division, and what happens when things go wrong, if they do; and what happens if things don't go wrong.

An e-mail arrived recently from somebody asking advice about this situation: The company and its partners had been doing business for years, this person had put money in at the start, apparently a lot, and others had put money in at various times of need during the history of the business. Now the e-mailer was worried about fairness. Shouldn't I get more because I was first? Isn't that normally what happens—people who invest later get fewer shares for their money?

Actually, yes, it is, but if it isn't written down and established, then there is a lot of battling to come.

Many fairness issues are infinitely easier to deal with when it's all hypothetical. After the fact, when there is real money at stake (or, heaven forbid, real debts), it's too late to easily determine what's fair.

Take this example: Three people hunt for the treasure in a shipwreck below the sea. One's the diving expert, one's the historian who discovered the map, and one owns the boat and the diving equipment. How should they divide the treasure? What if a fourth person puts up the money for the expedition? What's fair?

Imagine two scenarios. In the first, before they do any hunting, or spending, they sit down around a table and agree on how they are going to divide the treasure, if they find it. In the other, they leave all their ideas about fairness unspoken, each assuming the others understand what's right. Then they find a huge treasure worth a lot of money. How do they decide what's fair then? What if they don't find anything, but the boat sinks and all the gear goes down with it? Does the expedition sponsor have to repay the boat owner?

This example points out the huge difference between working fairness out ahead of time, compared to working it out after the fact of either success or failure.

Don't think, as you start your new business, that there are some rules somewhere that you can call on to decide issues of fairness when things get difficult. Fairness isn't defined anywhere. Different people have widely different assumptions about the comparative value of the original idea, the know-how, the actual work, the invested money, and other factors.

First, talk it out as well as you can, and get it in writing. Get help online if you can by asking a reasonable and useful question at one of the various ask-the-expert sites (sidebar). If you know the right attorney, get some help with the attorney. If you don't, start looking. And don't forget other sources such as the nearest Small Business Development Center (SBDC), SCORE office, or local business school.

TAKE NOTES!

WEEK 1

One good place to find discussion questions for ownership documents is in the "Starting a Business" section at nolo.com; another is incorporate.com.

Also, there are ask-the-expert sites that can help if you ask simple questions. Don't ask an expert to tell you what's fair in your specific case, or who's right. Ask the expert to tell you what questions to ask, what issues to discuss. We're online as experts at bplans.com and entrepreneur.com.

And all of that is just by way of introduction, before we get to the real legal discussion. And, before we do, an important disclaimer: We aren't attorneys. Laws change, often faster than books can change. We can't give you legal advice. We're merely trying to help you inform yourself before you take the proper legal steps. We want to help you to know what to ask.

Also, be aware that laws on corporate entities are different in different states. There are reasons that corporations go to Delaware, or, more recently, Nevada. In our experience, in this litigious business environment we live in, scrimping on attorney fees is not the best way to save money.

On the other hand, a lot of people do this using online facilities and are glad they did. We get different reports. It's been great for some, not so great for others. Be careful out there.

> ## TAKE NOTES!
>
> Your legal entity can change. You aren't stuck with it forever. Palo Alto Software, our company, started as Infoplan, a DBA, in 1983. That spawned Infoplan, a Delaware corporation, in 1987. That begat Palo Alto Software, Inc., a California corporation, in 1988. In 1992, we moved it to Oregon and created a new Oregon corporation that absorbed the assets. In 1994 the California corporation was dissolved.
>
> Don't get us wrong: We're not recommending a glib or casual attitude, but it's not necessarily going to be written on your tombstone, either.
>
> And just for the record, when we started as a sole proprietorship, we had a good professional attorney who said being a corporation was too much trouble until we got bigger. "If you do," he added.

Choosing a Business Structure

Of all the decisions you make when starting a business, probably the most important one relating to taxes is the type of legal structure you select for your company.

Not only will this decision have an impact on how much you pay in taxes, but it also will affect the amount of paperwork your business is required to do, the personal liability you face, and your ability to raise money.

The most common forms of business are sole proprietorship, partnership, corporation, and S corporation. A more recent development to these forms of business is the limited liability company (LLC) and the limited liability partnership (LLP). Because each business form comes with different tax consequences, you will want to make your selection wisely and choose the structure that most closely matches your business's needs.

If you decide to start your business as a sole proprietorship but later decide to take on partners, you can reorganize as a partnership or other entity. If you do this, be sure you notify the IRS as well as your state tax agency.

Sole Proprietorship

The simplest structure is the sole proprietorship, which usually involves just one individual who owns and operates the enterprise. If you intend to work alone, this structure may be the way to go.

The tax aspects of a sole proprietorship are appealing because the expenses and your income from the business are included on your personal income tax return, Form 1040. Your profits and losses are recorded on a form called Schedule C, which is filed with your 1040. The "bottom-line amount" from Schedule C is then transferred to your personal tax return. This is especially attractive because business losses you suffer may offset the income you have earned from your other sources.

As a sole proprietor, you must also file a Schedule SE with Form 1040. You use Schedule SE to calculate how much self-employment tax you owe. In addition to paying annual self-employment taxes, you must make estimated tax payments if you expect to owe at least $1,000 in federal taxes for the year and your withholding will be less than the smaller of: 1) 90 percent of your current year tax liability or 2) 100 percent of your previous year's tax liability if your adjusted gross income is $150,000 or less ($75,000 or less if you are married and filing separately). The federal government permits you to

> **TAKE NOTES!**
>
> If you operate as a sole proprietor, be sure you keep your business income and records separate from your personal finances. It helps to establish a business checking account and get a credit card to use only for business expenses.

> WEEK
> 1

pay estimated taxes in four equal amounts throughout the year on the 15th of April, June, September, and January. With a sole proprietorship, your business earnings are taxed only once, unlike other business structures.

Another big plus is that you will have complete control over your business—you make all the decisions.

There are a few disadvantages to consider, however. Selecting the sole proprietorship business structure means you are personally responsible for your company's liabilities. As a result, you are placing your assets at risk, and they could be seized to satisfy a business debt or a legal claim filed against you.

TAKE NOTES!

The sole proprietorship is also commonly called DBA (for doing business as) and fictitious business name. These common nicknames focus more on the use of the name than the business type.

Raising money for a sole proprietorship can also be difficult. Banks and other financing sources may be reluctant to make business loans to sole proprietorships. In most cases, you will have to depend on your financing sources, such as savings, home equity, or family loans.

Partnership

If your business will be owned and operated by several individuals, you'll want to take a look at structuring your business as a partnership. Partnerships come in two varieties: general partnerships and limited partnerships. In a general partnership, the partners manage the company and assume responsibility for the partnership's debts and other obligations. A limited partnership has both general and limited partners. The general partners own and operate the business and assume liability for the partnership, while the limited partners serve as investors only; they have no control over the company and are not subject to the same liabilities as the general partners.

Unless you expect to have many passive investors, limited partnerships are generally not the best choice for a new business because of all the required filings and administrative complexities. If you have two or more partners who want to be actively involved, a general partnership would be much easier to form.

One of the major advantages of a partnership is the tax treatment it enjoys. A partnership does not pay tax on its income but "passes through" any profits or losses to the individual partners. At tax time, the partnership must file a tax return (Form 1065) that reports its income and loss to the IRS. In addition, each partner reports his or her share of income and loss on Schedule K-1 of Form 1065.

TAKE NOTES!

WEEK 7

Partnerships are much less common now than they were 20 or 30 years ago. There are so many more LLCs these days. Why? That's a good question to ask your attorney.

Personal liability is a major concern if you use a general partnership to structure your business. Like sole proprietors, general partners are personally liable for the partnership's obligations and debts. Each general partner can act on behalf of the partnership, take out loans and make decisions that will affect and be binding on all the partners (if the partnership agreement permits). Keep in mind that partnerships are also more expensive to establish than sole proprietorships because they require more legal and accounting services.

Corporation

The corporate structure is more complex and expensive than most other business structures. A corporation is an independent legal entity, separate from its owners, and as such, it requires complying with more regulations and tax requirements.

TAKE NOTES!

WEEK 7

In our experience, having a corporation doesn't shield you from liability that much. Try getting a business loan as a small, closely held corporation, without giving owner personal guarantees. It doesn't happen often.

The biggest benefit for a business owner who decides to incorporate is the liability protection he or she receives. A corporation's debt is not considered that of its owners, so if you organize your business as a corporation, you are not putting your personal assets at risk. A corporation also can retain some of its profits without the owner paying tax on them. However, in practice, owners of small closely held corporations will almost always sign personal guarantees, pledging their personal assets, for any business loan. This reduces the real effective impact of the separation between liabilities and corporate liabilities.

WEEK 1

RED TAPE ALERT!

Rules for corporations vary by state. Not all of the details suggested here will necessarily apply to your corporation in your state. Make sure you ask; we aren't attorneys and not everything we say here applies to every state equally.

One of the major advantages is the ability of a corporation to raise money. A corporation can sell stock, either common or preferred, to raise funds. Corporations also continue indefinitely, even if one of the shareholders dies, sells the shares, or becomes disabled. The corporate structure, however, comes with a number of down sides. A major one is higher costs. Corporations are formed under the laws of each state with its own set of regulations. You will probably need the assistance of an attorney to guide you. In addition, because a corporation must follow more complex rules and regulations than a partnership or sole proprietorship, it requires more accounting and tax preparation services.

Another drawback to forming a corporation: Owners of the corporation pay a double tax on the business's earnings. Not only are corporations subject to corporate income tax at both the federal and state levels, but any earnings distributed to shareholders in the form of dividends are taxed at individual tax rates on their personal income tax returns.

One strategy to help soften the blow of double taxation is to pay some money out as salary to you and any other corporate shareholders who work for the company. A corporation is not required to pay tax on earnings paid as reasonable compensation, and it can deduct the payments as a business expense. However, the IRS has limits on what it believes to be reasonable compensation.

S vs. C Corporation

The S corporation is more attractive to small-business owners than a regular (or C) corporation. That's because an S corporation has some appealing tax benefits and still provides business owners with the liability protection of a corporation. With an S corporation, income and losses are passed through to shareholders and included on their individual tax returns. As a result, there's just one level of federal tax to pay.

In addition, owners of S corporations who don't have inventory can use the cash method of accounting, which some bookkeepers prefer. Under this method, income is taxable only when payments have been received and expenses are deductible when paid.

S corporations can also have up to 100 shareholders in some states. The limit varies. In Oregon, our state, they are allowed to have no more than 35. This makes it possible to have more investors and thus attract more capital, tax experts maintain.

S corporations do come with some down sides. For example, S corporations are subject to many of the same rules corporations must follow, and that means higher legal and tax service costs. They also must file articles of incorporation, hold directors and shareholders meetings, keep corporate minutes, and allow shareholders to vote on major corporate decisions. The legal and accounting costs of setting up an S corporation are also similar to those for a regular corporation.

RED TAPE ALERT!

WEEK 1

You can switch from S to C once in a while, if you do it right. Our company went from S to C in 1999. We did it because we were bringing in venture capital investment, and the investors needed to own shares as a corporation.

We haven't had a reason to switch back to S, but we've been told we could now if we wanted to. Five years had to pass. For the record, S would be more interesting to us if we were losing money, because then we could claim losses on our personal taxes.

Another major difference between a regular corporation and an S corporation is that S corporations can only issue one class of stock. Experts say this can hamper the company's ability to raise capital.

In addition, and probably more importantly, unlike in a regular corporation, S corporation stock can only be owned by individuals, estates, and certain types of trusts. In 1998, tax-exempt organizations such as qualified pension plans were added to the list. This change provides S corporations with even greater access to capital because a number of pension plans are willing to invest in closely held small-business stock.

Making It Real

To start the process of incorporating, first decide whether or not you want to do this online. We recommend that at the very least you jump online and contact two or three of the more interesting looking options. You can find them by doing a web search for "online incorporation." We have direct experience with the Company Corporation and Nolo Press, but look on the blog 3weeks2start for the latest. Things change.

If you don't like how that feels, or you decide for whatever reason that you want to do it the old-fashioned way, you still have another obvious choice. You can do it the way most of us do, using an attorney we trust, and paying a few hundred dollars for the fees to have him or her do it. Or, if you are a true adventurer, contact the secretary of state or the state office that is responsible for registering corporations in your state. Ask for instructions, forms, and fee schedules on incorporating. And close your eyes and forget about the old saying that an attorney who represents him- or herself has a fool for a client.

If you do it yourself, you will save the expense of using a lawyer, which can cost from $750 to $1,000. The disadvantage is that the process may take you some time to accomplish. There is also a chance you could miss some

> **WEEK 1**
>
> ## TAKE NOTES!
>
> Inform yourself first. That's what we're here for. Know the general trade-offs. Then get together with an attorney you trust—if you don't have one, find one, because you're going to need one as you get into business—and go over the options between corporations, LLCs, sole proprietorships, and so on. It seems like a luxury, but this is your business. It's worth it.

small but important detail in your state's law. Or, more importantly, there's also the chance that you make the wrong choice because you didn't have that talk with a knowledgeable expert about what the issues might be in your specific case.

One of the first steps in the incorporation process is to prepare a certificate or articles of incorporation. Some states provide a printed form for this, which either you or your attorney can complete. The information requested includes the proposed name of the corporation, the purpose of the corporation, the names and addresses of those incorporating, and the location of the principal office of the corporation. The corporation will also need a set of bylaws that describe in greater detail than the articles how the corporation will run, including the responsibilities of the company's shareholders, directors and officers; when stockholder meetings will be held; and other details important to running the company. Once your articles of incorporation are accepted, the secretary of state's office will send you a certificate of incorporation.

Rules of the Road

Once you are incorporated, be sure to follow the rules of incorporation. If you fail to do so, a court can pierce the corporate veil and hold you and the other business owners personally liable for the business's debts.

It is important to follow all the rules required by state law. You should keep accurate financial records for the corporation, showing a separation between the corporation's income and expenses and those of the owners.

The corporation should also issue stock, file annual reports, and hold yearly meetings to elect company officers and directors, even if they're the same people as the shareholders. Be sure to keep minutes of shareholders' and directors' meetings. On all references to your business, make certain to identify it as a corporation, using Inc. or Corp., whichever your state requires. You also want to make sure that whomever you will be dealing with, such as your banker or clients, knows that you are an officer of a corporation. (For more corporate guidelines, do an internet search for "Corporate Checklist."

This may sound like it's for a larger corporation, but it is necessary, and with small, privately-held corporations, it can be done with a simple meeting with the lawyer once a year and doesn't have to become bureaucratic.

If, by the way, you choose to establish your corporation using online offerings, we recommend you also follow up with them about additional web tools and services to help you with the resulting paperwork, such as annual minutes. Some of the more sophisticated vendors can offer you turnkey solutions to these problems.

Three weeks, remember? That's easier online. Look for the resource list at the end of this chapter.

Limited Liability Corporation

Limited liability corporations, often referred to as "LLCs," have been around since 1977, but their popularity among entrepreneurs is a relatively recent phenomenon. An LLC is a hybrid entity, bringing together some of the best features of partnerships and corporations. Some states also call them Limited Liability Companies.

Especially because these are a relatively recent phenomenon, be careful with the difference between LLCs in different states. Rules will vary.

LLCs were created to provide business owners with the liability protection that corporations enjoy without the double taxation. Earnings and losses pass through to the owners and are included on their personal tax returns.

Sound similar to an S corporation? It is, except that an LLC offers business owners even more attractions than an S corporation. For example, there is no limitation on the number of shareholders an LLC can have, unlike an S corporation, which has a limit of 100 shareholders. In addition, any member or owner of the LLC is allowed a full participatory role in the business's operation; in a limited partnership, on the other hand, partners are not permitted any say in the operation.

In most states, to set up an LLC you must file articles of organization with the secretary of state in the state where you intend to do business.

Some states also require you to file an operating agreement, which is similar to a partnership agreement. Like partnerships, LLCs do not have perpetual life. Some state statutes stipulate that the company must dissolve after 30 or 40 years. Technically, the company dissolves when a member dies, quits, or retires.

If you plan to operate in several states, you must determine how a state will treat an LLC formed in another state. If you decide on an LLC structure, be sure to use the services of an experienced accountant who is familiar with the various rules and regulations of LLCs.

> **TAKE NOTES!**
> **WEEK 1**
>
> If you anticipate several years of losses in your business, keep in mind you cannot deduct corporate losses on your personal tax return. Business structures such as partnerships, sole proprietorships, and S corporations allow you to take those deductions.

Another recent development is the limited liability partnership (LLP). With an LLP, the general partners have limited liability. For example, the partners are liable for their own malpractice and not that of their partners. This legal form works well for those involved in a professional practice, such as physicians.

The Nonprofit Option

Are you organizing your venture as a nonprofit corporation? Unlike a for-profit business, a nonprofit may be eligible for certain benefits, such as sales, property, and income tax exemptions at the state level. The IRS points out that while most federal tax-exempt organizations are nonprofit organizations, organizing as a nonprofit at the state level does not automatically grant you an exemption from federal income tax.

Another major difference between a profit and nonprofit business deals with the treatment of the profits. With a for-profit business, the owners and shareholders generally receive the profits. With a nonprofit, any money that is left after the organization has paid its bills is put back into the organization. Some types of nonprofits can receive contributions that are tax deductible to the individual who contributes to the organization. Keep in mind that nonprofits are organized to provide some benefit to the public.

Nonprofits are incorporated under the laws of the state in which they are established. To receive federal tax-exempt status, the organization must apply with the IRS. First, you must have an Employer Identification Number (EIN) and then apply for recognition of exemption by filing Form 1023 (Application for Recognition of Exemption Under Section 501(c)(3) of the Internal Revenue Code) or 1024 (Other Tax-Exempt Organizations), with the necessary filing fee. Both forms are available online at irs.gov.

The IRS identifies the different types of nonprofit organizations by the tax code by which they qualify for exempt status. One of the most common forms is 501(c)(3), which is set up to do charitable, educational, scientific, religious, and literary work. This includes a wide range of organizations, from continuing education centers to outpatient clinics and hospitals.

The IRS also mandates that there are certain activities tax-exempt organizations can't engage in if they want to keep their exempt status. For example, a section 50l(c)(3) organization cannot intervene in political campaigns.

Remember, nonprofits still have to pay employment taxes, but in some states they may be exempt from paying sales tax. Check with your state to make sure you understand how nonprofit status is treated in your area. In addition, nonprofits may be hit with unrelated business income tax. This is regular income from a trade or business that is not substantially related to the charitable purpose. Any exempt organization under Section 501(a) or Section 529(a) must file Form 990-T (Exempt Organization Business Income Tax Return) if the organization has gross income of $1,000 or more from an unrelated business and must pay tax on the income.

If your nonprofit has revenues of more than $25,000 a year (check this number, as it can change), be sure to file an annual report (Form 990) with the IRS. Form 990-EZ is a shortened version of 990 and is designed for use by small exempt organizations with total assets at the end of the year of less than $25,000.

Form 990 asks you to provide information on the organization's income, expenses and staff salaries. You also may have to comply with a similar state requirement. The IRS report must be made available for public review. If you use the calendar year as your accounting period, file Form 990 by May 15.

For more information on IRS tax-exempt status, download IRS Publication 557 (Tax-Exempt Status for Your Organization) at irs.gov.

Even after you settle on a business structure, remember that the circumstances that make one type of business organization favorable are always subject to changes in the laws. It makes sense to reassess your form of business from time to time to make sure you are using the one that provides the most benefits.

ONLINE TOOLS

Yes, it's a complicated area, and yes, you do need an attorney as a guide, but you can also reduce legal bills, improve your own understanding and streamline the process by working online to inform yourself before you walk into the attorney's office.

At Palo Alto Software, we've worked for years with the Company Corporation at incorporate.com. We chose them because they've been around for a long time and have a good track record with our customers. When you go to their website, you'll see they offer a wide range of related services, including not just incorporation but also LLC formation, corporate documents, and information and advice. Still, it's best to be cautious. We still recommend working with an attorney you know.

However, we don't want to limit our listing to the ones we know best. There are other online vendors offering similar services. We may not have personal experience with them, but they may be just as good.

- Bizfilings: bizfilings.com
- Legalzoom: legalzoom.com
- A Google search for "online incorporation" reveals a lot more.

Several of the online articles at bplans.com cover topics related to legal establishment. These are all online at bplans.com, in the Small Business Articles and Startups sections.

- "Nonprofit Corporation Basics"
- "How to Protect a Business Idea"
- "Choosing Your Business Name:" business plan help and small business articles, bplans.com
- "How to Form a Corporation"
- "How to Form a Limited Liability Company (LLC)"
- Check our site, 3weeks2start.com, for updates too.

Here are some other sites offering legal advice and legal information. Remember, don't take anything you read on the internet as necessarily true. Use this information as a head start, but be careful too.

Free legal advice, in general, can be found at these and many other sites.

- freeadvice.com
- law.com
- lawguru.com
- legal.com
- alllaw.com
- gigalaw.com

We've worked for years with Nolo Press, publisher of law-related books, legal forms, and legal software for people who aren't attorneys,

- nolo.com

For help finding a lawyer, try:

- legalmatch.com

Every state has their own website (see Table 4-1). Contact information for all the states can also be found at division-of-corporations.org/index.htm.

3 WEEKS TO STARTUP

Table 4-1: State Web Sources for Legal Information	
State	**Web Source**
Alabama	sos.state.al.us/businessservices/default.aspx
Alaska	dced.state.ak.us/occ
Arizona	azcc.gov/divisions/corporations
Arkansas	ark.org/sos/ofs/docs/index.php
California	sos.ca.gov/business
Colorado	sos.state.co.us/pubs/business/main.htm
Connecticut	ct.gov/sots
Delaware	corp.delaware.gov
Florida	sunbiz.org
Georgia	sos.georgia.gov/corporations
Hawaii	hawaii.gov/dcca/areas/breg
Idaho	idsos.state.id.us
Illinois	cyberdriveillinois.com/departments/business_services/home.html
Indiana	secure.in.gov/sos/bus_service/online_corps/name_search.aspx
Iowa	sos.state.ia.us
Kansas	kcc.state.ks.us
Kentucky	sos.ky.gov
Louisiana	sos.louisiana.gov
Maine	maine.gov/sos/cec/corp/incorporating.html
Maryland	blis.state.md.us
Massachusetts	sec.state.ma.us/cor/coridx.htm
Michigan	michigan.gov/dleg/0,1607,7-154-35299---,00.html
Minnesota	sos.state.mn.us/business/typeoffile.html
Mississippi	sos.state.ms.us/busserv/corp/corporations.asp
Missouri	sos.mo.gov/business/corporations
Montana	sos.mt.gov/bsb/index.asp

Table 4-1: State Web Sources for Legal Information

State	Web Source
Nebraska	sos.state.ne.us/business/corp_serv
Nevada	division-of-corporations.org/nevada-secretary-of-state-corporations.htm
New Hampshire	sos.nh.gov/corporate/index.html
New Jersey	state.nj.us/njbusiness
New Mexico	nmprc.state.nm.us
New York	dos.state.ny.us/corp/corphtml
North Carolina	secretary.state.nc.us/corporations
North Dakota	nd.gov/sos/businessserv/registrations/types/corporations/general/faq.html
Ohio	sos.state.oh.us/sos/businessservices/corp.aspx
Oklahoma	occ.state.ok.us
Oregon	filinginoregon.com
Pennsylvania	dos.state.pa.us/corps
Rhode Island	sec.state.ri.us/corps
South Carolina	scsos.com/corporations.htm
South Dakota	sdsos.gov
Tennessee	state.tn.us/sos
Texas	sos.state.tx.us/corp/index.shtml
Utah	corporations.utah.gov
Vermont	sec.state.vt.us/corps/index.htm
Virginia	scc.virginia.gov
Washington	secstate.wa.gov/corps
West Virginia	wvsos.com/business/startup/corporation.htm
Wisconsin	wdfi.org/corporations
Wyoming	soswy.state.wy.us/corporat/corporat.htm

CHAPTER 5

GETTING FINANCED

In Chapter 1, we suggested

you find yourself on the different scales and sizes of startup businesses. We set up at least three points on the scale, the simple self-financed bootstrapping business at the low end, the business requiring serious investment towards the middle of the range, and the business seeking serious professional investment at the high end. And then we suggested, as we discussed your business planning towards the end of that chapter, that you should make some educated guesses about how much money you'd need.

The sense of scale is important now as we look at raising money for your new business. What makes sense for financing changes as the amounts go up.

Starting a business almost always takes money. You have to spend money getting necessary startup assets like equipment, signs, and fixing up a location. You have to spend money renting a location while you fix it up, and paying the people involved. Usually you spend money on marketing as well. Furthermore, even after you're finally up and running, you're usually not breaking even month to month until the business acquires some momentum. So you need to finance your startup; that means either you invest your own money or you get somebody else's money. This chapter covers figuring out how much money you need and how to raise that money.

> ### RED TAPE ALERT!
>
> You're not likely to be fully financed in less than three weeks if you need to find outside investors. It's possible with some bank financing, and remotely possible with some banks using SBA guaranteed loans (but not likely). It's perfectly reasonable if you are using your own money or if you have friends and family investors already lined up, or even if you are going to borrow against personal assets. It's also reasonable to be legally established, have a team ready, and your planning done, and to have begun the process of seeking investors, all within three weeks.

There are exceptions. Let's say, for example, that you're an accomplished graphic artist. You resign from your job at the graphic arts firm and strike out on your own. You already own your computer equipment, and your first sales call results in a lucrative contract. You're on your way, and you haven't had to invest any money. The same might happen with an attorney (although office expenses can be daunting), management consultant, or freelance writer. Even with these businesses, however, you will need enough money to cover your personal expenses until your first client pays you.

Set the Right Scale

How much money you need has a big influence on how you're going to get it. The first thing to do is go back over your estimate. Make sure you've got as good an educated guess as you can get.

Understand that there's risk here. Your startup money is roughly equivalent to how much money you stand to lose, if your startup fails. That's not a guarantee, because with the wrong kind of management decisions—where you get into more debt as the company situation worsens—you can lose a lot more.

A second good reason to pay special attention to your estimated starting costs is that you need to have a good idea of what it costs to get it started —and started well. Factors like packaging, for example, can be critical for some kinds of startups. If you're starting one of those businesses that depends on good packaging, but you don't plan for enough money to get the packaging done, then the rest of your spending could be wasted. And that's just one example.

A Few Thousand Dollars or Less

If the amount you need is this small, try to raise it yourself from your personal assets. If that's too hard to do, it's okay; you can look for credit card financing or turn to friends and family. We understand. But it's so much better, especially when there's relatively little money involved, to just do it yourself, after which you own the business and you run it.

This is a typical three-week startup; more financing takes more time.

Tens of Thousands of Dollars

You're in between with this amount, unless you have it to spend. The legal work involved with dealing with outside investors is very expensive, making the economics hard to manage if you need only tens of thousands. Talk to your local bank about SBA guaranteed loans for these amounts, but you

TAKE NOTES!

WEEK 1

If there were a good time for a business plan, it's before you start talking to people—friends and family, professionals, bankers, whomever—about getting funded. A business plan sets out in writing the expectations for the company. It shows family members who are putting up the money that you are serious and that you plan to succeed. And it helps keep the entrepreneur—you—mindful of responsibilities to family members who backed you and keeps you on track to fulfill your obligations.

need to know that these typically require you to put in 30 percent of the total yourself. There are credit card programs to finance these amounts, but they come with high interest rates. A lot of people who have equity in their homes end up borrowing against that equity to finance the business. And a lot of times this money comes from friends and family.

Hundreds of Thousands

At this amount, you're probably looking at an SBA-guaranteed commercial loan through a business bank, or friends and family (if you can raise this much through friends and family), or local angel investment.

TAKE NOTES!

The best place to begin looking for financing is in the mirror. Self-financing is the number-one form of financing used by most business startups. In addition, when you approach other financing sources such as bankers, venture capitalists, or the government, they will want to know exactly how much of your own money you are putting into the venture. After all, if you don't have enough faith in your business to risk your own money, why should anyone else risk theirs?

Millions

When you need millions of dollars, you're at the high scale and probably need to seek professional investment, such as sophisticated high-end angel investment or venture capital.

Bootstrapping vs. Getting Financed

Begin by doing a thorough inventory of your assets. You are likely to uncover resources you didn't even know you had. Assets include savings accounts, equity in real estate, retirement accounts, vehicles, recreational equipment, and collections. You may decide to sell some assets for cash or to use them as collateral for a loan.

If you have investments, you may be able to use them as a resource. Low-interest-margin loans against stocks and securities can be arranged through your brokerage accounts.

The downside here is that if the market should fall and your securities are your loan collateral, you'll get a margin call from your broker, requesting you to supply more collateral. If you can't do that within a certain time, you'll be asked to sell some of your securities to shore up the collateral. Also take a look at your personal line of credit. Some businesses have success-fully been started on credit cards, although this is one of the most expensive ways to finance yourself.

If you own a home, consider getting a home equity loan on the part of the mortgage that you have already paid off. The bank will either provide a lump-sum loan payment or extend a line of credit based on the equity in your home. Depending on the value of your home, a home-equity loan could become a substantial line of credit. If you have $50,000 in equity, you could possibly set up a line of credit of up to $40,000. Home-equity loans carry relatively low interest rates, and all interest paid on a loan of up to $100,000 is tax-deductible. But be sure you can repay the loan—you can lose your home if you do not repay.

Consider borrowing against cash-value life insurance. You can use the value built up in a cash-value life insurance policy as a ready source of cash. The interest rates are reasonable because the insurance companies always get their money back. You don't even have to make payments if you do not want to. Neither the amount you borrow nor the interest that accrues has to be repaid. The only loss is that if you die and the debt hasn't been repaid, that money is deducted from the amount your beneficiary will receive.

If you have a 401(k) retirement plan through your employer and are start-ing a part-time business while you keep your full-time job, consider bor-rowing against the plan. It's very common for such plans to allow you to borrow a percentage of your money that doesn't exceed $50,000. The inter-est rate is usually about 6 percent with a specified repayment schedule. The downside of borrowing from your 401(k) is that if you lose your job, the loan has to be repaid in a short period of time—often 60 days. Consult the plan's documentation to see if this is an option for you.

Another option is to use the funds in your individual retirement account (IRA). Within the laws governing IRAs, you can actually withdraw money from an IRA as long as you replace it within 60 days. This is not a loan, so you don't pay interest. This is a withdrawal that you're allowed to keep for 60 days. It's possible for a highly organized entrepreneur to juggle funds among several IRAs. But if you're one day late—for any reason—you'll be hit with a 10 percent premature withdrawal fee, and the money you haven't returned becomes taxable.

If you are employed, another way to finance your business is by squirreling away money from your current salary until you have enough to launch the business. If you don't want to wait, consider moonlighting or cutting your full-time job back to part time. This ensures you'll have some steady funds rolling in until your business starts to soar.

> ## TAKE NOTES!
>
> Is this new business worth risking your personal relationships with friends and family?
>
> Think of this first: What if you fail? Then: What if you don't fail, but the business drags on, dragging you down, and you'd like to give up but you can't because it would mean telling friends and family they've lost their money?

People generally have more assets than they realize. Use as much of your own money as possible to get started; remember, the larger your own investment, the easier it will be for you to acquire capital from other sources.

Friends and Family

Your own resources may not be enough to give you the capital you need. After self-financing, the second most popular source for startup money is composed of friends, relatives, and business associates.

"Family and friends are great sources of financing," says Tonia Papke, president and founder of MDI Consulting. "These people know you have integrity and will grant you a loan based on the strength of your character."

Sometimes it makes sense. People with whom you have close relationships know you are reliable and competent, so there should be no problem in asking for a loan, right? Keep in mind, however, that asking for financial help isn't the same as borrowing the car. While squeezing money out of family and friends may seem an easy alternative to dealing with bankers, it can actually be a much more delicate situation. Papke warns that your family members or friends may think lending you money gives them license to meddle. "And if the business fails," she says, "the issue of paying the money back can be a problem, putting the whole relationship in jeopardy."

Clearly, this sounds good enough in a startup mode but later on relationships may be at stake. Fortunately, there are ways to work out the details and make the business relationship advantageous for all parties involved. If you handle the situation correctly and tactfully, you may gain more than finances for your business—you may end up strengthening the personal relationship as well.

Make sure to look at our Online Tools section for services that help you document these agreements with friends and family. Whether it's an investment or a loan, you should get it written in clear legal terms.

Loan or Investment

When considering asking friends and/or family to help finance your startup, distinguish in your mind whether you are borrowing money, seeking investment, or both. There are clear tradeoffs. You can't present this to friends and family unless you understand it yourself, and set your goals.

- Borrowing money means you will pay it back, regardless of success or failure of your new business. It's a loan, and loans need to be paid back.

- Investment means spending money to buy a portion of ownership of your company. Investment is not to be paid back if the company fails, and means permanent ownership of some percentage of the business, usually including some voting rights and dividends if the company does well. People who are part owners of your business have a right to know what you're doing and influence your decisions. They don't have a right to get their money back if you fail.

- There are mixes of both loans and investment. These require careful documentation. Many times a private person who lends money to a startup will receive some ownership shares and also have the full amount of the loan paid back. This is often fair compensation for a

risky loan. Another common option is to give the lender equity ownership unless the loan is paid back, or until the loan is paid back. There
are variations.

You may want to seek the advice of an attorney to distinguish between these
different options clearly, and develop the correct documentation. You can
also find additional information on this, and examples, at some of the websites listed in the Online Tools section at the end of this chapter.

The Right Source

As you approach friends and family, remember that mixing business and
personal relationships can threaten the personal relationships. Think about
the people you approach in those terms. Will they understand the separation between business and personal? Can you make them understand? Or
will this become a personal favor that requires paybacks, or a way to
demand favoritism and attention later? These are important questions.

A good way to approach people is to talk to them about your business
idea, and, after describing it, asking them whether or not they know anybody who might be interested. That makes things less awkward if they
aren't interested. And it makes it easy for them to show interest.

It there is interest, follow up professionally. Depending on your relationship and how you decide to proceed, you might want to meet with the
person in your office—make it a business setting—or send a summary
memo (see page 103), or, if it seems appropriate, a complete business plan.
You do want the follow-up to set the discussion to a business level, and
move it away from personal.

Normally a large part of informing this person is compiling a business
plan, which you should bring to your meeting. Explain the plan in detail,
and do the presentation just as you would in front of a banker or other
investor. Your goal is to get the other person on your side and make him or
her as excited as you are about the possibilities of your business.

During your meeting—and, in fact, whenever you discuss a business deal,
either loan or investment—try to separate the personal from the business as

much as possible. Difficult as this may sound, it's critical to the health of your relationship. You must make the distinction between business and personal as clear as possible.

Make sure you're able to take rejection. In fact, you should make it very easy for any friends and family to reject your offer. If you insist, you might have people joining you reluctantly, and that will cause problems later on.

Putting It On Paper

Now it's time to put the deal (loan or investment) in motion. First, you must state how much money you need, what you'll use it for, and how much of your company you are giving in exchange,

> ### TAKE NOTES!
>
> **WEEK 7**
>
> He was about 45 years old. He spoke to the class about starting a business, and running a business, and of his experience of 15 years manufacturing sailboats. He had started the business because he loved sailboats, but it hadn't gone well.
>
> "So why don't you just give up?" asked one of the students listening.
>
> "Because I can't face the family and friends who believed in me to tell them that it's over, and they've lost all their money."

or, if it is a loan, how you'll pay it back. Next, draw up the legal papers—an agreement stating that the person will indeed put money into the business.

In this particular area, there are some excellent online tools that have really improved and simplified the process of properly documenting business dealings with friends and family. CircleLending.com was started to focus in exactly this area; it was purchased and became virginmoneyus.com. Another option is prosper.com.

Too frequently, business owners fail to take the time to figure out exactly what kind of paperwork should be completed when they borrow or take investment from family or friends. "Often, small-business owners put more thought into figuring out what type of car to buy than how to structure this type of lending arrangement," says Steven I. Levey of accounting firm GHP Financial Group. Unfortunately, once you've made an error in this area, it's difficult to correct it.

Your loan agreement needs to specify whether the loan is secured (that is, the lender holds title to part of your property) or unsecured, what the payments will be, when they're due, and what the interest is. If the money is in the form of an investment, you have to establish whether the business is a part-

TAKE NOTES!

Don't do friends and family investment deals without defining your terms: How much ownership of the company do your investors get, for how much money.

nership or corporation, and what role, if any, the investor will play. To be sure you and your family and friends have a clear idea of what financial obligations are being created, you have a mutual responsibility to make sure everyone is informed about the process and decide together how best to proceed.

Make sure you deal specifically and concretely with the details. Both parties have legal responsibilities, and both parties have monetary responsibilities. If it is a loan, specify repayment terms, interest rates, and what happens on default. If it is an investment, make sure both sides understand the share of the business that changes ownership, and what that means in the future. What voice will shareholders have in important decisions?

All agreements should always be in writing. There are legal requirements and tax requirements as well.

Taxing Matters

Putting the agreement on paper also protects both you and your lender come tax time. Relying on informal and verbal agreements results in tax quagmires. "In these cases, you have a burden of proof to show the IRS that [the money] was not a gift," says Tom Ochsenschlager, vice president of taxation for the American Institute of Certified Public Accountants. If the IRS views it as a gift, then the lender becomes subject to the federal gift tax rules and will have to pay taxes on the money if it is more than the relatively small amount allowed ($12,000 as this is written, but that changes as the law changes). Also, make sure the person providing the money as a loan charges an interest rate that reflects a fair market value.

If your friend or family member wants to give you a no-interest loan, make sure the loan is not more than $100,000. If you borrow more, the IRS will slap on what it considers to be market-rate interest, better known as "imputed interest," on the lender. That means that while your friend or relative may not be receiving any interest on the money you borrowed, the IRS will tax them as if they were.

No interest is imputed if the aggregate loans are less than $10,000. Between $10,000 and $100,000, the imputed amount is limited to your net investment income, such as interest, dividends and, in some cases, capital gains. To determine the interest rate on these transactions, the IRS uses what it calls the applicable federal rate, which it sets on a regular basis. Keep in mind that if you don't put all the details of the loan in writing, it will be very difficult for you to deduct the interest you pay on it. Additionally, the relative who lent the money won't be able to take a tax deduction on the loss if you find you can't repay.

To be absolutely safe, Ochsenschlager recommends that you make the friend or relative who is providing the money one of the business's shareholders. This effectively makes the transaction an investment in your company and also makes it easier from a tax standpoint for your friend or relative to write off the transaction as an ordinary loss if the business fails. (This applies only if the total amount your company received for its stock, including the relative's investment, does not exceed $1 million.)

In addition, "if your company is wildly successful, your relative will have an equity interest in the business, and his or her original investment will be worth quite a bit more," Ochsenschlager says. In contrast, if a relative gives you a loan and your company goes under, the relative's loss would generally be considered a personal bad debt. This creates more of a tax disadvantage because personal bad debts can be claimed as capital losses only to offset capital gains. If the capital loss exceeds the capital gains, only $3,000 of the loss can be used against ordinary income in any given year. Thus, an individual making a large loan that isn't repaid may have to wait several years to realize the tax benefits from the loss.

If the loan that can't be repaid is a business loan, however, the lender receives a deduction against ordinary income and can take deductions even before the loan becomes totally worthless. (One catch: The IRS takes a very narrow view of what qualifies as a business loan. To qualify as a business loan, the loan would have to be connected to the lender's business.) This will be difficult, so consult an accountant about the best way to structure the loan for maximum tax benefits to both parties.

Making your relative a shareholder doesn't mean you'll have to put up with Mom or Pop in the business. Depending on your company's organizational structure, your friend or relative can be a silent partner if your company is set up as a partnership, or a silent shareholder if you are organized as an S corporation or limited liability company.

Keep 'Em Happy

Even with every detail documented, your responsibilities are far from over. Don't make assumptions or take people for granted just because they are friends or family members. Communication is key.

If your relative or friend is not actively involved in the business, make sure you contact him or her once every month or two to explain how the business is going. Beware of misunderstandings over how much interest and oversight is involved.

And, of course, there are the payments. Though friends or relatives who invest in your business understand the risks, you must never take the loan for granted. Payments must always be made. Don't slip on any payments, or the entire structure of the deal could fall apart.

Debt Financing

As we suggested earlier, many startups use money borrowed from local banks against the entrepreneur's personal assets. That involves you and your relationship with your bank, and the banker will do the explaining. We want to focus here, instead, on borrowing help from the government.

How To Get Government Loans

You've probably seen the nationally televised advertisements about free government money, in which a loud man with a loud sports coat (usually covered in dollar signs) promises "free government money." His name is Matthew Lesko, and what he sells is a database of government programs. It's a long list.

Unfortunately, the idea that the U.S. government has a lot of easy money is extremely exaggerated. While there are a few programs that apply to some entrepreneurs, they are rare. Most of what is available is help with borrowing money, like loan guarantees or subsidized interest rates, and most of that requires that you put in serious amounts of initial startup capital yourself.

In the real world, the main source of federal government startup help is the U.S. Small Business Administration (SBA). The federal government has a vested interest in encouraging the growth of small business. As a result, some SBA loans have less stringent requirements for owner's equity and collateral than do commercial loans, making the SBA an excellent financing source for startups. In addition, many SBA loans are for smaller sums than most banks are willing to lend.

TAKE NOTES!

If you have been laid off or lost your job, another source of startup capital may be available to you. Some states have instituted self-employment programs as part of their unemployment insurance systems.

People who are receiving unemployment benefits and meet certain requirements are recruited into entrepreneurial training programs that show them how to start businesses. This gives them an opportunity to use their unemployment funds for startup, while boosting their chances of success.

Contact the department in your state that handles unemployment benefits to see if such a program is available to you.

Of course, that doesn't mean the SBA is giving money away. In fact, the SBA does not actually make direct loans; instead, it provides loan guarantees to entrepreneurs, promising the bank to pay back a certain percentage of your loan if you are unable to.

Banks participate in the SBA program as regular, certified or preferred lenders. The SBA can help you prepare your loan package, which you then submit to banks. If the bank approves you, it submits your loan package to the SBA. Applications submitted by regular lenders are reviewed by the

SBA in an average of two weeks, certified lender applications are reviewed in three days, and approval through preferred lenders is even faster.

RED TAPE ALERT!

When seeking an SBA loan, choose your bank carefully. Look for one that is experienced in this type of loan.

The most basic eligibility requirement for SBA loans is the ability to repay the loan from cash flow, but the SBA also looks at personal credit history, industry experience, or other evidence of management ability, collateral, and owner's equity contributions. If you own 20 percent or more equity in the business, the SBA asks that you personally guarantee the loan. After all, you can't ask the government to back you if you're not willing to back yourself. The SBA offers a wide variety of loan programs for businesses at various stages of development. A closer look at these SBA programs follows.

7(a) Guaranty Loan Program

The biggest and the most popular SBA loan program is the 7(a) Guaranty Loan Program. The SBA does not lend money itself, but provides maximum loan guarantees of up to $1.5 million or 75 percent of the total loan amount, whichever is less. For loans that are less than $150,000, the maximum guarantee is 85 percent of the total loan amount. SBA policy prohibits lenders from charging many of the usual fees associated with commercial loans. Still, you can expect to pay a one-time guarantee fee, which the agency charges the lender and allows the lender to pass on to you.

A 7(a) loan can be used for many business purposes including real estate, expansion, equipment, working capital, and inventory. The money can be paid back over as long as 25 years for real estate and equipment and 7 years for working capital. Interest rates vary with the type of loan.

SBAExpress Program

A general 7(a) loan may suit your business's needs best, but the 7(a) program also offers several specialized loans. One of them, the SBAExpress

Program, promises quick processing for amounts less than $350,000. SBA Express can get you an answer quickly because approved SBAExpress lenders can use their own documentation and procedures to attach an SBA guarantee to an approved loan without having to wait for SBA approval. The SBA guarantees up to 50 percent of SBAExpress loans.

CAPLines

For businesses that need working capital on a short-term or cyclical basis, the SBA has a collection of revolving and nonrevolving lines of credit called CAPLines. A revolving loan is similar to a credit card, with which you carry a balance that goes up or down, depending on the payments and amounts you borrow. With nonrevolving lines of credit, you borrow a flat amount and pay it off over a set period of time.

CAPLine loans provide business owners short-term credit, with loans that are guaranteed up to $1.5 million. There are five loan and line-of-credit programs that operate under the CAPLines umbrella:

1. Seasonal line of credit: designed to help businesses during peak seasons, when they face increases in inventory, accounts receivable and labor costs

2. Contract line of credit: used to finance labor and material costs involved in carrying out contracts

3. Standard asset-based line of credit: helps businesses unable to meet credit qualifications associated with long-term credit; provides financing for cyclical, growth, recurring, or short-term needs

4. Small asset-based revolving line of credit: provides smaller, asset-based lines of credit (up to $200,000), with requirements that are not as strict as the standard asset-based program

5. Builder's line of credit: used to finance labor and materials costs for small general contractors and builders who are constructing or renovating commercial or residential buildings

Each of the five credit lines has a five-year maturity but can be tailored to the borrower's needs.

Pre-Qualification Program

The SBA's Pre-Qualification Loan Program helps pre-qualify low-income borrowers, disabled business owners, veterans, exporters, rural entrepreneurs, and specialized industries for loans. Under the program, entrepreneurs can apply for loans and get up to $250,000. With the aid of private intermediary organizations chosen by the SBA, eligible entrepreneurs prepare a business plan and complete a loan application. The intermediary submits the application to the SBA.

If the application is approved, the SBA issues you a pre-qualification letter, which you can then take, along with your loan package, to a commercial bank. With the SBA's guarantee attached, the bank is more likely to approve the loan.

MicroLoan Program

SBA financing isn't limited to the 7(a) group of loans. The MicroLoan Program helps entrepreneurs get very small loans, ranging from less than $100 up to $35,000. The loans can be used for machinery and equipment, furniture and fixtures, inventory, supplies and working capital, but they cannot be used to pay existing debts. This program is unique because it assists borrowers who generally do not meet traditional lenders' credit standards.

MicroLoans are administered through nonprofit intermediaries. These organizations receive loans from the SBA and then turn around and make loans to entrepreneurs. Small businesses applying for MicroLoan financing may be required to complete some business-skills training before a loan application is considered.

Maturity terms and interest rates for MicroLoans vary, although terms are usually short; the loans typically take less than a week to process.

504 Loan Program

On the opposite end of the loan size spectrum is the 504 Loan, which provides long-term, fixed-rate loans for financing fixed assets, usually real estate and equipment. Loans are most often used for growth and expansion.

504 Loans are made through Certified Development Companies (CDCs)—nonprofit intermediaries that work with the SBA, banks, and businesses looking for financing. There are CDCs throughout the country, each covering an assigned region.

If you are seeking funds up to $1.5 million to buy or renovate a building or put in some major equipment, consider bringing your business plan and financial statements to a CDC. Typical percentages for this type of package are 50 percent financed by the bank, 40 percent by the CDC, and 10 percent by the business.

In exchange for this below-market, fixed-rate financing, the SBA expects the small business to create or retain jobs or to meet certain public policy goals. Businesses that meet these public policy goals are those whose expansion will contribute to a business district revitalization, such as an empowerment zone; a minority-owned business; an export or manufacturing company; or a company whose expansion will contribute to rural development.

> ## TAKE NOTES!
>
> **WEEK 1**
>
> Women business owners have a friend in Washington: the Office of Women's Business Ownership (OWBO), part of the SBA. The OWBO coordinates federal efforts that support women entrepreneurs through business training and technical assistance, and by providing access to financing, federal contracts, and international trade opportunities.
>
> In addition, the office directs Women's Business Centers in 48 states. Women's Business Centers provide assistance, training, and business counseling through the SBA.
>
> For information about OWBO services, contact the OWBO at 409 Third St. SW, 6th Fl., Washington, DC 20416, (800) U-ASK-SBA, or visit SBA.gov/financing/special/women. html.

Empowerment Zones/Enterprise Communities

Since 1980, more than 35 states have established programs to designate enterprise zones, offering tax breaks and other incentives to businesses that locate in certain economically disadvantaged areas. States vary widely in the number of zones designated, incentives offered, and success of the programs. In some areas, businesses may also qualify for lower utility rates or low-interest financing from eligible government jurisdictions. To be eligible for any of these incentives, businesses must generally meet certain criteria, such as creating new jobs in a community.

The Empowerment Zone/Enterprise Communities initiative was set up to provide tax incentives and stimulate community investment and development. Specified urban and rural communities will receive grants and tax breaks for businesses in the area. The federal government's involvement means entrepreneurs in those areas can get federal (not just state) tax breaks.

If you choose to locate in an enterprise or empowerment zone, look beyond the tax breaks to consider long-term concerns such as availability of a work force and accessibility of your target market. Make sure the zone offers other support services, such as streamlined licensing and permitting procedures. Most zones that succeed have high development potential to begin with, with good highway access, a solid infrastructure, and a trainable labor force.

For more information on enterprise zones, contact your state's economic development department or call HUD's Office of Community Renewal at (202) 708-6339.

8(a) Program

The SBA's 8(a) program is a small-business set-aside program that gives companies certified as socially and economically disadvantaged (i.e., owned by minorities) access to government contracts as well as management and technical assistance to help them develop their businesses. The 8(a) program is envisioned as a starter program for minority-owned businesses, which must leave the program after nine years.

Entrepreneurs who participate in the 8(a) program are eligible for the 7(a) Guaranty Loan and the Pre-Qualification Programs. Socially disadvantaged categories include race, ethnicity, gender, or physical handicap. To qualify as economically disadvantaged, the person must have a net worth of less than $250,000.

3 WEEKS TO STARTUP

Export Working Capital Program

If you are planning to export, you should investigate the Export Working Capital Program. This allows a 90 percent guarantee on loans up to $1.5 million. If the loan is for a single transaction, the maximum loan term is 18 months. If the loan is for a revolving line of credit, loan maturities are typically 12 months, with two 12-month renewal options. Loans can be for single or multiple export sales and can be used for pre-shipment working capital or post-shipment exposure coverage; however, they can't be used to buy fixed assets.

> ### TAKE NOTES!
>
> **WEEK 7**
>
> If exporting is part of your business game plan, the Export-Import Bank of the United States (Ex-Im Bank) can be your biggest ally. The Ex-Im Bank is committed to supporting small exporters and provides many financing tools targeted to small businesses.
>
> Business owners can contact the Ex-Im Bank directly at (800) 565-3946 or through any commercial lender that works with the agency (see the Lender Locator at ExIm.gov). Based in Washington, DC, the Ex-Im Bank also has regional offices in Chicago, Houston, Miami, and New York City, as well as Long Beach, San Diego, and San Francisco, California.

Special Purpose Loans

If you believe you have a special case that requires extra help, you may be in luck. Of course, keep in mind that everybody believes they deserve extra help with financing, but in many situations, the SBA has a loan program tailor-made for your situation. If you're starting a business, for instance, that pollutes the environment, but you plan to spend additional money to reduce the toxins you're putting into the air, soil, or water, you may be eligible for a Pollution Control Loan, which is basically a 7(a) loan earmarked for businesses that are planning, designing, or installing a pollution control facility. The facility must prevent, reduce, abate, or control any form of pollution, including recycling.

If your business plans to be active in international trade or your top competition is cheap imports, the International Trade Loan Program is something you should look into. The SBA can guarantee up to $1.75 million for a combination of fixed-asset financing (facilities and equipment), as well as

Export Working Capital Program (see page 17.8) assistance. The fixed-asset portion of the loan guaranty cannot exceed $1.25 million, and the nonfixed-asset portion cannot exceed $1.25 million.

TAKE NOTES!

Worried your business acumen isn't as sharp is it could be? Wishing you had taken an accounting class instead of that film history course on John Wayne? Then the Small Business Training Network might be for you.

Also known as the E-Business Institute, the Small Business Training Network is an internet-based learning environment—functioning like a virtual campus. As their website says, they offer online courses, workshops, information resources, learning tools, and direct access to electronic counseling and other forms of technical assistance.

The national network of SBDCs (Small Business Development Centers) includes about 1,000 SBDCs that also have classes on starting and running a business.

The classes run the gamut from how to start your own business—with titles like "A Primer on Exporting" and "Identify Your Target Market"—to how to build a website, understand taxes, and plan for retirement. Most of these workshops are self-paced and usually extremely topical. Some classes were developed within the SBA, while others have been developed by academic institutions. For more information, log on to www.sba.gov/training. For SBDCs, try www.asbdc-us.org

As the SBA's website says, "Numerous variations of the SBA's basic loan programs are made available to support special needs." So if you believe your business might fall into a category in which the SBA can funnel additional loans to you, it's definitely an avenue worth checking out.

Making the Most of the SBA

The SBA is more than a source of financing. It can help with many aspects of business startup and growth. The SBA is an excellent place to get help with "getting your ducks in a row" before seeking financing. SBA services include free resources to help you with such tasks as writing a business plan and improving your presentation skills—all of which boost your chances of getting a loan.

For more information on other SBA programs, visit the SBA's website at sba.gov, call the SBA's Answer Desk at (800) U-ASK-SBA, or contact your local SBA district office. Your SBA district office can mail you a startup booklet and a list of lenders, and inform you about specialized loans tailored to your industry and where to go for help with your business plan or putting together financial statements.

Government Grants

When most people think of grants, they think of money given free to non-profit organizations. But for-profit companies, and frequently startups, can also win grant money. How do you find these grants? Unfortunately, locating a grant is a little like looking for your soul mate. The right grant is out

> **WEEK 1**
>
> **TAKE NOTES!**
>
> If you believe your future business could contribute to community development or empower a group of economically disadvantaged people, visit your state economic development office to find out what types of community development grants may be available.

there, but you're going to have to do a lot of looking to find a good match. Start at the government site at grants.gov.

Another good place to do research is at your local bookstore. There are a lot of books about getting grants, with titles like *Grant Writing for Dummies* (Wiley) by Beverly A. Browning, *Grantseeker's Toolkit* (Wiley) by Cheryl Carter New and James Quick, and *Demystifying Grantseeking* (Wiley) by Larissa Golden Brown and Martin John Brown. And then there's the bible of grant books: *The Grants Register* (Palgrave Macmillan), an annual publication that lists more than 3,500 grants.

There are other places to look, of course. The most logical place to get an infusion of cash is from Uncle Sam, but you can also win grants from foundations and even some corporations.

Even in the most economically challenged of times, the government is one of the best sources for grants. For instance, the National Institute of Standards and Technology's Advanced Technology Program offers grants to co-fund "high-risk, high-payoff projects" that will benefit American industry. Whatever the project is, you can bet it will be scrutinized by a board of qualified experts and academia.

The Small Business Innovation Research (SBIR) Program is another government program that gives grants. The SBIR Program specializes in small businesses looking for funding for high-risk technologies. The catch: Unlike the Advanced Technology Program, the technology must meet the research and development needs of the federal government. Founded in 1982, the SBIR recently awarded $2 billion to startups, with grants going to software, biotechnology, health-care, and defense companies. So if you're planning on opening a pizzeria, you might have trouble with this one.

WEEK 1

TAKE NOTES!

Experienced investors generally agree that legal costs and legal hassles are about the same for a $100,000 investment as for a $10 million investment.

But there are federal grants awarded to food and nutrition companies. For instance, a pizzeria that caters to children and specializes in serving nutritious, healthy pizzas may be able to win a grant. You can also check with your state or local government—start with your local or state chamber of commerce.

Of course, *finding* the grant is the easy part; the hard part is *getting* the grant. It's a lot like applying to college. You have to jump through the hoops of each organization, which usually involves writing an extensive essay on why you need the money. There are grantwriting businesses out there as well as grant brokers—people who try to find the right grant for you. You pay them regardless of whether they find you a grant; on the other hand, if they land you a $750,000 grant, you still pay them the flat fee, which is generally from $25 to $100 an hour, depending on their level of success. But if you don't have the funds to pay for a grantwriter or a broker, and you're a decent writer and have a passion for your business, then start researching, and fill out the forms and compose the essay yourself. There's no rule that says you can't try to get a grant on your own. And who knows—you might be successful!

Finding Outside Investors

Professional arms-length investors come in basically two categories: The so-called "angel investors," who are wealthy individuals or groups of wealthy individuals that invest hundreds of thousands of dollars in businesses they tend to know, and the "venture capitalists," who are partners in venture capital firms that invest other people's money professionally.

Venture Capital vs. Angel Investment

Until very recently, one of the simplest ways to separate angel investors from venture capital was the amount of investment. It used to be that angels would invest hundreds of thousands of dollars and venture capitalists would invest millions. That general rule has shifted somewhat lately, because venture capitalists have seen some very interesting web 2.0 companies, built by well-known teams with venture capital experience, start up for total investment of just a few hundred thousand dollars. Some venture capitalists will compete for shares of those startups, even though investment amounts are less.

Another traditional mode that seems to be changing is the rule that venture capitalists almost always invest in groups of three or more firms. Until the smaller startup requirements of even well known Web 2.0 startups changed the playing field, they wanted to be one of several such firms investing because with several professional investors involved, there was less risk. There was less chance the entrepreneurs would change their mind about exit. However, with some venture capitalist investments going for just a few hundred thousand dollars, this is not as iron clad as it was a few years ago.

The key thing to understand about outside investors of any type is that they invest to make money. Investors don't make money just because your startup is healthy and happy; they make money when your company

> **TAKE NOTES!**
>
> Don't say "venture capital" when you mean "outside investment" or "angel investment." Venture capital is a very small number of very specialized deals, maybe five to ten thousand per year.

either "goes public" (registers your stock on the public markets) or is acquired by another company. It has to generate liquidity by successfully executing an exit strategy. Part of the reason that professional early-stage investors almost always end up with controlling interest in a startup company is that they want to be sure that the owner doesn't take their money, create the company with it, and then decide to keep that company healthy forever and not sell stock. A minority interest in a small financially sound company doesn't necessarily generate money. That's why the exit is so important.

What You Need

To get any kind of outside investment you'll need to have an interesting business with a good chance of high growth and a financially attractive three-to-five year exit strategy.

Some areas of business are inherently more interesting to investors: high technology usually means a greater likelihood of high growth. That might be computer technology, web businesses, biomedicine, biotechnology, and, more recently, "green" technology including sustainable energy sources, waste disposal, and anything that might slow the onset of global warming.

Professional investors want to minimize risk so they look to management experience, which means you almost always need an experienced management team. That presents a Catch 22—outside investors want you to have a track record with successful startups as a requirement of investment, but you can't get a track record without investment. It's a difficult fact of life. Sometimes you get around it by working with a startup first, to get startup experience. Sometimes you have a special relationship with an angel investor who knows you and your industry very well. Often, however, you simply can't expect to get significant investment for your new business, no matter how interesting it might seem to you, if you don't have experienced management. If you're worried about this problem, start right now looking for partners, advisors, or management team members who can fill some gaps.

You'll also need a solid business plan. Don't be fooled by those who say investors don't read business plans, or that all you'll need is a pitch presentation; real investors and experts will say that sometimes because it's fun to be contrarian and surprising. The truth is that you can't do an effective pitch presentation, or a summary memo, or some of the other supposed alternatives to a business plan unless you have a business plan already done. These other options simply summarize and explain the plan; they don't substitute for the plan. You'll look foolish if a first contact, summary memo, or presentation inspires an investor to respond positively and request that you "send us your plan" and you don't have a plan to send. The investors may not read the plan, but they will expect to be able to assign a younger associate to read it, and they'll want to be able to refer to key points, key metrics, and information contained in the plan.

How It Works

The investment process varies depending on the habits of the investors you deal with. Be prepared for the details go differently each time you approach a new potential investor.

Usually, there is a first contact of some sort that generates a request—you hope—for more information. That means following up with a summary memo, after which, if the investors continue to be interested, you'll either send a business plan or set an appointment (the investors will decide; it's not your choice) for a pitch presentation. If that goes well, buckle your seat belt because you're on your way. You'd better have an attorney experienced with investment dealings on your side. You'll probably be delivering a series of presentations, and a series of business plans, each with revisions requested by investors.

Investors do not invest in business plans. They invest first and foremost in people. They look to invest in people who know how to build interesting new businesses, who have good track records, and who present business plans that make the information easy to find and compelling.

The Summary Memo

Formats for summary memos vary a lot. If you are asked to produce one, it's okay to ask about details. Don't be shy. "How many pages is ideal?"

is not an unusual question. Regardless of how few or how many pages, write the summary for the investors. What they want to know is everything that helps them see how investing in you and your business will generate money—lots of money—for them in three to five years time. They want to know about your track record because that helps them believe you'll make the right decisions to make them money. They want to know about your business and its potential growth because that's going to help them believe that investing with your company will make them money. Remember always that your success alone is not enough to make them money. There has to be a realistic exit strategy. You must plan to either go public or get acquired in three to five years, or investors will not be not interested.

The Pitch Presentation

Guy Kawasaki has practically defined the rules of the pitch presentation in his "The Art of the Pitch" chapter of his book *The Art of the Start*. If you're impatient and want to get going immediately, he summarized that book for you in "The 10-20-30 Rule of Powerpoint" on his blog; basically, in your presentation use 10 slides, 20 minutes, and nothing less than 30 point type.

Like the summary memo, the pitch presentation is built around how you will make the investors money. You show your business, its growth and profitability prospects, its management team, and its "secret sauce," meaning how it's different and what will make it grow fast and make money. For some businesses it's literally a secret sauce, for most it's proprietary technology, and for a few it's some brilliant new idea in marketing or distribution. All of this is about making money for investors.

The Business Plan

Don't risk a good opportunity on a poorly done business plan. Take that plan-as-you-go plan you started with in Chapter 2, and build around it to create a complete business plan document that covers all the main points.

While outline order isn't that important, this outline will pretty much cover you for a good standard formal business plan:

1. **Executive summary:** just a few pages, just the highlights.

2. **Company:** legal establishment, history, capitalization, ownership, location, facilities.

3. **Business offering:** features, benefits, sourcing, technology, secret sauce, intellectual property.

4. **Market analysis:** market size, growth rates, trends, segments, industry composition, competition, market focus.

5. **Strategy and implementation:** growth strategy, market strategy, sales strategy, distribution strategy, sales forecast, specific concrete milestones.

6. **Management team:** backgrounds, track records, organizational structure, personnel policies, estimated personnel costs.

7. **Financial strategy:** funding and financing strategy, investment offering, projected profit and loss, balance, cash flow, and basic business ratios monthly for the first year and annually for the two following years.

Keep your business plan short and simple. Illustrate your financial projections with bar graphs and pie charts. Use bullet points and plain English. Keep the format simple so it doesn't get in the way. Add additional illustrations—technical diagrams, pictures of floor plans and locations, for example—wherever they communicate and explain concepts.

Don't get lost in your technology. A business plan is about the business, not about the technology. Use other means—appendices, white papers, patents, or whatever—to lay out the technology.

The Deal

Investors trade their money for shares in your company. The deal struck will revolve around an assumed valuation of your company, which will be simple math and difficult negotiation. The simple math is just dividing the investment amount by the percentage ownership to determine the resulting valuation. For example, a $600,000 investment for 50 percent ownership implies a valuation of $1.2 million. When investors question your suggested terms (they will), the discussion might be around valuation. When they say they are questioning your valuation, what they mean is they want more ownership for the same amount of money, or the same amount of ownership for less money.

There are no magic formulas, no algorithms, no simple ways to determine what deal terms should be. The most powerful word in the investor's vocabulary is "no." The most powerful word in your vocabulary is also "no."

Choose an Investor As You Would a Spouse

An investment relationship is a lot like a marriage. Don't think any investment from any investor is a win. Incompatible investors can destroy your business. You are in fact much better off without investment than with an investment relationship with partners with whom you can't work.

═══ ONLINE TOOLS ═══

Commercial Borrowing

If you're looking for traditional loans, you can get a lot of information and even apply for and receive a commercial loan online. There is so much of this going on that it's hard for us to specify just a few sources; so, as with so many other elements of your three-week startup, search the internet well and go carefully, checking references often.

- Search more than 4,000 small business loan sources: businessfinance. com
- The American Bankers Association: aba.com
- Virgin Money, which absorbed the friends and family lending business Circlelending: virginmoneyus.com
- Direct commercial loans: commercialdirectloans.com

Government Grants

Be careful with the web searches in this area, because there are too many websites, and many of them are trying to take advantage of entrepreneurs enthusiasm and offering less value that we'd like.

- Always start with the government grants website: grants.gov and the SBA information site: sba.gov.

- Do the web search for "startup business grants" and brace yourself— there is a lot of noise in this market. Proceed with caution.

Seeking Investment

Where to start? We're biased towards bplans.com and its resources on the search for investment, but there are so many other sites. These are just a few that are prominent at present.

- There's a very interesting social networking website built around a database of comments from entrepreneurs about specific professional investment firms: thefunded.com.

- National Venture Capital Association website: nvca.org.

- The University of New Hampshire sponsors the Center for Venture Research: wsbe.unh.edu/cvr

- Venture Capital Access Online: the venture capital and private equity marketplace: vcaonline.com

- The Angel Investor Network: gobignetwork.com.

- Do a web search for "venture capital" and "angel investment."

Business Plans and Business Planning

One author is founder and president and the other is the current CEO of Palo Alto Software, which publishes Business Plan Pro. We believe very strongly that every business should start with Business Plan Pro. The product information is at BusinessPlanPro.com and the main company site is

PaloAlto.com. We also support two different websites offering Tim's books on business planning free for reading on the web:

- *The Plan-As-You-Go Business Plan:* planasyougo.com
- *Hurdle: the Book on Business Planning*: hurdlebook.com

Some Related Websites

In addition, we sponsor the world's largest and most-linked-to resource website for business planning, which is bplans.com. That site includes thousands of articles including dozens that we've cited in this book as good resources. It also has a startup costs calculator, sample business plans, and a database of previous questions and answers. We recommend it highly. Some of the related articles on bplans.com include:

- "How to Get Your Business Funded," business plan help and small business articles, bplans.com: articles.bplans.com/index.php/business-articles/starting-a-business/how-to-get-your-business-funded
- "Estimating Realistic Startup Costs," business plan help and small business articles, bplans.com: articles.bplans.com/index.php/business-articles/starting-a-business/estimating-realistic-start-up-costs

Beyond that, please check in with the 3weeks2startup.com companion site for updated links, and the *venture capital* and *angel investment* and *bootstrapping* categories of our blogs at blog.timberry.com, upandrunning.entrepreneur.com, and mommyceo.wordpress.com.

Additional Information

- Small Business Administration: sba.gov/services/financialassistance/sbaloantopics/snapshot/index.html
- EarlyBirdCapital, Inc: earlybirdcapital.com
- Prosper, online marketplace for people-to-people lending: prosper.com
- Loans from friends and family: entrepreneur.com/money/financing/loansfromfriendsandfamily/article51542.htm

WEEK 1 CHECKLIST

At this point, we'd like to pause and suggest taking stock of where you should be in our three-week timeframe.

	YES	NO
You've defined **success**, as explained in Chapter 1: What you want as success for your business.		
You understand your **business identity,** as explained in Chapter 1: You've defined strengths, weaknesses and core competencies, and you understand how that affects strategy.		
You have a clear **market focus**, as explained in Chapter 1: You have a clear aim at target market.		
You've gone over the discussion in Chapter 3 to determine whether or not you and your business need to develop **market research** to prove the market, support the sales forecast, or set the market strategy. If you've decided you do need the research, you've started it and you're on track to finish within the next two weeks.		
You've defined the **business offering** (product or service) focus as explained in Chapter 1.You know and understand what needs and/or wants of the target market that your business offering will address.		
You're comfortable with your overall **strategic focus**, as explained in Chapter 1. You can talk about how your new business is different from others, and what sets it apart.		
If you are working as a **partnership or team** and not a one-person business, you and other core founders have talked about and agreed on percentage of ownership and general responsibilities of each member. This was covered in Chapter 4.		

	YES	NO
You've got it in writing: You have a written document clarifying your agreements reached. This is not a legal document yet, but it will be used in Week 3 as the foundation of the eventual legal document. It does cover the issues brought up in Chapter 4.		
You've chosen your **business name**. You've gone through the discussion about business names in Chapter 4, decided on a name, and done the first checks on name availability.		
You have a preliminary **sales forecast** as explained in Chapter 2.		
You have a preliminary **expense budget** as explained in Chapter 2.		
You have estimated **startup costs** as explained in Chapter 5.		
You've gone over the options and tradeoffs of **raising money** (Chapter 5), and determined how much you need and how you intend to get it, so now you know whether or not you need a formal business plan as part of the process of raising money. If you need that document, you've started developing it and included your estimated sales forecast, expense budget, and startup costs.		

WEEK 2:
KEEP MOVING!

CHAPTER 6

GETTING PAID

A surprising and sad number of otherwise successful businesses run aground over simply not getting paid by their customers. This is not something you expect until you get into the middle of it. However, the standard in business-to-business (B2B) sales is turning over goods or services along with an invoice, and then waiting to get paid. The normal wait time is 30, 45, 60 days, or more.

If you're going to be selling only to individual consumers, then the problem of getting paid is a lot simpler.

Getting paid for your products or services is what business is all about. These days, there are more options than ever for accepting payment.

Whether you are in a B2B or consumer-oriented industry, your choices can include extending credit, taking checks, and accepting credit or debit cards. With so many options, it's easy for a new business owner to get caught up in the excitement of making sales and to forget the necessity of a well-thought-out credit policy. Deciding what forms of payment you will accept, how you will handle them, and what collection methods you'll use to ensure debts are paid is essential to any small business's success.

Establishing a Credit Policy

Credit can make or break a small business. A too-lenient credit policy can set the stage for collection and cash-flow problems later, while a creatively and carefully designed policy can attract customers and boost your business's cash flow.

Many small businesses are reluctant to establish a firm credit policy for fear of losing their customers. What they do not realize is that a consistent credit policy not only strengthens your company, but also creates a more professional image in your customers' eyes. A well-thought-out credit policy accomplishes four things:

1. Avoids both bad debts and hard feelings

2. Standardizes credit procedures, providing employees with clear and consistent directions

3. Demonstrates to employees and customers that the company is serious about managing credit

4. Helps the business owner define how credit fits into the overall sales and marketing plan

To establish a smart credit policy, start by investigating the way your competition handles credit. Your goal is to make it easy to buy your products. If your competition offers better terms, they have an advantage. You must meet your competitors' credit terms to attract customers.

At the same time, be cautious not to go too far with your credit policy. Novice entrepreneurs are often tempted to offer lower prices and longer payment terms to take business away from competitors. Credit is a double-edged sword. You want to attract customers with your credit policy, but you do not want to attract customers who are not credit-worthy. Be aware that some troubled companies routinely switch from supplier to supplier whenever they reach their credit limit with one. Others are outright con artists that take advantage of new and naive entrepreneurs.

> **TAKE NOTES!**
>
> **WEEK 2**
>
> Even the best customers can suddenly become deadbeats. Watch for these warning signs that a customer may be in financial trouble:
>
> - Changes in personnel, especially buyers or management
> - Changes in buying patterns, such as purchasing much larger amounts than usual or buying significant amounts off-season
> - Failure to return calls with the usual promptness

How to protect yourself? One good way to start is to write a short, simple statement that sums up the intent and spirit of your company's credit policy. For example, a liberal policy might read: "Our credit policy is to make every reasonable effort to extend credit to all customers recommended by sales management, provided a suitable credit basis can be developed."

A conservative policy might say: "Our company has a strict credit policy, and credit lines will be extended only to the most credit-worthy accounts. New customers who fail to meet our credit criteria will need to purchase using cash-on-delivery terms until they establish their ability and willingness to pay on our terms."

Base your policy selection—conservative or liberal—on your industry, the size and experience of your staff, the dollar amount of your transactions, your profit margins, and your tolerance for risk. Also consider the industry to which you're selling. If your customers are in "soft" industries such as construction or computers, for example, you would do well to use a conservative policy.

If you adopt a liberal credit policy for your business, make sure you are prepared to handle the collection calls. Liberal policies will require you to be aggressive when customers do not pay on time.

Give 'Em Credit

The simplest customer credit policy has two basic points: limiting credit risk, and diligently investigating each company's credit-worthiness.

No matter how credit-worthy a customer is, never extend credit beyond your profit margin. This policy ensures that if you aren't paid, at least your expenses will be paid. For example, if you mark up your product or service 100 percent, you can then safely risk that amount without jeopardizing your company's cash flow. To gauge a company's credit-worthiness, draft a comprehensive credit application that contains the following:

- Name of business, address, phone, and fax number
- Names, addresses, and Social Security numbers of principals
- Type of business (corporation, partnership, sole proprietorship)
- Industry
- Number of employees
- Bank references
- Trade payment references
- Business/personal bankruptcy history
- Any other names under which the company does business
- A personal guarantee that the business owners promise to pay you if their corporation is unable to

TAKE NOTES!

When dealing with a new client, it's a good idea to protect yourself by asking for part of your payment upfront. This is an especially good policy if the client is a new or fledgling business.

Your credit application should also specify what your credit terms are and the consequences of failing to meet them. Indicate what late fees you'll charge, if any; that the customer is responsible for any attorney's fees or collection costs incurred at any time, either during or prior to a lawsuit; and the venue where such a suit would be filed. Have your credit application form reviewed by an attorney specializing in creditors' rights to make sure it is in line with your state's regulations.

Once a potential customer has completed the application, how do you investigate the information? One way to verify the facts and assess the company's credit history is to call credit-reporting agencies. Some companies' payment histories will also be available through D&B. Because credit agencies' reporting can be unreliable, however,

> ## TAKE NOTES!
>
> Try this proactive approach to prompt a customer to pay faster: About 10 days before payment is due, call to ask if the customer received the bill. Make sure they are satisfied with the product; then politely ask, "Do you anticipate any problems paying your bill on time?"
>
> WEEK
> 2

it's also a good idea to call others in the industry and try to determine the company's payment record and reputation. Most industries have associations that trade credit information.

Also ask customers how much credit they think they will need. This will help you estimate the volume of credit and the potential risk to your business. Finally, simply use your intuition. If someone doesn't look you straight in the eye, chances are they won't let you see what's in their wallet, either.

Payment Due

Once you've set your credit policy, it's important to stick to it and do your part to ensure prompt payment. The cornerstone of collecting accounts receivable on time is making sure invoices go out promptly and accurately. If you sell a product, get the invoice out to the customer at the same time the shipment goes out. If you're in a service industry, track your billable hours daily or weekly, and bill as often as your contract or agreement with the client permits. The sooner the invoice is in the mail, the sooner you get paid.

To eliminate any possibility of confusion, your invoice should contain several key pieces of information. First, make sure you date it accurately and clearly state when payment is due, as well as any penalties for late payment. Also specify any discounts, such as discounts for payment in 15 days or for payment in cash.

Each invoice should give a clear and accurate description of the goods or services the customer received. Inventory code numbers may make sense to your computer system, but they don't mean much to the customer unless they are accompanied by an item description.

It's also important to use sequentially numbered invoices. Going this route helps make things easier when you need to discuss a particular invoice with a customer, and it also makes it easier for your employees to keep track of invoices.

Before sending out an invoice, call the customer to ensure the price is correct, and check to make sure prices on invoices match those on purchase orders and/or contracts.

Know the industry norms when setting your payment schedules. While 30 days is the norm in most industries, in others, 45- or 60-day payment cycles are typical. Learn your customers' payment practices, too. If they pay only once a month, for instance, make sure your invoice gets to them in plenty of time to hit that payment cycle. Also keep on top of industry trends and economic ups and downs that could affect customers' ability to pay.

Promptness is key not only in sending out invoices, but also in following up. If payment is due in 30 days, don't wait until the 60th day to call

---

WEEK 2

RED TAPE ALERT!

Having trouble collecting on a bill? Your Better Business Bureau (BBB) may be able to help. Many BBBs now assist with B2B disputes regarding payment as part of their dispute resolution service. BBBs do not operate as collection agencies, and there is no charge beyond standard membership dues.

When the BBB gets involved, there can be three possible outcomes. First, the account may be paid; second, the BBB can serve as a forum for arbitration; third, if the company refuses to pay or arbitrate, the complaint is logged in the BBB's files for three years.

Most businesses find a call from the BBB a powerful motivator to pay up. If the debtor belongs to the BBB and refuses to pay, its membership could be revoked.

To find out if the BBB in your area offers this service, visit bbb.org.

---

the customer. By the same token, however, don't be overeager and call on the 31st day. Being too demanding can annoy customers, and this could result in you losing a valuable client. Knowledge of industry norms plus your customers' payment cycles will guide you in striking a middle ground.

Constant communication trains customers to pay bills promptly and leads to an efficient, professional relationship between you and them. Usually, a polite telephone call to ask about a late payment will get the ball rolling, or at least tell you when you can expect payment. If any problems exist that need to be resolved before payment can be issued, your phone call will let you know what they are so you can start clearing them up. It could be something as simple as a missing packing slip or as major as a damaged shipment.

The first 15 to 20 seconds of the call are crucial. Make sure to project good body language over the phone. Be professional and firm, not wimpy. Use a pleasant voice that conveys authority, and respect the other person's dignity.

> **TAKE NOTES!**
>
> WEEK **2**
>
> To make sure you get paid for any work performed, it's a perfectly reasonable practice for a business that has out-of-pocket expenses to ask that the client make a deposit at least large enough to cover these expenses.

Remember the old saying "You catch more flies with honey than with vinegar"? It's true.

What if payment still is not made after an initial phone call? Don't let things slide. Statistics show that the longer a debt goes unpaid, the more difficult it will be to collect and the greater chance that it will remain unpaid forever. Most experts recommend making additional phone calls rather than sending a series of past-due notices or collection letters. Letters are easier to ignore, while phone calls tend to get better results.

If several phone calls fail to generate any response, a personal visit may be in order. Try to set up an appointment in advance. If this isn't possible, leave a message stating what date and time you will visit. Make sure to bring all the proper documentation with you so you can prove exactly what is owed. At this point, you are unlikely to get full payment, so see if you can get the customer to commit to a payment plan. Make sure, however, that you put it in writing.

If the customer refuses to meet with you to discuss the issue or won't commit to a payment plan, you may be facing a bad debt situation and need to take further action. There are two options: using the services of an attorney or employing a collection agency. Your lawyer can advise you on what is best to do.

TAKE NOTES!

Require employees to sign their initials on checks they accept. No one wants to have their initials on a check that might bounce, so employees will be extra careful about following your check acceptance policy.

If you decide to go with a collection agency, ask friends or business owners for referrals, or look in the Yellow Pages or online to find collectors who handle your type of claim. To make sure the agencies are reputable, contact the Better Business Bureau or the securities division of your secretary of state's office. Since all collection companies must be bonded with the state, this office should have them on file.

For more information on collection agencies, you can also contact the Association of Credit and Collection Professionals (acainternational.org). Most reputable collection firms are members of this international organization.

Many collection agencies take their fee as a cut of the collected money, so there is no upfront cost to you. Shop around to find an agency with a reasonable rate. Also compare the cost of using a collection agency to the cost of using your lawyer. You may be able to recover more of the money using one option or the other, depending on the total amount of the debt and the hourly rate or percentage the lawyer or agency charges.

Accepting Checks

Bounced checks can cut heavily into a small business's profits. Yet a business that doesn't accept personal checks can't expect to stay competitive.

How can you keep bad checks out of your cash register? Here are some steps to establishing a check-acceptance policy that works.

- **Start with the basics.** Since laws regarding the information needed to cash checks vary greatly among states (and even within states), begin by contacting your local police department. They can familiarize you with the laws and regulations that govern checks in your state. Some police departments have seminars instructing businesses on how to set up proper check-cashing policies.

  While rules vary among states, there are some good general rules of thumb to follow. When accepting a check, always ask to see the customer's driver's license or similar identification card, preferably one that has a photograph. Check the customer's physical characteristics against his identification. If you have reason to question his identity, ask the customer to write his signature on a separate piece of paper. Many people who pass bad checks have numerous false identifications and may forget which one they are using. Ask for the customer's home and work telephone numbers so you can contact him in case the check bounces. Don't cash payroll checks, checks for more than the amount of purchase or third-party checks.

- **Be observant.** Desktop-publishing software, laser printers and scanners have made it easier for people to alter, forge and duplicate checks. To avoid accepting a forged or counterfeit check, evaluate the document very carefully. Smudge marks on the check could indicate the check was rubbed with moist fingers when it was illegally made. Smooth edges on checks are another sign of a document that may be counterfeit; authentic checks are perforated either on the top or left side of the check. Smudged handwriting or signs that the handwriting has been erased are other warning signs that you might be dealing with an illegal check.

- **Be especially cautious with new checks.** A large majority of bad checks are written on new accounts. Many businesses will not accept checks that don't have a customer's name preprinted on them. If the check is written on a brand-new account (one with check number, say, below 300), protect yourself by asking to see two forms of ID.

- **Establish a waiting period for refunds.** Merchants can easily be stiffed when a customer makes a purchase by check and returns the merchandise the next day for a cash refund. When the check bounces, the merchant is out the cash paid for the refund. To avoid this scenario, many entrepreneurs require a five-to-seven-business-day grace period to allow checks to clear the bank before cash refunds are paid.

Electronic Help

If you process a large volume of checks, you might benefit from the services of a check-verification company. By paying a monthly fee, ranging from $50 to $100 (depending on your company's size and volume of checks), you can tap into a company's database of individuals who write bad, stolen, or forged checks. This is done by passing a customer's check through an electronic "check reader" at your checkout stand. If the check matches a name in the company's database, the check is refused.

Using a "check reader" from companies like TeleCheck, a check-verification and check-guarantee company, is quick and efficient. They can approve a check within seconds, which is generally as fast as, or faster than, a merchant getting acceptance for a credit card purchase.

Check-verification companies also offer a check-guarantee service. If a check is approved by a check-verification company and it later turns out to be a bad check, the merchant gets reimbursed for the value of the check. This guarantee service reduces the risk of accepting bad checks. Getting a handle on the bad checks that might pass through your business certainly has its benefits. For small merchants, one bad check can wipe out an entire day's profits.

Another option is an electronic check conversion/acceptance system, which allows merchants to accept checks as easily and safely as credit cards.

Here's how it works: When a customer makes a payment with a check, the paper check is run through a check reader, converting it into an electronic item much like the credit card terminal does when swiping a card. Once the transaction is approved, funds are electronically debited from the customer's account and deposited into the merchant's account, usually within 24 to 48 hours. This same technology allows businesses to process checks over the phone or the internet.

Follow Policy

Whatever check-acceptance policy you develop, make sure your employees clearly understand the procedure to follow. Also be sure to post your check-acceptance policy prominently where customers can see it. Specify any charges for bounced checks, what forms of ID are required, and what types of checks you will and will not accept. Posting signs helps prevent disgruntlement when customers wait in line, only to find at the register that you can't accept their check.

What if you do receive a bad check? In most cases, after a check bounces, the bank allows you another attempt to deposit it. After that, the responsibility for collecting the money falls on you.

Contact the customer, either by phone or mail. (Again, consult your local police on the proper procedure; some states require that a registered letter be sent and a specific amount of time elapse before other action can be taken.) Keep your cool; there's nothing gained by being angry or hostile about the situation. Most people bounce checks by accident. Explain the situation, and request immediate payment plus reimbursement for any bank charges you have incurred.

If the person still refuses to pay, or you cannot reach them, you have several options. The first, and probably the easiest, is to hold the check for a short time (up to six months) from the date it was written. Although banks will not allow the check to be deposited a third time after it bounced twice, many banks will nonetheless cash that same check for immediate cash if there are sufficient funds. Call the debtor's bank periodically to see if the funds are there. When they are, cash the check immediately.

Another option is going to the police. Since, through your check-acceptance procedure, you collected all the information needed to prosecute, you should be able to complete the proper paperwork. However, the hassle of hiring a lawyer, identifying suspects, and going to court may be more effort than you want to expend for a $200 check. In that case, your best bet is to use a collection agency as discussed in the section "Payment Due" on page 117.

Accepting Credit Cards

Why should a small-business owner accept credit cards? There are dozens of reasons. First and foremost, research shows that credit cards increase the probability, speed, and amount of customer purchases. Many people prefer not to carry cash, especially when traveling. Others prefer to pay with credit cards because they know that it will be easier to return or exchange the merchandise.

Accepting credit cards has several advantages for business owners as well. It gives you the chance to increase sales by enabling customers to make impulse buys even when they do not have enough cash in their wallets or sufficient funds in their checking accounts. Accepting credit cards can improve your cash flow, because in most cases you receive the money within a few days instead of waiting for a check to clear or an invoice to come due. Finally, credit cards provide a guarantee that you will be paid, without the risks involved in accepting personal checks.

Merchant Status

To accept major credit cards from customers, your business must establish merchant status with each of the credit card companies whose cards you want to accept. You'll probably want to start by applying for merchant status with American Express or Discover. For these cards, all you need to do is contact American Express or Discover directly and fill out an application.

However, chances are you'll want to accept Visa and MasterCard, too, since these are used more frequently. You cannot apply directly to Visa or MasterCard; because they are simply bank associations, you have to establish a merchant account through one of several thousand banks that set up such accounts, called "acquiring banks."

The first thing you need to understand about accepting credit cards, explains Debra Rossi of Wells Fargo Bank, is that the bank views this as an extension of credit. "When we give you the ability to accept credit cards, we're giving you the use of the funds before we get them. By the time the

TAKE NOTES!
Don't Skimp on Security

Thanks to the internet, small businesses have an unprecedented opportunity to market their products and services to a larger consumer audience than ever before. However, an online presence means little if customers don't feel safe making a transaction on your website. Because identity theft and credit card fraud are running rampant on the internet, many consumers will not buy from a site that doesn't provide secure transactions.

That's where a Secure Sockets Layer (SSL) certificate comes into play. Understanding how SSL affects online security can help unlock your business's e-commerce potential.

SSL technology encrypts your customers' payment information as it travels to you over the internet, protecting credit card data and other sensitive information from hackers during the transaction process. It also verifies to customers that you are who you say you are (a padlock icon is visible, indicating that a secure transaction is underway). This prevents a third party from accepting orders while disguised as your business.

SSL certificates are issued by a Certificate Authority such as VeriSign, Thawte, GeoTrust and others. The cost of a standard one-year certificate is $200 to $400.

If you store your customers' data or credit card numbers on your server, a firewall is another vital tool for protecting this information. Many companies expose their customers to hackers by neglecting to implement a proper firewall. If you are uncertain how to install a firewall on your site, consult your web hosting company.

For more information, check out VeriSign's "What Every E-Business Should Know About SSL Security and Consumer Trust." You can request a free copy at Verisign.com.

WEEK
2

money arrives in the cardholder's account, it could be another 30 days," Rossi says. There's also the real concern that if your company goes out of business before merchandise is shipped to customers, the bank will have to absorb losses.

While the requirements vary among banks, in general a business does not have to be a minimum size in terms of sales. However, some banks do have minimum requirements for how long you've been in business. This doesn't mean a startup can't get merchant status; it simply means you may have to look a little harder to find a bank that will work with you.

While being considered a "risky business"—typically a startup, mail order or homebased business—is one reason a bank may deny your mer-

TAKE NOTES!

MasterCard, Visa, and American Express all have their place. But there's another option you may not have considered: issuing a private-label credit card with your company's name on it.

In addition to all the usual advantages of credit cards, a private-label credit card program allows businesses to focus on who their customers are. For example, your program can gather data about customer purchases, buying patterns, income, and demographics.

Small businesses can save money and eliminate hassles by using an outside administrator that specializes in private-label credit cards. A number of banks have entered this arena; ask your banker if he or she administers such programs. If not, the banker may be able to recommend a private-label credit card administration company.

Administration companies can do everything from setting up the operation to developing specialized marketing programs, designing the credit cards, training employees, and developing lists of potential customers. Fees vary depending on the number of services provided and the size of your customer base.

Before choosing an administration company, talk to other business owners who use private-label credit card programs to see if they're happy with the service and if the administration company does a good job handling customer applications, payments, and the like. Weigh the cost of any program against the benefits you expect to get from it.

chant status request, the most common reason for denial is simply poor credit. Approaching a bank for a merchant account is like applying for a loan. You must be prepared with a solid presentation that will persuade the bank to open an account for you.

You will need to provide bank and trade references, estimate what kind of credit card volume you expect to have, and what you think the average transaction size will be. Bring your business plan and financial statements, along with copies of advertisements, marketing pieces, and your catalog, if you have one. If possible, invite your banker to visit your store or operation. Banks will evaluate your product or service to see if there might be potential for a lot of returns or customer disputes. Called "chargebacks," these refunds are very expensive for banks to process. They are more common among mail order companies and are one reason why these businesses typically have a hard time securing merchant status.

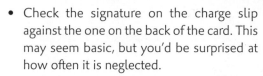

TAKE NOTES!

To prevent credit card fraud, follow these steps every time a credit purchase is made:

- Check the signature on the charge slip against the one on the back of the card. This may seem basic, but you'd be surprised at how often it is neglected.

- Verify the card's expiration date.

- Check frequently the credit card companies' updated bulletins listing canceled card numbers.

In your initial presentation, provide a reasonable estimate of how many chargebacks you will receive, and then show your bank why you do not expect them to exceed your estimates. Testimonials from satisfied customers or product samples can help convince the bank that your customers will be satisfied with their purchases. Another way to reduce the bank's fear is to demonstrate that your product is priced at a fair market value.

Rossi at Wells Fargo says the bank's goal is to find out if your business is profitable and if it will be around for a long time to come. "We approve a lot of startup businesses, and in those cases, we rely on the personal financial picture of the business principals," she says. "We look at [their personal] tax returns and at where they got the money to start the business. We also look to see if you're a customer at Wells Fargo and at your relationship with Wells."

TAKE NOTES!

Don't ask another merchant to deposit your sales slips for you, and never let another business deposit slips through your account. This practice is called "laundering" sales slips, and not only is it prohibited by Visa and MasterCard, but it is also illegal in some states. Honest business owners have been wiped out by scam artists who ask them to deposit their sales slips, then rack up thousands of dollars in phony sales, which later turn into chargebacks.

As Rossi's comment suggests, the best place to begin when trying to get merchant status is by approaching the bank that already holds your business accounts. If your bank turns you down, ask around for recommendations from other business owners who accept plastic. You could look in the Yellow Pages for other businesses in the same category as yours (home-based, retail, mail order). Call them to ask where they have their merchant accounts and whether they are satisfied with the way their accounts are handled. When approaching a bank with which you have no relationship, you may be able to sweeten the deal by offering to switch your other accounts to that bank as well.

If banks turn you down for merchant status, another option is to consider independent credit card processing companies, which can be found in the Yellow Pages. While independents often give the best rates because they have lower overhead, their application process tends to be more time-consuming, and startup fees are sometimes higher.

You can also go through an independent sales organization (ISO). These are field representatives from out-of-town banks who, for a commission, help businesses find banks willing to grant them merchant status. Your bank may be able to recommend an ISO, or you can look in the Yellow Pages or online under "Credit Cards." An ISO can match your needs with those of the banks he or she represents without requiring you to go through the application process with all of them.

Money Matters

Enticing your bank with promising sales figures can also boost your case since the bank makes money when you do. Every time you accept a credit card for payment, the bank or card company deducts a percentage of the sale—called a "merchant discount fee"—and then credits your account with the rest of the sale amount.

Here are some other fees you can expect to pay. All of them are negotiable except for the discount fee:

- Startup fees of around $200 to $500

- Equipment costs of $250 to $1,000, depending on whether you lease or buy a handheld terminal or go electronic

- Monthly statement fees of $10 to $20

- Transaction fees of 25 to 70 cents per purchase

- The discount rate—the actual percentage you are charged per transaction based on projected card sales volume, the degree of risk, and a few other factors (the percentage ranges from 1.5 to 3 percent; the higher your sales, the lower your rate)

- Chargeback fees of up to $25 per return transaction

There may also be some charges from the telephone company to set up a phone line for the authorization and processing equipment. Before you sign on with any bank, consider the costs carefully to make sure the anticipated sales are worth the costs.

> **TAKE NOTES!**
>
> **WEEK 2**
>
> Even after you have obtained merchant status, keep looking for ways to lower your fee. Your bank can suggest options. Also, ask other merchants who process transactions similar to yours how much they are paying. If you find a better deal, let your bank know and see if it will match it.

Getting Equipped

Once your business has been approved for credit, you will receive a startup kit and personal instruction in how to use the system. You don't need fancy equipment to process credit card sales. You can start with a phone and a simple imprinter that costs under $30. However, you'll get a better discount rate (and get your money credited to your account faster) if you process credit card sales electronically.

Although it's a little more expensive initially, purchasing or leasing a terminal that allows you to swipe the customer's card through for an instant authorization of the sale (and immediate crediting of your merchant account) can save you money in the long run. Cash registers can also be adapted to process credit cards. Also, using your personal computer as opposed to a terminal to get authorization can cut costs per transaction even more.

Once you obtain merchant account status, make the most of it. The credit card and bank industries hold seminars and users' conferences covering innovations in the industry, fraud detection techniques, and other helpful subjects. You can ask a credit card company's representatives for details, and keep on top of ways to get more from your customers' credit cards.

Online Payments

Are you selling on the web? If so, you'll need an internet merchant account to accept payments online. An internet merchant account costs more than a regular merchant account because the risk of credit card fraud is greater in an online environment, where no card is physically presented at the point of sale. To cover this risk, your bank or account issuer may charge a higher discount rate (3 to 5 percent per transaction vs. 1.5 to 3 percent for regular merchant accounts). The service provider may also charge an application fee of $50 to $300, as well as monthly statement fees and transaction fees on each purchase. When you apply, you'll likely need to estimate the average order size and the average monthly amount you expect to run through the account. You may be asked to keep a percentage of that amount in your account to cover fraud.

It's possible to accept payments over the internet without establishing your own merchant account. Third-party payment processors like PayPal will accept credit card payments on your behalf in return for a percentage of the cost of the transaction. While this percentage is relatively higher than it would be if you had your own merchant account, you only pay these fees if you sell your product. What's more, you don't have to pay the startup fees and mandatory monthly fees charged by most merchant account providers. Keep in mind, however, that third-party processors are cheaper as long as your monthly sales volume is below $1,000. If your business has significant sales volume, it's usually cheaper to process payments through a merchant account.

Accepting Debit Cards

In addition to credit cards and checks, there's a newer form of payment that more and more small businesses are accepting these days: ATM or debit cards. Consumers like the cards because they eliminate the hassle of writing checks, offset the need to carry wads of cash, and ensure security, thanks to a customer-activated PIN.

Many merchants, too, prefer accepting debit cards over credit cards or checks. Debit cards can even be better than cash. Debit is less expensive than a credit card or check and is not vulnerable to employee theft like cash is. Debit is also a guaranteed transaction: Money is immediately debited from the customer's account and deposited into yours—giving you instant access to funds. Finally, debit gives you access to consumers who don't have credit cards.

> **TAKE NOTES!**
>
> If you accept debit cards, be sure you educate customers about it. Many cardholders don't understand they can use their cards at a merchant's point-of-sale terminal just as they would at an ATM. Stickers and signs by the cash register help, as does placing the PIN-pad terminal in an easily accessible location. Training your clerks to ask customers "Will you be using your ATM card today?" also encourages debit card use.
>
> **WEEK 2**

Installing a debit system in your business can be as easy as walking into your bank, filling out an application requesting debit acceptance capabilities, and clearing some counter space next to your cash register for a debit terminal and printer (some banks can interface directly with your cash register).

You can purchase equipment for as little as $200 to $500, or check out monthly leasing options. You may find that you already have most of the necessary equipment. Some merchants' existing credit terminals can simply be reprogrammed to accept debit cards as well. If your terminals don't already have printers, however, you'll need to install them, since federal regulations require merchants to provide receipts for debit card transactions.

Electronic devices that accept both credit and debit cards are available on the market. Some are even integrated with the cash register. Because the debit PIN-pad terminal needs to be within easy reach of the customer and clerk, however, smaller businesses may opt for a stand-alone POS debit system. When you buy the service from a bank or other payment service provider, look for a system that accepts both credit and debit cards. A joint system takes up less counter space and is usually less confusing for clerks and customers to handle.

Another consideration is where your POS takes place. Restaurants, for example, may choose to collect the bill from patrons while they are still seated at their tables. In this case, you'll need the capability to take the PIN pad to each table for customers to key in their PIN. Such technology is available through most major financial institutions that provide debit equipment.

Beware, however, that not all banks are experienced in debit card services. Although sticking with your current financial institution when setting up a debit card system may have its advantages, make sure your bank understands debit before signing on with them.

Once you find a bank to service your debit needs, you will most likely be required to fill out a simple one-page application. Applying for debit is not like requesting merchant status, which is an extension of credit, and thus is a risk for the bank. Since debit cards are a guaranteed transaction, the credit of the applicant merchant is not evaluated as stringently.

Once you've set up your POS terminal, the fee you pay for its use depends on which debit network you're connected to. Banks typically don't charge merchants a percentage of each debit card sale. Instead, the bank might charge merchants up to 40 cents for each transaction.

While there's no doubt the cost per debit transaction adds up, it's still significantly less than some other options. For example, check processing typically runs from 18 to 50 cents per check, not taking into account the costs of bounced checks. Cash handling can also be expensive. Entrepreneurs who accept debit cards say they like the safety and security of this method. The bottom line: Debit offers your customers another way to pay…and the easier you make it for customers to buy, the more sales your business will ring up.

ONLINE TOOLS

The biggest and quickest gain online is the online billing and collection facilities. Particularly if you're going to be billing your clients individually (which is common for business services, for example, such as business consulting, graphic design, or bookkeeping), look at online tools to simplify this process.

- Blinksale "The easiest way to send invoices online:" blinksale.com
- Invoice templates for Microsoft Office: office.microsoft.com
- Freshbooks "The Fastest Way to Track Time and Invoice Your Clients:" freshbooks.com
- Vebio "Because time is money:" vebio.com
- Online invoices for small businesses; Intuit Billing Manager from the makers of QuickBooks: billingmanager.intuit.com
- Credit card merchant accounts and payment gateways: transactmoney.com
- Google Search: google.com/search?q=online+invoices

If your business will involve selling to consumers, you'll probably be looking online for help establishing the merchant accounts that allow you to accept credit cards.

- Chase Platinum Business Card: creditcard.chase.com

- Compare prices: uscreditcenter.net

- Merchant account, accept credit cards and credit card processing—First Data Independent Sales: charge-it-now.com

If you're going to have to approve credit for your clients, some of these websites may help.

- Standard and Poor's: standardandpoors.com

- D&B Small Business Credit Solutions (Dun & Bradstreet): smallbusiness.dnb.com

- Nationwide Collection Agency: pcmholdings.com

- Credit rating agencies (the full global list): defaultrisk.com

And finally, a helpful article: "How to Accept Credit Cards Online:"

- bplans.com

CHAPTER 7

COVER YOUR ASSETS

A common mistake that startup business owners make is failing to buy adequate insurance for their businesses. It's an easy error to make: Money is tight, and with so many things on your mind, protecting yourself against the possibility of some faraway disaster just doesn't seem that important. "Oh, I will get insurance," you promise yourself, "one of these days." Soon, "one of these days" comes and goes, and you're still uninsured. Only now, your business has gotten much bigger, you've put a lot more into it, and you have a lot more to lose. Everything, to be exact.

It doesn't take much. A fire, a burglary, the long-term illness of a key employee—any one of these could destroy everything you've worked so hard to build.

When you think of all the time, effort, and money you're investing in building your business, doesn't it make sense to invest a little extra to protect it?

Following is a closer look at the types of business insurance available and what most entrepreneurs need, plus tips for keeping costs under control.

Basic Insurance Needs

The basic business insurance package consists of four fundamental coverages—workers' compensation, general liability, auto, and property/casualty—plus an added layer of protection over those, often called an umbrella policy. In addition to these basic needs, you should also consider purchasing business interruption coverage and life and disability insurance.

TAKE NOTES!

Depending on how many employees you have when you first start, you may or may not have to get insurance like worker's compensation. There are state laws that mandate at what point you need to get worker's compensation, so be sure to check to see what the law is in your state. In New York, for instance, you don't need to get worker's compensation insurance until you have more than three people in your company.

If you are running a service business and initially you are the only employee, you will want to make sure that you are getting the right amount of insurance—but not over insuring yourself from day one.

In some cases, a payroll services company can help you navigate and figure out what you need to be legal, and what you need to be safe.

Workers' Compensation

Workers' compensation, which covers medical and rehabilitation costs and lost wages for employees injured on the job, is required by law in all 50 states, although not for all company sizes. If you employ fewer than five people you should double check and see what the actual law is in your state.

Workers' comp insurance consists of two components, with a third optional element. The first part covers medical bills and lost wages for the injured employee; the second encompasses the employer's liability, which covers the business owner if the spouse or children of a worker who's permanently disabled or killed decides to sue. The third and optional element of workers' compensation insurance is employment practices liability, which insures against lawsuits arising from claims of sexual harassment, discrimination, and the like.

"Employment practices liability protects the unknowing corporation from the acts of the individual," according to a spokesperson at the Independent Insurance Agents of America (IIAA), an industry association. "Whether you need it depends on the size of your business and how much control you have over the daily work of employees." Although you may not need to include employment practices liability insurance at first, it is something you may need to consider as your company grows.

According to the IIAA, it is often hard for small companies to get workers' compensation insurance. Consequently, some states have a risk-sharing pool for firms that can't buy from the private market. Typically state-run and similar to assigned risk pools for car insurance, these pools generally don't provide the types of discounts offered in the voluntary market and thus are an "insurance of last resort."

Because insurance agents aren't always up-to-date on the latest requirements and laws regarding workers' comp, you should check with your state, as well as your agent, to find out exactly what coverage you need. Start at your state's department of insurance or insurance commissioner's office.

Generally, rates for workers' comp insurance are set by the state, and you purchase insurance from a private insurer. The minimum amount you need is also governed by state law. When you buy workers' comp, be sure to

TAKE NOTES!

WEEK 2

Understanding what your general liability insurance covers and what it does not is very important. Different industries may have different insurance options available to help mitigate the risk of doing business in your particular industry. It definitely pays to do some research online and find out as much as you can about the types of liability insurance available to you. Check the trade organizations for your industry. Most have great websites that can help you understand what's available and what is necessary.

Getting the right insurance is all a balance between what you MUST to get insured on, what you CAN get insured on, and what you SHOULD get insured on.

choose a company licensed to write insurance in your state and approved by the insurance department or commissioner.

If you are purchasing insurance for the first time, the rate will be based on your payroll and the average cost of insurance in your industry. You'll pay that rate for a number of years, after which an experience rating will kick in, allowing you to renegotiate premiums.

Depending on the state you are located in, the business owner will be either automatically included or excluded from coverage; if you want something different, you'll need to make special arrangements. While excluding yourself can save you several hundred dollars, this can be penny-wise and pound-foolish. Review your policy before choosing this option, because in most states, if you opt out, no health benefits will be paid for any job-related injury or illness by your health insurance provider.

A better way to reduce premiums is by maintaining a good safety record. This could include following all the Occupational Health and Safety Administration guidelines related to your business, creating an employee safety manual, and instituting a safety training program.

Another way to cut costs is to ensure that all jobs in your company are properly classified. Insurance agencies give jobs different classification ratings depending on the degree of risk of injury.

General Liability

Comprehensive general liability coverage insures a business against accidents and injury that might happen on its premises as well as exposures related to its products.

For example, suppose a visiting salesperson slips on a banana peel while taking a tour of your office and breaks her ankle. General liability covers her claim against you. Or let's say your company is a window-sash manufacturer, with hundreds of thousands of its window sashes installed in people's homes and businesses. If something goes wrong with them, general liability covers any claims related to the damage that results.

The catch is that the damage cannot be due to poor workmanship. This points to one difficulty with general liability insurance: It tends to have a lot of exclusions. Make sure you understand exactly what your policy covers—and what it doesn't.

You may want to purchase additional liability policies to cover specific concerns. For example, many consultants purchase "errors and omissions liability," which protects them in case they are sued for damages resulting from a mistake in their work. A computer consultant who accidentally deletes a firm's customer list could be protected by this insurance, for example.

Companies with a board of directors may want to consider "directors' and officers' liability" (D&O), which protects top executives against personal financial responsibility due to actions taken by the company.

How much liability coverage do you need? Experts say $2 million to $3 million of liability insurance should be plenty. The good news is that liability insurance isn't priced on a dollar-for-dollar basis, so twice the coverage won't be twice the price.

The price you'll have to pay for comprehensive general liability insurance depends on the size of your business (measured either by square footage or by payroll) and the specific risks involved.

Auto Insurance

If your business provides employees with company cars, or if you have a delivery van, you need to think about auto insurance. The good news here is that auto insurance offers more of an opportunity to save money than most other types of business insurance. The primary strategy is to increase your deductible; then your premiums will decrease accordingly. Make sure, however, that you can afford to pay the deductibles should an accident happen. For additional savings, remove the collision and comprehensive coverage from older vehicles in your fleet.

Pay attention to policy limits when purchasing auto coverage. Many states set minimum liability coverages, which may be well below what you need. If you don't have enough coverage, the courts can take everything you have, and then attach your future corporate income, thus possibly causing the company severe financial hardship or even bankruptcy. You should carry at least $1 million in liability coverage.

TAKE NOTES!

If you are running a business where you will be employing people to drive company vehicles, do a little homework. Get DMV driving records for your potential employee BEFORE you hire them. Think about instituting NO TOLERANCE policies towards DUIs or moving violations.

For instance, in the car rental industry most companies will fire any employee ON THE SPOT if they get a DUI. It doesn't matter if that employee ever drives company cars, or if that employee is an Executive Vice President. If they get a DUI at any time while they are your employee, they lose their job.

Property/Casualty Coverage

Most property insurance is written on an all-risks basis, as opposed to a named-peril basis. The latter offers coverage for specific perils spelled out in the policy. If your loss comes from a peril not named, then it isn't covered.

Make sure you get all-risks coverage. Then go the extra step and carefully review the policy's exclusions. All policies cover loss by fire, but what about such crises as hailstorms and explosions? Depending on your geographic location and the nature of your business, you may want to buy coverage for all these risks.

Whenever possible, you should buy replacement cost insurance, which will pay you enough to replace your property at today's prices, regardless of the cost when you bought the items. It's protection from inflation. (Be sure your total replacements do not exceed the policy cap.)

For example, if you have a 30,000-square-foot building that costs $50 per square foot to replace, the total tab will be $1.5 million. But if your policy has a maximum replacement of $1 million, you're going to come up short. To protect yourself, experts recommend buying replacement insurance with inflation guard. This adjusts the cap on the policy to allow for inflation. If that's not possible, then be sure to review the limits of your policy from time to time to ensure you're still adequately covered. A good, honest insurance broker will help make sure that you keep your policies up to date. Ask around in your community and you will likely get some good word-of-mouth recommendations.

Beyond the Basics

The previous four types of insurance represent the fundamental insurance coverage you should have for your business right from the startup. The following are some additional insurances you should consider depending on your business type and other individual circumstances.

Umbrella Coverage

In addition to the four basic "food groups," many insurance agents recommend an additional layer of protection, called an umbrella policy. This protects you for payments in excess of your existing coverage or for liabilities not covered by any of your other insurance policies.

Business Interruption Coverage

When a hurricane or earthquake puts your business out of commission for days—or months—your property insurance has your building covered. But while property insurance pays for the cost of repairs or rebuilding, who pays for all the income you're losing while your business is unable to function?

For that, you'll need business interruption coverage. Many entrepreneurs neglect to consider this important type of coverage, which can provide enough to meet your overhead and other expenses during the time your business is out of commission. Premiums for these policies are based on your company's income.

Life Insurance

Many banks require a life insurance policy on the business owner before lending any money. Such policies typically take the form of term life insurance, purchased yearly, which covers the cost of the loan in the event of the borrower's death; the bank is the beneficiary.

Term insurance is less costly than permanent insurance at first, although the payments increase each year. Permanent insurance builds equity and should be considered once the business has more cash to spend. The life insurance policy should provide for the families of the owners and key management. If the owner dies, creditors are likely to take everything, and the owner's family will be left without the income or assets of the business on which to rely.

Another type of life insurance that can be beneficial for a small business is "key person" insurance. If the business is a limited partnership or has a few key stockholders, the buy-sell agreement should specifically authorize this type of insurance to fund a buyback by the surviving leadership. Without a provision for insurance to buy capital, the buy-sell agreement may be rendered meaningless.

The company is the beneficiary of the key person policy. When the key person dies, creating the obligation to pay, say, $100,000 for his or her stock, the cash with which to make that purchase is created at the same time. If

WEEK 2

RED TAPE ALERT!

If you are considering purchasing Key Person Insurance, and want to figure out the best way to set up this type of insurance to fund a buy-back by the surviving leadership you will NEED to contact a lawyer. This is NOT something you want to do on your own. As discussed in Chapter 3, having the right legal contract in place with partners and fellow owners is vital and should be done correctly.

Ask around and find a good business attorney who is used to dealing with small businesses to help you get these agreements in place. You may want to check with your local SBDC (Small Business Development Center) as they will tend to have good recommendations for small business service providers. Check out their website to find your local chapter: asbdc-us.org

you don't have the cash to buy the stock back from the surviving family, you could find yourself with new "business partners" you never bargained for—and wind up losing control of your business.

In addition to the owners or key stockholders, any member of the company who is vital to operations should also be insured.

3 WEEKS TO STARTUP

Disability Insurance

It's every businessperson's worst nightmare—a serious accident or a long-term illness that lays you up for months, or even longer. Disability insurance, sometimes called "income insurance," can guarantee a fixed amount of income—usually 60 percent of your average earned income—while you're receiving treatment or are recuperating and unable to work. Because you are your business's most vital asset, many experts recommend buying disability insurance for yourself and key employees from day one.

There are two basic types of disability coverage: short term (anywhere from 12 weeks to a year) and long term (more than a year). An important element of disability coverage is the waiting period before benefits are paid. For short-term disability, the waiting period is generally seven to 14 days. For long-term disability, it can be anywhere from 30 days to a year. If being unable to work for a limited period of time would not seriously jeopardize your business, you can decrease your premiums by choosing a longer waiting period.

Another optional add-on is "business overhead" insurance, which pays for ongoing business expenses such as office rental, loan payments, and employee salaries if the business owner is disabled and unable to generate income.

Choosing an Insurance Agent

Given all the factors that go into business insurance, deciding what kind of coverage you need typically requires the assistance of a qualified insurance agent.

Selecting the right agent is almost as important, and sometimes as difficult, as choosing the types of coverage you need. The most fundamental question regarding agents is whether to select a direct writer—that is, someone who represents just one insurance company—or a broker, who represents many companies.

Some entrepreneurs feel they are more likely to get their money's worth with a broker because he or she shops insurance companies for them. Others feel brokers are more efficient because they compare the different policies and give their opinions, instead of the entrepreneur having to talk to several direct writers to evaluate each of their policies. Another drawback to direct writers: If the insurance company drops your coverage, you lose your agent, too, and all his or her accumulated knowledge about your business.

Still, some people prefer direct writers. Why? An agent who writes insurance for just one company has more clout there than an agent who writes for many. So when something goes wrong, an agent who works for the company has a better chance of getting you what you need. Finally, direct writers often specialize in certain kinds of businesses and can bring a lot of industry expertise to the table.

To find an insurance agent, begin by asking a few of your peers whom they recommend. If you want more names, a trade association in your state may have a list of recommended agencies or offer some forms of group coverage with attractive rates.

Once you have a short list of agencies to consider, start looking for one with whom you can develop a long-term relationship. As your business grows and becomes more complicated, you'll want to work with someone who understands your problems. You don't want to spend a lot of time teaching the agent the ins and outs of your business or industry.

Find out how long the agency has been in business. An agency with a track record will likely be around to help you in the future. If the agency is new, ask about the principals; have they been in the industry in general long enough that you feel comfortable with their knowledge and stability?

One important area to investigate is loss-control service (which includes everything from fire-safety programs to reducing employees' exposures to injuries). The best way to reduce your premiums over the long haul is to minimize claims, and the best way to do that is through loss-control services. Look for a broker who will review and analyze which of the carriers offer the best loss-control services.

Another consideration is the size of the agency. The trend in insurance is consolidation. If you're looking for a long-term relationship, you want to avoid an agency that is going to get bought out. One way to get a handle on whether the agency you are considering is a likely acquiree is by looking at the agency's owner. If he or she is older and is not grooming a successor, there's a chance the agency will get bought out.

Verify the level of claims service each agency provides. When a claim arises, you don't want the agent telling you to call some toll-free number. If that's his or her idea of claims service, keep looking. An agency that gets involved in the claims process and works with the adjuster can have a positive impact on your settlement, while an agency that doesn't get involved tends to minimize your settlement.

You want an insurance agency that will stay on top of your coverage and be on the spot to adjust it as your business changes. Of course, it's always difficult to separate promises from what happens after the sale is closed. However, you might ask would-be agents how often they will be in touch.

> ## RED TAPE ALERT!
>
> **WEEK 2**
>
> Although it may take some time to put together, keep detailed records of the value of your office or store's contents off-premises. Include photos of equipment plus copies of sales receipts, operating manuals, and anything else that proves what you purchased and how much was paid. That way, in case of a fire, flood, or other disaster, you can prove what was lost. It's also important to be able to prove your monthly income so you are properly reimbursed if you have to close down temporarily.

Even for the most basic business situation, the agent should still meet with you at least twice a year. For more complex situations, the agent should call you monthly to make sure your coverage is adequate.

You also want to make sure the company your agent selects or represents is highly rated. While there are numerous rating agencies, the most respected is A.M. Best, which rates the financial strength of insurance companies from A++ to F, according to their ability to pay claims and their size. You can find their rating book, Best Rating Guide, at your local library or you can search Best's ratings online at ambest.com. You will have to register with the site for access, but searching is free. Look for a carrier rated no lower than B+.

Also make sure the agent you choose is licensed by the state. The best way to find out is by calling your state insurance department, listed in the telephone book. If you can't find a number there, call the National Insurance Consumer helpline at (800) 942-4242.

Ask for references, and check them. This is the best way to predict how an agent will work with you.

Last but not least, trust your gut. Does the agent listen to you and incorporate your concerns into the insurance plan? Does he or she act as a partner or just a vendor? A vendor simply sells you insurance. Your goal is to find an agent who functions as a partner, helping you analyze risks and decide the best course of action. Of course, partnership is a two-way street. The more information you provide your agent, the more he or she can do for you.

Insurance Costs

As with most other things, when it comes to insurance, you get what you pay for. Don't pay to insure against minor losses, but don't ignore real perils just because coverage carries hefty premiums.

You can lower your insurance premiums with a higher deductible. Many agents recommend higher deductibles on property insurance and putting the money you save toward additional liability coverage.

How much can you afford for a deductible or uninsured risk? Look at your cash flow. If you can pay for a loss out of cash on hand, consider not insuring it.

You can also save money on insurance by obtaining it through a trade group or an association. Many associations offer insurance tailored to your industry needs—everything from disability and health to liability and property coverage. You can also help keep insurance costs down by practicing these good insurance habits:

- Review your needs and coverage once a year. If your circumstances or assets have changed, you may need to adjust your insurance coverage.

- Ask your insurance agent for risk-reduction assistance. He or she should be able to visit your premises and identify improvements that would create a safer facility.

- Check out new insurance products. Ask your agent to keep you up-to-date on new types of coverage you may want.

- Take time to shop for the best, most appropriate coverage. A few hours invested upfront can save thousands of dollars in premiums or claims down the road.

Package Deal

If figuring out what insurance you need makes your head spin, calm down; chances are, you won't have to consider the whole menu. Most property and casualty companies now offer special small-business insurance policies.

A standard package policy combines liability; fire, wind and vehicle damage; burglary; and other common coverages. That's enough for most small offices and stores, such as an accounting firm or a gift shop. Some common requirements for a package policy are that your business occupy less than 15,000 square feet and that the combined value of your office building, operation, and inventory be less than $3 million.

> **TAKE NOTES!**
>
> The IRS now allows self-employed businesspeople to deduct 100 percent of health insurance premium costs. For more information on specific IRS guidelines, request IRS Publication 533, Self-Employment Tax, and IRS Publication 502, Medical and Dental Expenses, by calling (800) TAX-FORM.
>
> WEEK 2

Basic package policies typically cover buildings, machinery, equipment, and furnishings. That should protect computers, phones, desks, inventory, and the like against loss due to robbery and employee theft, in addition to the usual risks such as fire. A good policy pays full replacement cost on lost items.

A package policy also covers business interruption, and some even offer you liability shelter. You may also be covered against personal liability. To find out more about package policies, ask your insurance agent; then shop around and compare.

The Name's Bond

Sometimes confused with insurance, bonding is a guarantee of performance required for any business, either by law or by consumer demand. The most common businesses that bond employees are general contractors, temporary personnel agencies, janitorial companies, and companies with government contracts. Bonding helps ensure that the job is performed and that the customer is protected against losses from theft or damage done by your employees.

Although you still have to pay on claims if your employees are bonded, bonding has the side benefit of making your business more desirable to customers. They know that if they suffer a loss as the result of your work, they can recover the damages from the bonding company. The difference between a bond and insurance is that a bonding company ensures your payment by requiring security or collateral in case a claim is made against you.

Staking Your Claim

Though you hope it never happens, you may someday have to file an insurance claim. These tips should make it easier:

- **Report incidents immediately.** Notify your agent and carrier right away when anything happens—such as a fire, an accident, or theft—that could result in a claim.

- **Take steps to protect your property from further damage.** Most policies cover the cost of temporary repairs to protect against further damage, such as fixing a window to prevent looting.

- **If possible, save damaged parts.** A claims adjuster may want to examine them after equipment repairs have been made.

- **Get at least two repair estimates.** Your claims adjuster can tell you what kind of documentation the insurance company wants for bids on repairs.

- **Provide complete documentation.** The insurance company needs proof of loss. Certain claims require additional evidence. For example, a claim for business interruption will need financial data showing income before and after.

- **Communicate with your agent and claims adjuster.** Though your claim is against the insurance company, your agent should be kept informed so he or she can help if needed.

ONLINE TOOLS

While asking around, and going to your local SBDC office are definitely great ways to find the right agent or broker for your business insurance, you may also want to do some research online. Using the web will help you understand what you need, and be better prepared when you talk to an agent or broker.

There are some easy to use websites where you can fill in information about your business and get quotes from different agencies. Once you have the quotes, you will also be connected to an agent. You can start to work with the different agents, asking lots of questions, getting as much information as you want and need, and then comparing rates. The more information you have, the more understanding of different services provided by agents, the better your choice will be when you pick the agent or broker who will provide you with your business insurance. Here are a few websites to check out:

These websites help you get quotes for business insurance from various companies:

- insurancefinder.com
- findalocalcommercialagent.com
- businessinsurancenow.com

This site puts business insurance news and facts and figures at your fingertips.

- ambest.com (click on "Business" to start)

This site supplies business insurance news and puts facts and figures at your fingertips:

- iii.org (click on "Business" to start. From there, "News" gives you recent developments, sorted by topic)

Designed for small businesses, this site has a ton of resources including guides, bulletins, online training programs, and CD-ROMs. You'll also find worksheets to help you determine the value of your business property and how much insurance you need:

- travelerspc.com

These companies cover computers against damage, theft, power surges, and other high-tech disasters:

- safeware.com
- coveragelink.com

Despite its bent toward larger companies, this user-friendly site contains a slew of informative and entertaining insurance-related resources:

- cigna.com

While its technical language requires you to be well versed in insurance lingo to fully comprehend it, this site has a "Commercial Insurance for Small and Medium-Sized Businesses" section that breaks down insurance coverage by industry:

- cna.com (click on "Products & Services" to find information on commercial insurance)

CHAPTER 8

BUILD YOUR TEAM

To hire or not to hire?

That is the question in the mind of the new entrepreneur. Hiring even one employee changes everything. Suddenly, you need payroll procedures, rules regarding hours, and a policy for vacation pay. You're hit with a multitude of legal requirements and management duties you'd never have to deal with if you worked solo.

To decide whether or not you need employees, take a closer look at your ultimate goals. Do you want to create the next Starbucks, or do you simply want a business where you work on your own terms without having to manage others or put up with a boss looking over your shoulder?

If your goals are modest, then adding staff may not be the best solution for you. If you do need employees, there are plenty of ways to meet your staffing needs without driving yourself nuts. From temporary workers and independent contractors to employee leasing, the following chapter takes a closer look at the dos and don'ts of staffing your business. Read it over, and you will have a better idea whether hiring is the right solution for you.

Defining Your Staffing Needs

The employees you hire can make or break your business. While you may be tempted to hire the first person who walks in the door "just to get it over with," doing so can be a fatal error. A small company cannot afford to carry dead wood on staff, so start smart by taking time to figure out your staffing needs before you even begin looking for candidates.

Job Analysis

Begin by understanding the requirements of the job you are looking to fill. What kind of personality, experience, and education are needed? To determine these attributes, sit down and do a job analysis covering the following areas:

- The reason the job exists (including an explanation of job goals and how they relate to other positions in the company)
- How the job will be done (the methods and equipment used)
- The physical/mental tasks involved (ranging from judging, planning, and managing to cleaning, lifting, and welding)
- The qualifications needed (training, knowledge, skills, and personality traits)

If you are having trouble, one good way to get information for a job analysis is to talk to employees and supervisors at other companies that have similar positions.

Job Description

Use the job analysis to write a job description and job specifications. Drawing from these concepts, you can then create your recruitment materials, such as a classified ad.

The job description is basically an outline of how the job fits into the company. It should point out in broad terms the job's goals, responsibilities, and duties. First, write down the job title and to whom that person will report. Next, develop a job statement or summary describing the position's major and minor duties. Finally, define how the job relates to other positions in the company. Which are subordinate and which are of equal responsibility and authority?

For a one-person business hiring its first employee, these steps may seem unnecessary, but remember, you are laying the foundation for your personnel policy, which will be essential as your company grows. Keeping detailed records from the time you hire your first employee will make things a lot easier when you hire your 50th.

The job specifications describe the personal requirements you expect from the employee. Like the job description, specifications should includes the job title, to whom the person reports, and a summary of the position. However, it also lists any educational requirements, desired experience, and specialized skills or knowledge required. Include salary range and benefits. Finish by listing any physical or other special requirements associated with the job, as well as any occupational hazards.

Writing the job description and job specifications will also help you determine whether you need a part- or full-time employee, whether the person should be permanent or temporary, and whether you could use an independent contractor to fill the position (more on all these options later).

Writing the Ad

Use the job description and specifications to write an ad that will attract candidates to your company. The best way to avoid wasting time on interviews with people who do not meet your needs is to write an ad that will lure qualified candidates and discourage others. Consider this example:

> Interior designer seeks inside/outside salesperson. Flooring, drapes (extensive measuring), furniture, etc. In-home consultations. Excellent salary and commission. PREVIOUS EXPERIENCE A NECESSITY. San Francisco Bay Area. Send resume to G. Green at P.O. Box 5409, San Francisco, CA 90842.

This job description is designed to attract a flexible salesperson and eliminate those who lack the confidence to work on commission. The advertiser asks for expertise in "extensive measuring," the skill he has had the most difficulty finding. The job location should be included to weed out applicants who don't live in the area or aren't willing to commute or relocate. Finally, the capitalized "PREVIOUS EXPERIENCE A NECESSITY" underscores that he will hire only candidates with previous experience.

To write a similarly targeted ad for your business, look at your job specifications and pull out the top four or five skills that are most essential to the job. Don't, however, list requirements other than educational- or experience-related ones in the ad. Nor should you request specific personality traits (such as outgoing, detail-oriented) since people are likely to come in and imitate those characteristics when they don't really possess them. Instead, you should focus on telling the applicants about the excitement and challenge of the job, what they will get out of it, and what it will be like working for you. You can include a salary range with the posting, but you might want to just wait and see the applicants you get and their experience before limiting the job posting with a salary.

WEEK 2

TAKE NOTES!

Posting a job on an online job site offers you advantages like 24-hour access to job postings, unlimited text for postings, and quick turnaround. They also allow you to screen candidates, search resume databases, and keep your ad online for a long period of time—30 to 60 days—vs. a newspaper ad, which runs for only one weekend.

Finally, specify how applicants should contact you. Depending on the type of job (professional or nonskilled) you are trying to fill, you may want

3 WEEKS TO STARTUP

to have the person send a cover letter and a resume, or simply call to set up an appointment to come in and fill out an application.

Recruiting Employees

The obvious first choice for recruiting employees is the classified ad section of your local newspaper, both print and online versions. Place your ad in the Sunday or weekend edition of the largest-circulation local papers.

Beyond this, however, there are plenty of other places to recruit good employees. Here are some ideas:

- **Tap into your personal and professional network.** Tell everyone you know—friends, neighbors, professional associates, customers, vendors, colleagues from associations—that you have a job opening. Someone might know the perfect candidate.

- **Contact school placement offices.** List your openings with trade and vocational schools, colleges, and universities. Check with your local school board to see if high schools in your area have job training and placement programs.

- **Use an employment agency.** Private and government-sponsored agencies can help with locating and screening applicants.

Often their fees are more than justified by the amount of time and money you save in the hiring process.

TAKE NOTES!

WEEK 2

Looking to fill an important position but dreading the hassle of hunting for candidates? Executive recruitment firms, also known as "headhunters" or search firms, can find qualified professional, managerial, or technical candidates for you. Search firms typically charge a percentage of the executive's first-year salary. Because these are expensive services (sometimes you will be charged tens of thousands of dollars) we suggest you only use this type of service if:

- You are hiring a very high-level executive. If you are looking for a CTO or a VP of Marketing, you will want to make sure you make a thorough search and you may find that the best way to find the right candidate is through a headhunter.

- You have tried all of the online options and have yielded no results.

- **List your opening with an appropriate job bank.** Many professional associations have job banks for their members. Contact groups related to your industry, even if they are outside your local area, and ask them to alert their members to your staffing needs.

- **Use industry publications.** Trade association newsletters and industry publications often have classified ad sections where members can advertise job openings. This is a very effective way to attract skilled people in your industry.

- **Go online.** There are a variety of online job banks and databases that allow employers to list openings. These databases can be searched by potential employees from all over the country. You can even receive resumes online.

- **Post notices at senior citizen centers.** Retirees who need extra income or a productive way to fill their time can make excellent employees.

Pre-Screening Candidates

Two important tools in pre-screening job candidates are the resume and the employment application. If you ask applicants to send in a resume, that will be the first tool you use to screen them. You can then have qualified candidates fill out an application when they come in for an interview. If you don't ask for a resume, you will probably want to have prospective employees come in to fill out applications, then review the applications and call qualified candidates to set up an interview.

In either case, it is important to have an application form ready before you begin the interview process. You can buy generic application forms at most office-supply stores or you can develop your own to meet your specific needs. Make sure any application form you use conforms to Equal Employment Opportunity Commission (EEOC) guidelines regarding questions you can and cannot ask (see "Off Limits" on page 162 for more on this).

Your application should ask for specific information such as name, address, and phone number; educational background; work experience, salary history; awards or honors; whether the applicant can work full or part time as well as available hours; and any special skills relevant to the job (foreign languages, familiarity with software programs, etc.). Be sure to ask for names and phone numbers of former supervisors to check as references; if the candidate is currently employed, ask whether it is OK to contact his or her current place of employment. You may also want to ask for personal references. Because many employers these days hesitate to give out information about an employee, you may want to have the applicant sign a waiver that states the employee authorizes former and/or current employers to disclose information about him or her.

> **TAKE NOTES!**
>
> Ask employees to send samples of their work with their resumes or to bring them to the interview. Or ask them to complete a project similar to the actual work they'd be doing (and pay them for it). This gives you a strong indication of how they would perform on the job, and gives them a clear picture of what you expect from them.
>
> At our company, we often ask web and software development potential hires to complete a short (less than two hour) assignment to test their coding skills. This gives our engineering team a much better sense of whether a potential employee has the skills we need.
>
> WEEK **2**

When screening resumes, it helps to have your job description and specifications in front of you so you can keep the qualities and skills you are looking for clearly in mind. Since there is no standard form for resumes, evaluating them can be very subjective. However, there are certain components that you should expect to find in a resume. It should contain the prospect's name, address, and telephone number at the top and a brief summary of employment and educational experience, including dates. Some resumes include a "career objective" that describes what kind of job the prospect is pursuing; other applicants state their objectives in their cover letters. Additional information you may find on a resume or in a cover letter includes references, achievements, and career-related affiliations.

Look for neatness and professionalism in the applicant's resume and cover letter. A resume riddled with typos raises some serious red flags. If a person can't be bothered to put his or her best foot forward during this crucial stage of the game, how can you expect him or her to do a good job if hired?

There are two basic types of resumes: the "chronological" resume and the "functional" resume. The chronological resume, which is what most of us are used to seeing, lists employment history in reverse chronological order, from most recent position to earliest. The functional resume does not list dates of employment; instead, it lists different skills or "functions" that the employee has performed.

Although chronological resumes are the preferred format among HR professionals and hiring managers, functional resumes have increased in popularity in recent years. In some cases, they are used by downsized executives who may be quite well-qualified and are simply trying to downplay long periods of unemployment or are making a career change. In other cases, however, they can signal that the applicant is a job-hopper or has something to hide.

Because it's easy for people to embellish resumes, it's a good idea to have candidates fill out a job application, by mail or in person, and then compare it to the resume. Because the application requires information to be completed in chronological order, it gives you a more accurate picture of an applicant's history.

Beyond functional and chronological resumes, there is another type of resume that's more important to be on the lookout for. That's what one consultant calls an "accomplishment" vs. a "responsibility" resume.

The responsibility resume is just that. It emphasizes the job description, saying things like "Managed three account executives; established budgets; developed departmental contests." An accomplishment resume, on the other hand, emphasizes accomplishments and results, such as "Cut costs by 50 percent" or "Met quota every month." Such a resume tells you that the person is an achiever and has the bottom line firmly in mind.

When reading the resume, try to determine the person's career patterns. Look for steady progress and promotions in past jobs. Also look for stability in terms of length of employment. A person who changes jobs every year is probably not someone you want on your team. Look for people with three-to four-year job stints.

At the same time, be aware of how economic conditions can affect a person's resume. During a climate of frequent corporate downsizing, for example, a series of lateral career moves may signal that a person is a survivor. This also shows that the person is interested in growing and willing to take on new responsibilities, even if there was no corresponding increase in pay or status.

By the same token, just because a resume or a job application has a few gaps in it doesn't mean you should overlook it entirely. You could be making a big mistake. Stay focused on the skills and value the job applicant could bring to your company.

Interviewing Applicants

Once you've narrowed your stack of resumes down to five or so top candidates, it's time to start setting up interviews. If you dread this portion of the process, you're not alone. Fortunately, there are some ways to put both yourself and the candidates at ease—and make sure you get all the information you need to make a smart decision. Start by preparing a list of basic interview questions in advance. While you won't read off this list like a robot, having it in front of you will ensure you cover all the bases and also make sure you ask all the candidates the same questions.

The initial few moments of an interview are the most crucial. As you meet the candidate and shake his or her hand, you will gain a strong impression of his or her poise, confidence, and enthusiasm (or lack thereof). Qualities to look for include good communication skills, a neat and clean appearance, and a friendly and enthusiastic manner.

Put the interviewee at ease with a bit of small talk on neutral topics. A good way to break the ice is by explaining the job and describing the company—its business, history, and future plans.

Then move on to the heart of the interview. You will want to ask about several general areas, such as related experience, skills, educational training or background, and unrelated jobs. Open each area with a general, open-ended question, such as "Tell me about your last job." Avoid questions that can be answered with a "yes" or "no" or that prompt obvious responses, such as "Are you detail-oriented?" Instead, ask questions that force the candidate to go into detail. The best questions are follow-up questions such as "How did that situation come about?" or "Why did you do that?" These queries force applicants to abandon pre-planned responses and dig deeper.

Here are some interview questions to get you started:

- If you could design the perfect job for yourself, what would you do?

- What kind of supervisor gets the best work out of you?

- How would you describe your current supervisor?

- How do you structure your time?

- What are three things you like about your current job?

- What were your three biggest accomplishments in your last job? In your career?

- What can you do for our company that no one else can?

- What are your strengths/weaknesses?

- How far do you think you can go in this company? Why?

- What do you expect to be doing in five years?

- What interests you most about this company? This position?

- Describe three situations where your work was criticized.

- Have you hired people before? If so, what did you look for?

Your candidate's responses will give you a window into his or her knowledge, attitude, and sense of humor. Watch for signs of "sour grapes" about former employers. Also be alert for areas people seem reluctant to talk about. Probe a little deeper without sounding judgmental.

Pay attention to the candidate's nonverbal cues, too. Does she seem alert and interested, or does she slouch and yawn? Are his clothes wrinkled and stained or clean and neat? A person who can't make an effort for the interview certainly won't make one on the job if hired.

Finally, leave time at the end of the interview for the applicant to ask questions—and pay attention to what he or she asks. This is the time when applicants can really show they have done their homework and researched your company—or, conversely, that all they care about is what they can get out of the job. Obviously, there is a big difference between the one who says, "I notice that your biggest competitor's sales have doubled since launching their website in January. Do you have any plans to develop a website of your own?" and the person who asks, "How long is the lunch break?" Similarly, candidates who can't come up with even one question may be demonstrating that they can't think on their feet.

End the interview by letting the candidate know what to expect next. How much longer will you be interviewing? When can they expect to hear from you? You are dealing with other people's livelihoods, so the week that you take to finish your interviews can seem like an eternity to them. Show some consideration by keeping them informed.

During the interview, jot down notes (without being obvious about it). After the interview, allow five or ten minutes to write down the applicant's outstanding qualities and evaluate his or her personality and skills against your job description and specifications.

> ## RED TAPE ALERT!
>
> **WEEK 2**
>
> The Americans With Disabilities Act of 1990 makes it illegal for employers with 15 or more employees to refuse to hire qualified people with disabilities if making "reasonable accommodations" would enable the person to carry out the duties of the job. That could mean making physical changes to the workplace or reassigning certain responsibilities.
>
> While the law is unclear on exactly how far an employer must go to accommodate a person with disabilities, what is clear is that it's the applicant's responsibility to tell the employer about the disability. Employers are not allowed to ask whether an applicant has a disability or a history of health problems. However, after the applicant has been given a written or verbal explanation of the job duties, you may then ask whether he or she can adequately perform those duties or would need some type of accommodation.
>
> For further clarification, read the laws, regulations, and enforcement guidance documents available online from the Equal Employment Opportunity Commission at eeoc.gov.

Off Limits

Equal Employment Opportunity Commission (EEOC) guidelines, as well as federal and state laws, prohibit asking certain questions of a job applicant, either on the application form or during the interview. What questions should you sidestep? Basically, you can't ask about anything not directly related to the job, including:

- Age or date of birth (except when necessary to satisfy applicable age laws)
- Sex, race, creed, color, religion, or national origin
- Disabilities of any kind
- Date and type of military discharge
- Marital status
- Maiden name (for female applicants)
- If a person is a citizen (however, you can ask if he or she, after employment, can submit proof of the legal right to work in the United States)

Other questions to avoid:

- How many children do you have? How old are they? Who will care for them while you are at work?
- Have you ever been treated by a psychologist or a psychiatrist?
- Have you ever been treated for drug addiction or alcoholism?
- Have you ever been arrested? (You may ask if the person has been convicted if it is accompanied by a statement saying that a conviction will not necessarily disqualify an applicant for employment.)
- How many days were you sick last year?
- Have you ever filed for workers' compensation? Have you ever been injured on the job?

In doubt whether a question (or comment) is offensive or not? Play it safe and zip your lip. In today's lawsuit-happy environment, an offhand remark could cost you plenty.

3 WEEKS TO STARTUP

Checking References

After preliminary interviews, you should be able to narrow the field to three or four top candidates. Now's the time to do a little detective work.

It's estimated that up to one-third of job applicants lie about their experience and educational achievements on their resumes or job applications. No matter how sterling the person seems in the interview process, a few phone calls upfront to check out their claims could save you a lot of hassle—and even legal battles—later on. Today, courts are increasingly holding employers liable for crimes employees commit on the job, such as drunk driving, when it is determined that the employer could have been expected to know about prior convictions for similar offenses.

Unfortunately, getting that information has become harder and harder to do. Fearful of reprisals from former employees, many firms have adopted policies that forbid releasing detailed information. Generally, the investigating party is referred to a personnel department, which supplies dates of employment, title, and salary—period.

There are ways to dig deeper, however. Try to avoid the human resources department if at all possible. Instead, try calling the person's former supervisor directly. While the supervisor may be required to send you to personnel, sometimes you'll get lucky and get the person on a day he or she feels like talking.

Sometimes, too, a supervisor can tip you off without saying anything that will get him or her in trouble. Consider the supervisor who, when contacted by one potential employer, said, "I only give good references." When the employer asked, "What can you tell me about X?" the supervisor repeated, "I only give good references." Without saying anything, he said it all.

> **TAKE NOTES!**
>
> **WEEK 2**
>
> Whenever possible, look for employees you can cross-train for different jobs. Someone with HR experience can come in and be an office manager and handle all of your employee benefits. Cross-trained employees can fill in when others are absent, helping keep costs down.

Depending on the position, you may also want to do education checks. You can call a college or university's admissions department to verify degrees and dates of attendance, although some universities will require a written request or a signed waiver from the applicant before releasing any kind of information to you.

WEEK 2 TAKE NOTES!

Motivating independent contractors can be tough. How do you make them feel like part of your business? Communication is key. Send regular e-mails and think about using an online project management tool like 37 Signal's BaseCamp project management tool (basecamphq.com) or think about using a service like Google Docs (docs.google.com) where you can share spreadsheets, word documents, and presentations online for free.

The more you can communicate regularly and make sure that they have access to the right resources internally, the more you will get for your money.

If the person is going to be driving a company vehicle, you may want to do a motor vehicle check with the department of motor vehicles. In fact, you may want to do this even if he or she will not be driving for you. Vehicle checks can uncover patterns of negligence or drug and alcohol problems that he or she might have.

If your company deals with property management, such as maintenance or cleaning, you may want to consider a criminal background check as well. Unfortunately, national criminal records and even state records are not coordinated. The only way to obtain criminal records is to go to individual courthouses in each county. Although you can't run all over the state to check into a person's record, it's generally sufficient to investigate records in three counties—birthplace, current residence, and residence preceding the current residence.

For certain positions, such as those that will give an employee access to your company's cash (a cashier or an accounting clerk, for instance), a credit check may be a good idea as well. You can find credit reporting bureaus in any Yellow Pages. They will be able to provide you with a limited credit and payment history. While you should not rely on this as the sole reason not to hire someone (credit reports are notorious for containing errors), a credit report can contribute to a total picture of irresponsible behavior. And if the person will have access to large sums of money at your company, hiring someone who is in serious debt is probably not a very good idea.

Be aware, however, that if a credit check plays any role in your decision not to hire someone, you must inform them that they were turned down in part because of their credit report.

If all this background-checking seems too time-consuming to handle yourself, you can contract the job out to a third-party investigator. Look in the Yellow Pages for firms in your area that handle this task. The cost averages about $100—a small price to pay when you consider the damages it might save you.

After the Hire

Congratulations! You have hired your first employee. Now what?

As soon as you hire, call or write the applicants who you did not choose to hire and tell them you'll keep their applications on file. That way, if the person you hired isn't the best—or is so good that business doubles—you won't have to start from scratch in hiring your second employee.

For each applicant you interviewed, create a file including your interview notes, the resume, and the employment application. For the person you hire, that file will become the basis for his or her personnel file. Federal law requires that a job application be kept at least three years after a person is hired.

Even if you don't hire the applicant, make sure you keep the file. Under federal law, all recruitment materials, such as applications and resumes, must be kept for at least six months after the employment decision has been made. In today's climate, where applicants sometimes sue an employer who decides not to hire them, it's a good idea to maintain all records related to a hire (or nonhire). Especially for higher-level positions where you narrow the field to two or three candidates, put a brief note or memo in each applicant's file explaining why he or she was or wasn't hired.

The hiring process doesn't end with making the selection. Your new employee's first day is critical. People are most motivated on their first day. Build on the momentum of that motivation by having a place set up for them to work, making them comfortable and welcome. Don't just dump them in an office and shut your door. Be prepared to spend some time with them explaining job duties, introducing them to their office mates, getting them started on tasks, or even taking them out to lunch. By doing so, you are building rapport and setting the stage for a long and happy working relationship.

Alternatives to Full-Time Employees

The traditional full-time employee is not your only hiring option. More employers are turning to alternative arrangements including leased employees, temporary employees, part-timers, and interns. All these strategies can save you money—and headaches, too.

Leased Employees

If payroll paperwork, personnel hassles, and employee manuals sound like too much work to deal with, consider an option that's growing in popularity. Employee leasing—a means of managing your human resources without all the administrative hassles—first became popular in California in the early '80s, driven by the excessive cost of health-care benefits in the state. By combining the employees of several companies into one larger pool, employee leasing companies (also known as professional employer organizations, or PEOs) could offer business owners better rates on health-care and workers' compensation coverage.

Today, there are more than two million leased employees in the United States, and the employee leasing industry is projected to continue growing at a rate of more than 20 percent each year, according to the National Association of Professional Employer Organizations (NAPEO).

But today, employee leasing firms do a lot more than just offer better healthcare rates. They manage everything from compliance with state and federal regulations to payroll, unemployment insurance, W-2 forms, and claims processing—saving clients time and money. Some firms have even branched out to offer "extras" such as pension and employee assistance programs. While many business owners confuse employee leasing companies with temporary agencies, the two organizations are quite different. Generally speaking, temporary help companies recruit employees and assign them to client businesses to help with short-term work overload or special projects on an as-needed basis, according to a spokesperson with the American Staffing Association. With leasing companies, on the other hand, a client business generally turns over all its personnel functions to an outside company, which will administer these operations and lease the employees back to the client.

TAKE NOTES!

Be sure you understand the precise legal relationship between your business and a leasing company. Some people consider the leasing company the sole employer, effectively insulating the client from legal responsibility. Others consider the client and the leasing company joint employers, sharing legal responsibility. Have an attorney review your agreement to clarify any risks.

According to the NAPEO, leasing services are contractual arrangements in which the leasing company is the employer of record for all or part of the client's work force. Employment responsibilities are typically shared between the PEO and the client, allowing the client to retain essential management control over the work performed by the employees.

Meanwhile, the PEO assumes responsibility for a wide range of employer obligations and risks, among them paying and reporting wages and employment taxes out of its own accounts as well as retaining some rights to the direction and control of the leased employees. The client, on the other hand, has one primary responsibility: writing one check to the PEO to cover the payroll, taxes, benefits, and administrative fees. The PEO does the rest.

Who uses PEOs? According to the NAPEO, small businesses make up the primary market for leasing companies since—due to economies of scale—they typically pay higher premiums for employee benefits. If an employee hurts his or her back and files a workers' compensation claim, it could literally threaten the small business's existence. With another entity as the employer of record, however, these claims are no longer the small-business owner's problem. PEOs have also been known to help business owners avoid wrongful termination suits and negligent acts in the workplace, according to an NAPEO spokesperson.

Having to comply with a multitude of employment-related statutes, which is often beyond the means of smaller businesses, is another reason PEOs are so popular with entrepreneurs. According to the NAPEO, with a leasing company, you basically get the same type of human resources department you would get if you were a Fortune 500 firm.

Before hiring a professional employer organization, be sure to shop around since not all offer the same pricing structures and services. Fees may be based on a modest percentage of payroll (2 to 6 percent) or on a per-employee basis. When comparing fees, consider what you would pay a full-time employee to handle the administrative chores the PEO will take off your hands.

Look Before You Lease

How do you decide if an employee leasing company is for you? The National Association of Professional Employer Organizations (NAPEO) suggests you look for the following:

- **Services that fit your human resources needs.** Is the company flexible enough to work with you?
- **Investigate the company's administrative competence.** What experience does it have?

TAKE NOTES!

How do you make the most of your temporary workers once they've come on board? For one, don't treat them any differently from your other employees. Introduce them to your full-time workers as people who are there to help you complete a project, to relieve some overtime stress, or to bring in some skills you might not have in-house.

And don't expect temporary workers to be so well-trained that they know how to do all the little (but important) things, such as operating the copier or answering the phone. Spend some time giving them a brief overview of these things, just as you would any new employee.

One strategy for building a better relationship with your temporary workers is to plan ahead as much as possible so you can use the same temporaries for an extended period of time—say, six months. Or try to get the same temporaries back when you need help again. This way, they'll be more productive, and you won't have to spend time retraining them.

3 WEEKS TO STARTUP

- **Banking and credit references.** Look for evidence that the company's payroll taxes and insurance premiums are up-to-date. Request to see a certificate of insurance.

- **Understand how employees' benefits are funded.** Do they fit your workers' needs? Find out who the third-party administrator or carrier is and whether it is licensed if your state requires this.

- **Make sure the leasing company is licensed** or registered if required by your state.

- **Ask for client and professional references,** and call them.

- **Review the agreement carefully** and try to get a provision that permits you to cancel at short notice—say, 30 days.

For a list of NAPEO member organizations in your area, search their directory online at napeo.org/find/members.cfm.

Temporary Employees

If your business's staffing needs are seasonal—for example, you need extra workers during the holidays or during busy production periods—then temporary employees could be the answer to your problem. If the thought of a temp brings to mind a secretary, think again. The services and skills temporary agencies offer small businesses have expanded.

Today, some companies specialize in medical services; others find their niche in professional or technical fields, supplying everything from temporary engineers, editors, and accountants to computer programmers, bankers, lab support staff, and even attorneys.

With many temporary agencies now offering specialized employees, many business owners have learned that they don't have to settle for low skill levels or imperfect matches. Because most temporary agencies screen—and often train—their employees, entrepreneurs who choose this option stand a better chance of obtaining the quality employees they need for their business.

In addition to pre-screened, pre-trained individuals, temporary agencies offer entrepreneurs other benefits. For one, they help keep your overhead low. For another, they save you time and money on recruiting efforts. You don't have to find, interview, or relocate workers. Also, the cost of health and unemployment benefits, workers' compensation insurance, profit-sharing, vacation time, and other benefits doesn't come out of your budget since many temporary help companies provide these resources to their employees.

How do you find the temporary agency that best suits your needs—from light secretarial to specialized technical support? Look in the Yellow Pages under "Employment Contractors—Temporary Help" or ask around for recommendations. Call a few and ask some questions, including:

- How do you recruit your temporary employees?

- Do you check references of your temporary employees?

- Do you have insurance? Look for adequate liability and workers' compensation coverage to protect your company from a temporary worker's claim.

- How often do you check the progress of your temporary employees while on an assignment?

- Do you offer training for your temporary employees? (According to the American Staffing Association, nearly 90 percent of the temporary work force receives free skills training of some kind.)

- What benefits do you offer your temporary employees?

- Should a temporary employee fail to work out, does the firm offer any guarantees? Look for a firm that can provide a qualified replacement temp right away.

- How quickly can you provide a temporary employee? (When you need one, you'll usually need one right away.)

Also ask the company to provide references. Contact references and ask their opinions of the temporary agency's quality level, reliability, reputation, service, and training.

Before securing the services of a temporary agency, also consider your staffing needs. Do you need a part- or full-time temporary employee? What are your expectations? Clearly defining your needs helps the company understand and provide what you are looking for.

Defining the expected duration of your needs is also very important. While many entrepreneurs bring on a temporary worker for just that—temporary work—some may eventually find they would like to hire the worker full time. Be aware that, at this point, some temporary agencies require a negotiated fee for hiring the temporary employee on a permanent basis. Defining your needs upfront can help you avoid any surprises.

Because a growing number of entrepreneurs purposely use temporary workers part-time to get a feel for whether they should hire them full-time, many temporary help companies offer an option: temporary-to-permanent programs, which allow the prospective employer and employee to evaluate each other. Temp-to-perm programs match a temporary worker who has expressed an interest in permanent work with an employer who has like interests. The client is encouraged to make a job offer to the employee within a predetermined time period, should the match seem like a good one. According to the American Staffing Association, 74 percent of temporary workers decide to become temporary employees because it's a way to get a permanent job.

Last, but not least, before contracting with a temporary agency, make sure it is a member of a trade association such as the American Staffing Association. This means:

1. The company has agreed to abide by a code of ethics and good practices.

2. It is in the business for the long haul—meaning it has invested in its industry by becoming a member of its trade association.

3. It has access to up-to-date information on trends that impact its business.

Part-Time Personnel

Another way to cut overhead costs and benefits costs while gaining flexibility is by hiring part-time workers. Under current law, you are not required to provide part-timers with medical benefits. What are the other benefits to you? By using permanent part-timers, you can get more commitment than you'd get from a temp but more flexibility than you can expect from a nine-to-fiver. In some industries, such as fast food, retail, and other businesses that are open long hours, part-timers are essential to fill the odd hours during which workers are needed.

A traditional source of part-time employees is students. They typically are flexible, willing to work odd hours, and do not require high wages. High school and college kids like employers who let them fit their work schedule to the changing demands of school.

Although students are ideal for many situations, there are potential drawbacks to be aware of. For one thing, a student's academic or social demands may impinge on your scheduling needs. Some students feel that a manicure or a tennis game is reason enough to change their work schedules. You'll need to be firm and set some standards for what is and is not acceptable.

Students are not the only part-timers in town, however. One often-overlooked source of employees is retired people. Often, seniors are looking for a way to earn some extra money or fill their days, and many have years of valuable business experience that could be a boon to your company.

Seniors offer many of the advantages of other part-time employees without the realiability issues that sometimes plague younger workers. They typically have an excellent work ethic and can add a note of stability to your organization. If a lot of your customers are seniors, they may prefer dealing with employees their own age.

Parents of young children, too, offer a qualified pool of potential part-time workers. Many stay-at-home moms and dads would welcome the chance to get out of the house for a few hours a day. Often, these workers are highly skilled and experienced.

Finally, one employee pool many employers swear by is people with disabilities. Workers from a local shelter or nonprofit organization can excel at assembling products or packaging goods. In most cases, the non-profit group will work with you to oversee and provide a job coach for the employees. To find disabled workers in your area, contact the local Association of Retarded Citizens office or the Easter Seals Society.

Outsourcing Options

One buzzword you are probably hearing more often is "outsourcing." Simply put, this refers to sending certain job functions outside a company instead of handling them in-house. For instance, instead of hiring an in-house bookkeeper, you might outsource the job to an independent accountant who comes in once a month or does all the work off-site.

More and more companies—large and small—are turning to outsourcing as a way to cut payroll and overhead costs. Done right, outsourcing can mean you never need to hire an employee at all!

How to make it work? Make sure the company or individual you use can do the job. That means getting (and checking) references. Ask former

WEEK 2

TAKE NOTES!

Some colleges encourage students to work, for a small stipend or even for free, through internship programs. Student interns trade their time and talents in exchange for learning marketable job skills. Every year, colleges match thousands of students with businesses of all sizes and types. Since they have an eye on future career prospects, the students are usually highly motivated.

Does your tiny one-person office have anything to offer an intern? Actually, small companies offer better learning experiences for interns since they typically involve a greater variety of job tasks and offer a chance to work more closely with senior employees.

Routine secretarial or "gofer" work won't get you an intern in most cases. Colleges expect their interns to learn specialized professional skills. Hold up your end of the bargain by providing meaningful work. Can you delegate a direct-mail campaign? Have an intern help on photo shoots? Ask her to put together a client presentation?

Check with your local college or university to find out about internship programs. Usually, the school will send you an application, asking you to describe the job's responsibilities and your needs in terms of skill level and other qualifications. Then the school will send you resumes of students it thinks could work for you. The best part of hiring interns? If you're lucky, you'll find a gem who'll stay with your company after the internship is over.

or current clients about their satisfaction. Find out what industries and what type of workload the firm or individual is used to handling. Can you expect your deadlines to be met, or will your small business's projects get pushed aside if a bigger client has an emergency?

Make sure you feel comfortable with who will be doing the work and that you can discuss your concerns and needs openly. Ask to see samples of work if appropriate (for example, if you're using a graphic design firm).

TAKE NOTES!

Like the idea of part-time workers but got a full-time slot to fill? Try job sharing—a strategy in which two part-timers share the same job. To make it work, hire people who are compatible in skills and abilities, and keep lines of communication open.

If your outsourcing needs are handled by an individual, you're dealing with an independent contractor. The IRS has stringent rules regulating exactly who is and is not considered an independent contractor. The risk: If you consider a person an independent contractor and the IRS later reclassifies him or her as an employee, you could be liable for that person's Social Security taxes and a wide range of other costs and penalties.

If you're still in doubt about hiring independent contractors, it always pays to consult your accountant. Making a mistake in this area could cost you big.

A Family Affair

Want to get good employees and tax savings, too? Consider putting your family members to work for you. Hiring family, especially children, enables you to move family income out of a higher tax bracket into a lower one. It also enables you to transfer wealth to your kids without incurring federal gift or estate taxes.

Even preteen children can be put to work stuffing envelopes, filing, or sorting mail. If their salary is reasonable, it is considered earned income and not subject to the "kiddie tax" rules that apply to kids under 14. And if your business is unincorporated, wages paid to a child under 18 are not subject to Social Security or FICA taxes. That means neither you nor your child has to pay these taxes. Finally, employed youngsters can make tax-deductible contributions to an individual retirement account.

Be sure to document the type of work the family member is doing and pay them a comparable amount to what you'd pay another employee, or the IRS will think you're putting your family on the payroll just for the tax breaks. Keep careful records of time worked, and make sure the work is necessary to the business. Your accountant can suggest other ways to take advantage of this tax situation without getting in hot water.

There are more considerations to think about when hiring family members. There are some great articles online about family business, as well as a whole industry in business education that deal with the ins and outs of running a family business. It would be useful for you to read about running a family business. Think about some of these items and make sure to discuss them with your family before your jump into a family business:

1. What do you do if you need to fire a family member?

2. What happens if a family member is not performing?

3. Is your family all on the same page when it comes to your business objectives?

4. Have you outlined a plan for family members who might be interested about an on-going career opportunity?

5. Be prepared to deal with other employees who are jealous or annoyed by what they may perceive as family members getting preferential treatment.

ONLINE TOOLS

Use the internet for many of your Human Resource needs; there are a number of online tools that can assist you in recruiting, hiring and managing your employees.

These sites allow you to post open positions and search resumes of potential candidates:

- careerbuilder.com
- monster.com
- hotjobs.com

This site may not be as easy to use, but is a fantastic place to post job openings:

- craigslist.com

If you want to obtain driving records, criminal records, background checks, or credit reports for potential employees, this site will provide you with all the necessary resources:

- dmv.org/reports-records.php

A site with an abundance of recruiting tools including recruiting news, daily articles, a recruiting blog, and much more:

- ere.net

Learn about the various types of interviews and get ideas of interview questions you can and cannot ask here:

- jobinterviewquestions.org

The American Staffing Association website provides answers to FAQs about staffing agencies, definitions of staffing services, and allows you to easily search for staffing agencies near you. Complete their brief questionnaire and get a list of all staffing agencies in your area:

- americanstaffing.net/jobseekers/find_company.cfm

For legal information on various Human Resource topics:

- nolo.com

The Society for Human Resource Management (SHRM) site offers comprehensive Human Resource guidance, although you have to become a member to take advantage of their resources:

- shrm.org

Need to find an employee for your specific industry? Try a trade association's website, many of which have classified sections or job boards. These sites allow you to post job listings at a low cost and receive responses from a targeted pool of candidates.

CHAPTER 9

MANAGE YOUR TEAM

Once you've gotten great employees on board, how do you keep them from jumping ship? One way is by offering a good benefits package.

Many small-business owners mistakenly believe they cannot afford to offer benefits. But while going without benefits may boost your bottom line in the short run, that penny-wise philosophy could strangle your business's chance for long-term prosperity. "There are certain benefits good employees feel they must have," says Ray Silverstein, founder of PRO, President's Resource Organization, a small-business advisory network.

Heading the list of must-have benefits is medical insurance, but many job applicants also demand a retirement plan, disability insurance, and more. Tell these applicants no benefits are offered, and they will often head for the door.

The positive side: Offer the right benefits, and your business may just jump-start its growth. Give employees the benefits they value, and they'll be more satisfied, miss fewer workdays, be less likely to quit, and have a higher commitment to meeting the company's goals. Research shows that when employees feel their benefits needs are satisfied, they're more productive.

Create a Culture

Besides looking into all the different benefits you should offer your employees, you should also think about creating a company culture. You will learn more about branding and what it means for your company in the next chapter, but part of branding is your company culture. What kind of work place environment do you want to encourage? What kind of people would best fit and match that environment?

At Palo Alto Software, we serve start-ups, small businesses, and entrepreneurs. Although we are a company that has been around for over 20 years, we have an entrepreneurial culture. We hire people who understand entrepreneurs, who are fascinated by start-ups, and who are excited about working in an entrepreneurial environment. If someone comes to a job interview at our company and is concerned with titles, closed-door offices, and whether they get executive perks, we know that person is not for us.

Figure out the personality of your company and create your culture. Be able to articulate to current employees and potential hires what culture you are cultivating. If people understand the type of environment you want to create, and they agree and like that environment, they will be happier employees. Happier employees tend to be more loyal, and tend to stay longer—all good things for your company.

Benefit Basics

Employers are required to provide employees with certain benefits. You must:

- Give employees time off to vote, serve on a jury, and perform military service
- Comply with all workers' compensation requirements (see Chapter 7)
- Withhold FICA taxes from employees' paychecks and pay your own portion of FICA taxes, providing employees with retirement and disability benefits
- Pay state and federal unemployment taxes, thus providing benefits for unemployed workers

> **TAKE NOTES!**
>
> As a boss, are you a saint—or a Scrooge? Read Jim Miller's *Best Boss, Worst Boss* (Fireside Books) to get an idea how you rate. Miller collected real-life stories, like the tightwad boss who charges employees 30 cents per personal call. Good bosses, by contrast, are generous, compassionate, and empowering. Result? Happier, more productive, and loyal employees.

- Contribute to state short-term disability programs in states where such programs exist
- Comply with the federal Family and Medical Leave Act

You are not required to provide:

- Retirement plans
- Health plans (except in Hawaii)
- Dental or vision plans
- Life insurance plans
- Paid vacations, holidays or sick leave

In reality, however, most companies offer some or all of these benefits to stay competitive. Most employers provide paid holidays for Christmas Day, New Year's Day, Memorial Day, Independence Day, Labor Day and Thanksgiving Day. Many employers also allow their employees to either take time off without pay or let them use vacation days for religious holidays.

Most full-time employees will expect one to two weeks' paid vacation time per year. In explaining your vacation policy to employees, specify how far in advance requests for vacation time should be made, and whether these requests should be in writing or can be done verbally.

There are no laws that require employers to provide funeral leave, but most allow two to four days' leave for deaths of close family members. Companies that don't do this generally allow employees to use some other form of paid leave, such as sick days or vacation.

Legally Speaking

Complications quickly arise as soon as a business begins offering benefits. That's because key benefits such as health insurance and retirement plans fall under government scrutiny, and it is very easy to make mistakes in setting up a benefits plan.

And don't think nobody will notice. The IRS can discover in an audit that what you are doing does not comply with regulations. So can the U.S.

RED TAPE ALERT!

What does COBRA mean to you? No, it's not a poisonous snake coming back to bite you in the butt. The Consolidated Omnibus Budget Reconciliation Act (COBRA) extends health insurance coverage to employees and dependents beyond the point at which such coverage traditionally ceases.

COBRA allows a former employee after he or she has quit or been terminated (except for gross misconduct) the right to continued coverage under your group health plan for up to 18 months. Employees' spouses can obtain COBRA coverage for up to 36 months after divorce or the death of the employee, and children can receive up to 36 months of coverage when they reach the age at which they are no longer classified as dependents under the group health plan.

The good news: Giving COBRA benefits shouldn't cost your company a penny. Employers are permitted by law to charge recipients 102 percent of the cost of extending the benefits (the extra 2 percent covers administrative costs).

The federal COBRA plan applies to all companies with more than 20 employees. However, many states have similar laws that pertain to much smaller companies, so even if your company is exempt from federal insurance laws, you may still have to extend benefits under certain circumstances. Contact the U.S. Department of Labor to determine whether your company must offer COBRA or similar benefits, and the rules for doing so.

Department of Labor, which has been beefing up its audit activities of late. Either way, a goof can be very expensive. You can lose any tax benefits you have enjoyed, retroactively, and penalties can also be imposed.

The biggest mistake? Leaving employees out of the plan. Examples range from exclusions of part-timers to failure to extend benefits to clerical and custodial staff. A rule of thumb is that if one employee gets a tax-advantaged benefit—meaning one paid for with pretax dollars—the same benefit must be extended to everyone. There are loopholes that may allow you to exclude some workers, but don't even think about trying this without expert advice.

Such complexities mean it's good advice never to go this route alone. You can cut costs by doing preliminary research yourself, but before setting up any benefits plan, consult a lawyer or a benefits consultant. An upfront investment of perhaps $1,000 could save you far more money down the road by helping you sidestep legal potholes.

Expensive Errors

Providing benefits that meet employee needs and mesh with all the laws isn't cheap—benefits probably add 30 to 40 percent to base pay for most employees—and that makes it crucial to get the most from these dollars. But this is exactly where many small businesses fall short, because often their approach to benefits is riddled with costly errors that can get them in financial trouble with their insurers or even with their own employees. The most common mistakes:

- **Absorbing the entire cost of employee benefits.** Fewer companies are footing the whole benefits bill these days. The size of employee contributions varies from a few dollars per pay period to several hundred dollars monthly, but one advantage of any co-payment plan is that it eliminates employees who don't need coverage. Many employees are covered under other policies—a parent's or spouse's, for instance—and if you offer insurance for free, they'll take it. But even small co-pay requirements will persuade many to skip it, saving you money.

- **Covering nonemployees**. Who would do this? Lots of business owners want to buy group-rate coverage for their relatives or friends. The trouble: If there is a large claim, the insurer may want to investigate. And that investigation could result in disallowance of the claims, even cancellation of the whole policy. Whenever you want to cover somebody who might not qualify for the plan, tell the insurer or your benefits consultant the truth.

- **Sloppy paperwork.** In small businesses, administering benefits is often assigned to an employee who wears 12 other hats. This employee really isn't familiar with the technicalities and misses a lot of important details. A common goof: not enrolling new employees in plans during the open enrollment period. Most plans provide a fixed time period for open enrollment. Bringing an employee in later requires proof of insurability. Expensive litigation is sometimes the result. Make sure the employee overseeing this task stays current with the paperwork and knows that doing so is a top priority.

- **Not telling employees what their benefits cost.** "Most employees don't appreciate their benefits, but that's because nobody ever tells them what the costs are," says PRO's Silverstein. Many experts suggest you annually provide employees with a benefits statement that spells out what they are getting and at what cost. A simple rundown of the employee's individual benefits and what they cost the business is very powerful.

- **Giving unwanted benefits.** A work force composed largely of young, single people doesn't need life insurance. How can you know what benefits your employees value? You can survey employees and have them rank benefits in terms of desirability. Typically, medical and financial benefits, such as retirement plans, appeal to the broadest cross-section of workers.

If workers' needs vary widely, consider the increasingly popular "cafeteria plans," which give workers lengthy lists of possible benefits plus a fixed amount to spend.

3 WEEKS TO STARTUP

Health Insurance

Health insurance is one of the most desirable benefits you can offer employees. There are several basic options for setting up a plan:

- **A traditional indemnity plan, or fee for service.** Employees choose their medical care provider; the insurance company either pays the provider directly or reimburses employees for covered amounts.

- **Managed care.** The two most common forms of managed care are the Health Maintenance Organization (HMO) and the Preferred Provider Organization (PPO). An HMO is essentially a prepaid health-care arrangement, where employees must use doctors employed by or under contract to the HMO and hospitals approved by the HMO. Under a PPO, the insurance company negotiates discounts with the physicians and the hospitals. Employees choose doctors from an approved list, then usually pay a set amount per office visit (typically $10 to $25); the insurance company pays the rest.

- **Self-insurance.** When you absorb all or a significant portion of a risk, you are essentially self-insuring. An outside company usually handles the paperwork, you pay the claims, and sometimes employees help pay premiums. The benefits include greater control of the plan design, customized reporting procedures and cash-flow advantages. The drawback is that you are liable for claims, but you can limit liability with "stop loss" insurance—if a claim exceeds a certain dollar amount, the insurance company pays it.

- **Health savings accounts.** HSAs allow workers with high-deductible health insurance to make pre-tax contributions to cover health-care costs. A high-deductible plan is one that has at least a $1,050 annual deductible for self-only coverage and a $2,100 deductible for family coverage in 2006. Furthermore, annual out-of-pocket costs paid under the plan must be limited to $5,250 for individuals and $10,500 for families.

Employer contributions to HSAs are tax deductible, excludable from gross income, and are not subject to employment taxes. Employees can use these tax-free withdrawals to pay for most medical expenses not covered by the high-deductible plan.

HSAs are broader than the Archer Medical Savings Accounts, which were available only to individuals working for small employers (50 or fewer employees) or to the self-employed. Archer Medical Savings Accounts expired in 2005. No new Archer accounts can be set up, but those accounts already established may continue to be used.

Cost Containment

The rising costs of health insurance have forced some small businesses to cut back on the benefits they offer. Carriers that write policies for small businesses tend to charge very high premiums. Often, they demand extensive medical information about each employee. If anyone in the group has a pre-existing condition, the carrier may refuse to write a policy. Or if someone in the company becomes seriously ill, the carrier may cancel the policy the next time it comes up for renewal.

Further complicating matters, states are mandating certain health-care benefits so that if an employer offers a plan at all, it has to include certain types of coverage. Mandated benefits increase the cost of basic health coverage from less than 20 percent to more than 50 percent, depending on the state, according to a recent analysis from the Council of Affordable Health Insurance. Employers who can't afford to comply often have to cut insurance altogether.

The good news: Some states have tried to ease the financial burden by passing laws that offer incentives to small-business owners who provide their employees with coverage. There are also ways to cut costs without cutting into your employees' insurance plan. A growing number of small businesses band together with other entrepreneurs to enjoy economies of scale and gain more clout with insurance carriers.

Many trade associations offer health insurance plans for small-business owners and their employees at lower rates. Your business may have only five employees, but united with the other, say, 9,000 association members and their 65,000 employees, you have substantial clout. The carrier issues a policy to the whole association; your business's coverage cannot be terminated unless the carrier cancels the entire association.

Associations are able to negotiate lower rates and improved coverage because the carrier doesn't want to lose such a big chunk of business. This way, even the smallest one-person company

> **TAKE NOTES!**
>
> **WEEK 2**
>
> Want a quick way to save on workers' comp insurance premiums? Some companies offer a 5 percent discount for simply having a written policy prohibiting drugs in the workplace. It's a simple way to save big. Ask your workers' comp provider for details.

can choose from the same menu of health-care options as big companies.

Associations aren't the only route to take. In some states, business owners or groups have set up health insurance networks among businesses that have nothing in common but their size and their location. Check with your local chamber of commerce to find out about such programs in your area.

Some people have been ripped off by unscrupulous organizations supposedly peddling "group" insurance plans at prices 20 to 40 percent below the going rate. The problem: These plans don't pay all policyholders' claims because they're not backed by sufficient cash reserves. Such plans often have lofty-sounding names that suggest a larger association of small employers.

How to protect yourself from a scam? Here are some tips:

- **Compare prices.** If it sounds too good to be true, it probably is. Ask for references from other companies that have bought from the plan. How quick was the insurer in paying claims? How long has the reference dealt with the insurer? If it's less than a few months, it's not a good sign.

- **Check the plan's underwriter.** The underwriter is the actual insurer. Many scam plans claim to be administrators for underwriters that really have nothing to do with them. Call the underwriter's headquarters and the insurance department of the state in which it's registered to see if it is really affiliated with the plan. To check the underwriter's integrity, ask your state's insurance department for its "A.M. Best" rating, which grades companies according to their ability to pay claims. Also ask for its "claims-paying ability rating," which is monitored by services like Standard & Poor's. If the company is too new to be rated, be wary.

- **Make sure the company follows state regulations.** Does the company claim it's exempt? Check with your state's insurance department.

- **Ask the agent or administrator to show you what his or her commission, advance, or administrative cost structure is.** Overly generous commissions can be a tip-off; some scam operations pay agents up to 500 percent commission.

- **Get help.** Ask other business owners if they have dealt with the company. Contact the Better Business Bureau to see if there are any outstanding complaints. If you think you're dealing with a questionable company, contact your state insurance department or your nearest Labor Department Office of Investigations.

Retirement Plans

A big mistake some business owners make is thinking they can't fund a retirement plan and put profits back into the business. But less than half of the employees at small companies participate in retirement plans. And companies that do offer this benefit report increased employee retention and happier, more efficient workers. Also, don't forget about yourself: Many business owners are at risk of having insufficient funds saved for retirement.

To encourage more businesses to launch retirement plans, the Economic Growth and Tax Relief Reconciliation Act of 2001 provides a tax credit for costs associated with starting a retirement plan, including a 401(k) plan, SIMPLE or Simplified Employee Pension (SEP) plan. The credit equals 50 percent of the first $1,000 of qualified startup costs, including expenses to set up and administer the plan and educate employees about it. For more information, see IRS Form 8881, Credit for Small Employer Pension Plan

Start-Up Costs. You can download a PDF of Form 8881 online at irs.gov/formspubs/index.html

Don't ignore the value of investing early. If, starting at age 35, you invested $3,000 each year with a 14 percent annual return, you would have an annual retirement income of nearly $60,000 at age 65. But $5,000 invested at the same rate of return beginning at age 45 only results in $30,700 in annual retirement income. The benefit of retirement plans is that savings grow tax-free until you withdraw the funds—typically at age 59. If you withdraw funds before that age, the withdrawn amount is fully taxable and also subject to a 10 percent penalty. The value of tax-free investing over time means it's best to start right away, even if you start with small increments.

Besides the long-term benefit of providing for your future, setting up a retirement plan also has an immediate payoff—cutting your taxes.

Here is a closer look at a range of retirement plans for yourself and your employees.

Individual Retirement Account (IRA)

An IRA is a tax-qualified retirement savings plan available to anyone who works and/or their spouse, whether the individual is an employee or a self-employed person. One of the biggest advantages of these plans is that the earnings on your IRA grow on a tax-deferred basis until you start withdrawing the funds. Whether your contribution to an IRA is deductible will depend on your income level and whether you are covered by another retirement plan at work.

You also may want to consider a Roth IRA. While contributions are not tax-deductible, withdrawals you make at retirement will not be taxed. For 2006 to 2007, the contribution limit for both single and joint filers was $4,000 per person and increased to $5,000 per person in 2008. After that, contributions are indexed to inflation. Individuals who are 50 or older may make an additional contribution of $1,000 a year.

To qualify for Roth IRA contributions, a single person's adjusted gross income (AGI) must be less than $95,000, with benefits phasing out completely at $110,000. For married couples filing jointly, the AGI must be less than $150,000. The contribution amount is decreased by 40 percent (50 percent if 50 or older) until it is eliminated completely at $160,000 for joint filers.

There's also a new retirement savings option known as a Roth 401(k) to consider. It is a 401(k) plan that allows employees to designate all or part of their elective deferrals as qualified Roth 401(k) contributions. Qualified Roth 401(k) contributions are made on an after-tax basis, just like Roth IRA contributions. Employees' contributions and earnings are free from federal income tax when plan distributions are taken. Unless extended, this option will expire at the end of 2010.

Regardless of income level, you can qualify for a deductible IRA as long as you do not participate in an employer-sponsored retirement plan, such as a 401(k). If you are in an employer plan, you can qualify for a deductible IRA if you meet the income requirements. Keep in mind that it's possible to set up or make annual contributions to an IRA any time you want up to the date your federal income tax return is due for that year, not including extensions. The contribution amounts for deductible IRAs are the same as for Roth IRAs.

For joint filers, even if one spouse is covered by a retirement plan, the spouse who is not covered by a plan may make a deductible IRA contribution if the couple's adjusted gross income is $150,000 or less. Like the Roth IRA, the amount you can deduct is decreased in stages above that income level and is eliminated entirely for couples with incomes over $160,000. Nonworking spouses and their working partners can contribute up to $8,000 to IRAs ($4,000 each), provided the working spouse earns at least $8,000. It's possible to contribute an additional $1,000 for each spouse who is at least 50 years old at the end of the year, as long as there is the necessary earned income. For example, two spouses over 50 could contribute a total of $10,000 if there is at least $10,000 of earned income.

Savings Incentive Match Plan for Employees (SIMPLE)

SIMPLE plans are an attractive option for small-business owners. With these plans, you can choose to use a 401(k) or an IRA as your retirement plan.

3 WEEKS TO STARTUP

A SIMPLE plan is just that—simple to administer. This type of retirement plan doesn't come with a lot of paperwork and reporting requirements.

You can set up a SIMPLE IRA only if you have 100 or fewer employees who have received $5,000 or more in compensation from you in the preceding year. Generally, the employer must make contributions to the plan by either matching each participating employee's contribution, dollar for dollar, up to 3 percent of each employee's pay, or by making an across-the-board 2 percent contribution for all employees, even if they don't participate in the plan, which can be expensive.

The maximum amount each employee can contribute to the plan is $10,000 for 2008. After that, the amount will be indexed for inflation. Participants in a SIMPLE IRA who are age 50 or over at the end of the calendar year can also make a catch-up contribution of an additional $2,500 in 2008.

Simplified Employee Pension (SEP) Plan

As its name implies, this is the simplest type of retirement plan available. Essentially, a SEP is a glorified IRA that allows you to contribute a set percentage up to a maximum amount each year. Paperwork is minimal, and you don't have to contribute every year. And regardless of the name, you don't need employees to set one up.

If you do have employees—well, that's the catch. Employees do not make any contributions to SEPs. Employers must pay the full cost of the plan, and whatever percentage you contribute for yourself must be applied to all eligible employees. Generally, the maximum contribution is 25 percent of an employee's annual salary (up to $225,000 for 2007, subject to cost-of-living adjustments for later years) or $45,000, whichever is less.

As your company grows, you may want to consider other types of retirement plans, such as Keogh or 401(k) plans.

Where to Go

With so many choices available, it's a good idea to talk to your accountant about which type of plan is best for you. Once you know what you want, where do you go to set up a retirement plan? Banks, investment companies, full-service or discount brokers, and independent financial advisors can all help you set up a plan that meets your needs. Many of these institutions also offer self-managed brokerage accounts that let you combine investments in mutual funds, stocks, bonds, and certificates of deposit (CDs).

TAKE NOTES!

Taking time to thank your employees pays off in perform-ance. Some ways to show appreciation: Send birthday cards to workers' homes. Write congratulatory notes for a job well done. Use food to boost morale—Popsicles on a hot day or hot choco-late in the winter. Small things make a big dif-ference in making employees feel valued.

Low-Cost Benefits

In addition to the standard benefits discussed above, there are plenty of benefits that cost your company little or nothing but reap huge rewards in terms of employee satisfaction and loyalty. Consider these ideas:

- **Negotiate discounts with local merchants for your employees.** Hotels, restaurants, and amusement parks may offer discounts on their various attractions, including lodging and food, through corporate customer programs. Warehouse stores, such as Sam's Club and Costco, allow discounted membership to employees of their corporate members. Movie theaters provide reduced-rate tickets for companies' employees.

- **Ask a local dry cleaner for free pickup and delivery of your employees' clothes.** Or ask a garage for free transportation to and from work for employees having their cars serviced there. Many businesses are willing to provide this service to capture—and keep—new customers.

- **Offer healthy drinks and snack to employees.** Usually the money you spend on snacks and drinks comes back to you two-fold in employee productivity. That employee under deadline who is starving can grab a healthy granola bar and bottle of juice and not have to run out to find food. Making sure you stock high quality tea and coffee in the office can also make people happier and more productive.

- **Offer free lunchtime seminars to employees.** Health-care workers, financial planners, safety experts, attorneys, and other professionals will often offer their speaking services at no charge. Education is beneficial for both your employees and your business.

- **Offer supplemental insurance plans** that are administered through payroll but are paid for by the employee. Carriers of health, life, auto, and accident insurance typically offer these plans at a lower rate to employers, so everybody benefits.

- **Offer a prepaid legal services plan** administered through payroll but paid for by the employee. Like insurance, the purpose of the prepaid legal service is to provide protection against the emotional and financial stress of an employee's legal problems. Such services include phone consultations regarding personal or business-related legal matters, contract and document review, preparation of wills, legal representation in cases involving motor vehicle violations, trial defense services, and IRS audit legal services.

The employer deducts the monthly service fee from the paychecks of those employees who want to take advantage of the service. Typical fees range from $17 to $30 per month per employee and cover most routine and preventive legal services at no additional cost. More extensive legal services are provided at a lower rate when offered in this manner, saving employees money.

- **How about an interest-free computer loan program?** Making it easier for employees to purchase computers for their personal use increases the technical productivity of employees on the job. The employee chooses the computer and peripherals based on the employer's parameters. For example, the computer must be a

TAKE NOTES!

Bob Nelson's book, *1001 Ways to Reward Employees,* is an encyclopedic survey of employee rewards. With more than 1,000 innovative ideas for rewarding employees, this book should give you plenty of inspiration on ways to offer rewards in any situation.

WEEK **2**

Macintosh, and the entire package may not exceed $3,000. The company purchases the system, allows the employee to take it home, and deducts the payments from his or her paycheck. Although there's some initial capital outlay, it is recouped quickly. Any computer experience an employee can gain at home will most likely enhance his or her proficiency in the workplace.

- **Offer employee discounts.** Let employees purchase excess inventory from your business at a significant discount via sample sales or employee auctions.

One of the most appreciated but most overlooked benefits is membership in a credit union. There are some 6,000 well-established, state-chartered credit unions throughout the United States and Canada that accept startup businesses as members—at no charge.

The benefits to your employees are threefold: Most likely they'll increase their savings rates (especially if you offer automatic payroll deduction), they'll have access to lower loan rates, and they'll pay lower fees—if any—for services. Services that credit unions frequently offer include:

- Automatic payroll deductions
- Individual retirement accounts
- Savings certificates
- Personal and auto loans
- Lines of credit
- Checking accounts
- Christmas club accounts

Only state-chartered credit unions are allowed to add new companies to their membership rosters. To find a credit union that will accept your company, call your state's league of credit unions. You can also write to the National Credit Union Administration, 1775 Duke St., Alexandria, VA 22314-3428, or call (703) 518-6300 for more information, or visit their website at ncua.gov for a list of consumer resources.

3 WEEKS TO STARTUP

When comparing credit unions, get references and check them. Find out how communicative and flexible the credit union is. Examine the accessibility. Are there ATMs? Is there a location near your business? Consider the end users—your employees.

Once your company is approved, designate one person to be the primary liaison with the credit union. That person will maintain information about memberships as well as enrollment forms and loan applications. Kick things off by asking a credit union representative to conduct on-site enrollment and perhaps return periodically for follow-up or new sign-ups.

Employee Policies

Now that you have employees, you'll need to set policies on everything from pay rates to safety procedures. Many of these policies are regulated by federal and state laws. Here's what you need to know.

Paying Employees

There are many state and federal laws that regulate the paying of employees, including the calculation of overtime, minimum wage, frequency of payment, and rules for payment upon termination. Because your business may be subject to both state and federal laws (the primary federal law being the Fair Labor Standards Act, or FLSA), which are often quite different and conflicting, you should check with the applicable government agencies, your local chamber of commerce, and

RED TAPE ALERT!

WEEK 2

Before you write an employee manual from scratch, check with a business lawyer, or check online to see if you can get a basic template to use as a starting point. Check out our online tools sections for more information. As you write your employee manual, focus on making sure the manual is easy to read and understand. Think of the simplest, shortest way to convey information. Use bullet points and numbered lists, where possible, for easier reading.

A lawyer or a human resources consultant can be invaluable throughout the process. At the very least, you'll want your attorney to review the finished product for loopholes.

Finally, ensure all new employees receive a copy of the manual and read it. Include a page that employees must sign, date, and return to you stating they have read and understood all the information in the manual and agree to abide by your company's policies. Maintain this in their personnel file.

appropriate financial and legal experts to determine which laws apply and how to correctly apply them.

Nonexempt and Exempt Employees

Under the FLSA, all employees are classified as either exempt or nonexempt. A nonexempt employee is entitled to a minimum wage and overtime pay as well as other protections set forth in the FLSA.

Exempt employees are not protected under these rules. However, if you wish to classify an employee as exempt, you must pay him or her a salary. Anyone paid on an hourly basis is automatically considered nonexempt; however, there can be nonexempt employees who are paid a salary.

If salary is not the determining factor, what factors determine whether an employee is exempt? Under FLSA and most state laws, an exempt employee is one whose job responsibilities, more than 50 percent of the time, involve the regular exercise of discretionary powers and can be characterized as:

- **Executive**: usually a manager who directs the work of other employees and has the authority to make recommendations affecting the status of those employees (e.g., hiring, firing, promotions, etc.).

- **Administrative**: a person who performs office or non-manual work under general supervision and whose work primarily involves special assignments or requires specialized training, experience, or education.

- **Professional**: a person who is engaged in a recognized profession such as medicine or law or in a field of learning that is specialized and predominantly intellectual or creative.

There are additional exempt categories for more specialized employees, such as professional artist, computer professional, or outside salesperson. In addition, your business may be subject to both federal and often more restrictive state laws governing the exempt status of employees. In those instances, an employee must meet the requirements for exemption under both federal and state law.

Tip Credits

States sometimes set minimum wage laws above or below the federal minimum wage standard. If your business is subject to both state and federal wage laws, you'll have to pay the higher of the two.

Under federal law (the Small Business Job Protection Act of 1996), you may apply tips received by an employee against the employee's minimum hourly wage, provided that:

- the employee makes at least $30 per month in tips,

- the employer pays at least 50 percent of the federal minimum wage,

- the employee has been informed of the applicable law governing minimum wage and tip credits, and

- the employee retains all the tips received by him or her (unless there's tip pooling with other employees). However, if the hourly wage paid by the employer when added to the tip credit is less than the minimum wage, the employer must make up the difference.

Once again, you will need to make sure there are no contrary state laws governing if and when you can use tip credits to meet your minimum wage obligations. For example, California law requires a higher minimum wage than federal law and thus applies to California employers and employees. Because California law prohibits crediting tips against minimum wage payments, tip credits are unavailable in California. For a table of state laws on tip credits, see dol.gov/esa/programs/whd/state/tipped.htm.

Overtime Requirements

Outside of certain industry-specific exceptions, federal and state law requires that nonexempt employees be paid overtime. Under the FLSA, nonexempt employees must be paid one and a half times their normal rate of pay for hours worked in excess of 40 hours during a work week. A work week is defined as seven consecutive 24-hour periods. Although a work week can begin on any day, it must be fixed for that employee and cannot be changed so as to evade applicable overtime laws. Most states also have their own overtime laws, and if they are more favorable to employees, those are the ones you must follow. For example, under California law, employees who work more than eight hours during a single day are entitled to overtime, even if they do not work more than 40 hours during a given work week (the federal requirement).

Remember, nonexempt employees can be salaried as well as hourly. So don't make the mistake of assuming that because employees are salaried, they are exempt from overtime.

Workplace Safety

Why worry about safety? Because failing to do so could literally destroy your business. Besides the human loss, workplace accidents cost money and time. You could be liable for substantial penalties that could wipe out your business's cash flow. The Occupational Safety and Health Administration (OSHA) can assess huge fines for willful violations of safety rules, especially when they could result in death or serious physical harm. In 2005, BP Products North America Inc. had to pay $21 million in penalties for safety and health violations after a fatal explosion at its plant in Texas City, Texas, that killed 15 workers and injured more than 170. So paying attention to safety is definitely worth your time.

OSHA Regulations

All employers, whether they have one employee or 1,000, are subject to federal OSHA requirements. However, in states where a federally certified plan

> **WEEK 2**
>
> ## TAKE NOTES!
>
> Sooner or later, every entrepreneur needs to write a manual. Employee policy manuals, procedures manuals, and safety manuals are just a few of the more important ones. Even if you only have one employee, it's not too soon to start putting policies in writing. Doing so now—before your staff grows—can prevent bickering, confusion, and lawsuits later when Steve finds out you gave Joe five sick days when he only got four.
>
> How to start? As with everything, begin by planning. Write a detailed outline of what you want to include.

has been adopted, the state plan governs. State standards must be at least as strict as the federal standards.

Businesses that use nonemployee workers, such as independent contractors or volunteers, are not subject to OSHA. Workers are considered employees under OSHA if the employer:

- controls the actions of the employee
- has the power to control the employee's actions
- is able to fire the employee or modify employment conditions.

Small employers (with 10 or fewer employees) don't have to report injuries and illnesses. However, that doesn't mean they are exempt from OSHA regulations.

Compliance With OSHA

The first step in complying with OSHA is to learn the published safety standards. The standards you must adhere to depend on the industry you're in.

Every business has to comply with general industry standards, which cover things like safety exits, ventilation, hazardous materials, personal protective equipment like goggles and gloves, sanitation, first aid, and fire safety.

Under OSHA, you also have a general duty to maintain a safe workplace, which covers all situations for which

> **TAKE NOTES!**
>
> **WEEK 2**
>
> Beware the practice of "cherry picking." Health insurance carriers often woo companies with young, healthy employees away from their existing policies by promising substantially lower rates. All too often, however, those rates rise dramatically after the first year. Sticking with one carrier rather than renegotiating your health insurance coverage every year saves time and effort. In the end, that's money, too.

there are published standards. In other words, just because you complied with the standards that specifically apply to your industry doesn't mean you're off the hook. You also need to keep abreast of possible hazards from new technology or rare situations the government may have thought of and published standards for.

Sound exhausting? Help is available. Start with your insurance carrier. Ask if an insurance company safety specialist can visit your business and make recommendations. Insurers are typically more than happy to do this since the safer your business is, the fewer accident claims you'll file. The government can also help you set up a safety program. Both OSHA and state safety organizations conduct safety consultation programs. Check to see what programs your state safety department offers, too. You'll find local offices of government agencies as well as state organizations listed in the government pages of your phone book, usually under "Labor Department," "Department of Commerce" or a similar name.

Don't forget to tap into the resources of your chamber of commerce, industry trade association, and other business groups. Many offer safety seminars and provide literature free or for a nominal charge. In addition, there are private consultants who can help small businesses set up safety programs that meet OSHA regulatory standards. Your lawyer may be able to recommend a good one in your area.

Put It In Writing

When you have a safety program in place, put it in writing with a safety manual. Your safety manual should explain what to do in the event of a fire, explosion, natural disaster, or any other catastrophe your business may face. In addition to emergency procedures, your safety manual should explain proper procedures for performing any routine tasks that could be hazardous. Ask employees for input here; they are closest to the jobs and may know about dangerous situations that aren't obvious to you. Finally, have an insurance professional, a government representative, and an attorney review the finished manual. You're putting your company's commitment to safety on the line, so make sure you get it right.

Other important safety tips: Emphasize the importance of safety with meetings, inspections, and incentive programs. These don't have to cost a lot (or anything). Make sure you keep well-stocked fire extinguishers and first-aid kits at convenient locations throughout your building. Make sure employees know where these are located and how to use them. Try establishing a "Safe Employee of the Month" award or giving a certificate for a free dinner for winning suggestions on improving safety.

Discriminatory Treatment?

Although sexual harassment is one of the biggest issues facing employers these days, it's not the only type of discrimination you need to be concerned about. Under the Civil Rights Act of 1991, employees who believe they were victims of job discrimination due to race, religion, sex, or disability are entitled to a trial by jury.

While companies with fewer than 15 employees are generally exempt from federal discrimination laws, most states have their own laws prohibiting discrimination, which, in addition to protecting a wider range of categories of employees, include smaller businesses within their scope and procedural and evidentiary standards more favorable to claimants. Apart from the tendency of some juries to award plaintiffs disproportionately high monetary damages, litigation in this area of the law can be extremely costly, even if you prevail. One attorney estimates the average legal fees for defense in a sexual harassment suit, regardless of the verdict, are upwards of $75,000.

> **TAKE NOTES!**
>
> WEEK **2**
>
> The federal Family and Medical Leave Act (FMLA) requires employers to give workers up to 12 weeks off to attend to the birth or adoption of a baby, or the serious health condition of the employee or an immediate family member.
>
> After 12 weeks of unpaid leave, you must reinstate the employee in the same job or an equivalent one. The 12 weeks of leave does not have to be taken all at once; in some cases, employees can take it a day at a time.
>
> In most states, only employers with 50 or more employees are subject to the Family and Medical Leave Act. However, some states have family leave laws that place family leave requirements on businesses with as few as 10 employees; in the District of Columbia, all employees are covered. To find out your state's requirements, visit the Labor Department's website at dol.gov/esa/programs/whd/state/fmla.

Concerns over discrimination are more important than ever in today's increasingly diverse business world. If you run a small business, chances are you will be dealing with employees from many cultures, races, and age groups. How can you keep things running harmoniously and protect your business from legal risk? The best policy is to make sure that everyone in your workplace understands what constitutes harassment and discrimination—and also understands the benefits of a diverse workplace.

TAKE NOTES!

Learn to spot some of the signs that sexual harassment may be occurring in your company. Increased absenteeism, drop-offs in productivity, and lackluster performance are all signs that something may be wrong.

Big companies may spend thousands on diversity training, but there are plenty of low-cost options:

- Learn as much as you can from books on the subject and from exposure to people who are different from you.

- Investigate video series on managing diversity. Many are available for rental or purchase.

- Consider public programs. A growing number of Urban League, chamber of commerce, Small Business Administration, and community college seminars and courses are bringing business owners together to learn about diversity issues.

As the business owner, it's important to set a good example. Some ground rules to help keep you out of trouble are:

- Don't touch employees inappropriately.

- Never date someone who works for you.

- Don't demean others or make suggestive comments. Watch your mouth; what seems humorous to some may offend others.

- Be sensitive to diversity of all kinds. Are employees in their 50s making condescending remarks about the "young upstarts" in their 20s? Two white women in their 40s might face a cultural conflict if one is from the Midwest and the other is from the West Coast, or if one has children and the other doesn't.

- If you decorate your office for the holiday season, don't include some religious symbols and leave out others. Many employers use nonreligious décor such as snowflakes and candles.

- Put policies regarding discrimination and harassment in writing as part of your employee manual. Outline the disciplinary action that will be taken and the process by which employees can make their complaints known.

- Hold a brief orientation meeting to introduce employees to your new policy or reacquaint them with the one already in place. Spell out very plainly what is and isn't acceptable. Many employees are especially confused about what constitutes sexual harassment. You don't want your staff walking around afraid to say hello to one another.

Even if an incident does arise, the good news for business owners: Most complaints can be solved at the company level, before the issue comes close to a courtroom. To make this work, however, time is of the essence. Don't put off dealing with complaints, or the victim is likely to stew.

Give both parties a chance to tell their side of the story. Often, the cause is a simple misunderstanding. To cover all your bases, you may want to have a neutral consultant or human resources professional from outside the company investigate the matter.

ONLINE TOOLS

To choose an insurance provider, you can check out Standard & Poor's insurance ratings at:

- funds-sp.com

Small-business owners can evaluate their options and consult with insurance brokers online—and at no charge at:

- benefitmall.com

For more on employee benefits visit:

- ebri.org

Get access to lots of great information about managing your employees:

- work.com/employees

When figuring out what to pay your employees, there are plenty of online resources. Check out the following salary guides to make sure you are offering competitive packages:

- rhii.com
- salary.com
- payscale.com

Want to get an idea what others in your industry are paying workers? The Bureau of Labor Statistics offers the National Compensation Survey for most regions of the country at:

- stats.bls.gov/ncs

Learn about drug-testing laws, read model employer guides and more at

- drugfreeworkplace.org.

IRS Publication 560, Retirement Plans for Small Business, describes rules for SEP, SIMPLE and other qualified plans. Visit:

- irs.gov

Use an online payroll service to streamline payroll and make it easy to implement. To get the most current results, go to:

- google.com and type "online payroll service"

Use online time tracking and attendance services. Why hassle with this if there are affordable services that do it better? This website outlines the various services you can use:

- timetrackingresearch.com

Don't write your own employee manual. Instead type "employee manual" into a search engine and peruse the results. There are companies that offer manuals for every state in the U.S. and websites that offer free templates. Because an employee manual is a legal document, have a lawyer look over the final document to make sure you have covered all the legal aspects.

CHAPTER 10

BRAND AID

You're really excited about your concept for a new product or service. But do you have a potential brand in the making?

Unfortunately, it's a question too many small-business owners ask far too late, or never ask at all—not a good idea in a world full of savvy consumers and big companies that have mastered the branding game. Great brands are all around us, and it's no accident they make us think of certain things. Think FedEx, and think overnight delivery. Apple Inc. brings to mind cutting-edge products and now, music. Even celebrities are brands. Would you describe Paris Hilton the same way you would Jennifer Aniston?

Their differences—socialite vs actress, party girl vs. good girl—helped to define their particular acting "brands" and let the public get a grasp on their personas. Corporate brands are no different. They have their own "personalities."

> **RED TAPE ALERT!**
>
> You may want to talk to an Intellectual Property lawyer about your branding efforts. There are traps you can fall into if you start using a brand that someone has trademarked, or a slogan or image that another company has already legally claimed as their own. Be aware and talk to a lawyer about the steps involved in branding and protecting your brand.

We like to categorize everything, whether we're talking about people, printers, or pizza places. Test this theory yourself. What draws you to one local business instead of another selling a similar product? One local restaurant might strike you as cute and inviting; another might make you lose your appetite without setting a foot inside—even though both restaurants serve the same type of food. You're not alone if you find yourself categorizing each business you pass.

As a startup entrepreneur, you'll be branding whether or not you're even trying. If you don't have a clear idea of what your new company is about, your potential customers will decide on their own—a risky move for a new company without many, or any, customers. You'll need to have a branding strategy in place before you hang out your shingle. However, before we start strategizing, let's answer the most basic question of all.

What Is Branding, Exactly?

Branding is a very misunderstood term. Many people think of branding as just advertising or a really cool-looking logo, but it's much more complex—and much more exciting, too. John Jantsch, an expert marketing consultant and author of *Duct Tape Marketing*, defines branding as "the art of becoming knowable, likable, and trustable." John goes on to say, "If marketing is doing, then branding is being. A small business brand is everything the business does and has done, much like a biography—or in this case, maybe a brandography."

- **Branding should be your company's foundation.** Branding is more than an element of marketing, and it's not just about awareness, a trademark, or a logo. Branding is your company's reason for being, the synchronization of everything about your company that leads to consistency for you as the owner, your employees and your potential customers. Branding meshes your marketing, public relations, business plan, packaging, pricing, customers, and employees.

- **Branding creates value.** If done right, branding makes the buyer trust and believe your product is somehow better than those of your competitors. Generally, the more distinctive you can make your brand, the less likely the customer will be willing to use another company's product or service, even if yours is slightly more expensive. In fact, a recent J.D. Power and Associates web-based survey of nearly 7,500 consumers who purchased or leased a new vehicle within the last six years found 93 percent of them willing to pay more for a leading brand name. "Branding is the reason why people perceive you as the only solution to their problem," says Rob Frankel, a branding expert and author of *The Revenge of Brand X: How to Build a Big-Time Brand on the Web or Anywhere Else.* "Once you clearly can articulate your brand, people have a way of evangelizing your brand."

TAKE NOTES!

A lot of new companies try to be everything to everyone, but this strategy will make it impossible to communicate your brand. Instead, identify your most likely customer and build your brand on what this person wants and how you can fill his or her needs in a unique way.

WEEK
2

- **Branding clarifies your message.** You have less money to spend on advertising and marketing as a startup entrepreneur, and good branding can help you direct your money more effectively. "The more distinct and clear your brand, the harder your advertising works," Frankel says. "Instead of having to run your ads eight or nine times, you only have to run them three times."

- **Branding is a promise.** At the end of the day, branding is the simple, steady promise you make to every customer who walks through your door—today, tomorrow and 10 years from now. Your company's ads and brochures might say you offer speedy, friendly service, but if customers find your service slow and surly, they'll walk out the door feeling betrayed. In their eyes, you promised something that you didn't deliver, and no amount of advertising will ever make up for the gap between what your company says and what it does. Branding creates the consistency that allows you to deliver on your promise over and over again.

Building a Branding Strategy

Your business plan should include a branding strategy. This is your written plan for how you'll apply your brand strategically throughout the company

TAKE NOTES!

It can be hard to put a dollar figure on what you're getting in return for your investment in branding. Branders talk about this dilemma in terms of "brand equity": The dollar value your brand generates over decades in terms of the demand it drives and the customer loyalty it creates. Coca-Cola's brand equity, for example, is estimated in the billions of dollars.

Think about conducting a simple "brand audit" at least once a year. This means looking at how your product or service is marketed and branded (your marketing messages, etc.), analyzing your brand positioning (i.e., asking customers what they think of your brand), and then comparing the two (your branding efforts vs. customer perceptions) to see how well the two connect.

A simple customer survey with questions like, "When you think about our company and our product, what words come to mind?" can tell you volumes about the strengths and weaknesses of your branding. A new coffee shop owner, for example, might think she serves the best coffee in town, while convenience or ambience—say, the type of music played over the sound system—turns out to be as much, or more, of a selling point from the customer's perspective. A brand audit will help keep you on track and help you build on what you already do well.

over time. At its core, a good branding strategy lists the one or two most important elements of your product or service, describes your company's ultimate purpose in the world, and defines your target customer. The result is a blueprint for what's most important to your company and to your customer.

Don't worry; creating a branding strategy isn't nearly as scary or as complicated as it sounds. Here's how:

Step One: Set Yourself Apart

Why should people buy from you instead of the same kind of business across town? Think about the intangible qualities of your product or service, using adjectives from "friendly" to "fast" and every word in between. Your goal is to own a position in the customer's mind so they think of you differently than the competition. "Powerful brands will own a word—like Volvo [owns] safety," says Laura Ries, an Atlanta marketing consultant and co-author of *The 22 Immutable Laws of Branding: How to Build a Product or Service into a World-Class Brand.* Which word will your company own? A new hair salon might focus on the adjective "convenient" and stay open a few hours later in the evening for customers who work late—something no other local salon might do. How will you be different from the competition? The answers are valuable assets that constitute the basis of your brand.

Step Two: Know Your Target Customer

Once you've defined your product or service, think about your target customer. You've probably already gathered demographic information about the market you're entering, but think about the actual customers who will walk through your door. Who is this person, and what is the one thing he

> **TAKE NOTES!**
> **WEEK 2**
>
> Make your company's website more than just a boring online brochure by adding a company blog, or a monthly podcast from the founder—anything that conveys your company's personality and humanizes your company in the eyes of potential customers. People want to know from whom they're buying, especially if it's a new company.

or she ultimately wants from your product or service? After all, the customer is buying it for a reason. What will your customer demand from you?

Step Three: Develop a Personality

How will you show customers every day what you're all about? A lot of small companies write mission statements that say the company will "value" customers and strive for "excellent customer service." Unfortunately, these words are all talk, and no action. Dig deeper and think about how you'll fulfill your brand's promise and provide value and service to the people you serve. If you promise quick service, for example, what will "quick" mean inside your company? And how will you make sure service stays speedy? Along the way, you're laying the foundation of your hiring strategy and how future employees will be expected to interact with customers. You're also creating the template for your advertising and marketing strategy.

Your branding strategy doesn't need to be more than one page long at most. It can even be as short as one paragraph. It all depends on your

TAKE NOTES!

Many companies large and small stumble when it comes to incorporating employees into their branding strategies. But to the customer making a purchase, your employee is the company. Your employees can make or break your entire brand, so don't ever forget them. Here are a few tips:

Hire based on brand strategy. Communicating your brand through your employees starts with making the right hires. Look to your brand strategy for help. If your focus is on customer service, employees should be friendly, unflappable, and motivated, right? Talk about this brand with your employees.

Set expectations. How do you expect employees to treat customers? Make sure they understand what's required. Reward employees who do an exceptional job or go above and beyond the call of duty.

Communicate, then communicate some more. Keeping employees clued in requires ongoing communication about the company's branding efforts.

product or service and your industry. The important thing is that you answer these questions before you open your doors.

Bringing It All Together

Congratulations—you've written your branding strategy. Now you'll have to manage your fledgling brand. This is when the fun really begins. Remember, FedEx was once a startup with an idea it had to get off the ground, too. Here are some tips:

- **Keep ads brand-focused.** Keep your promotional blitzes narrowly focused on your chief promise to potential customers. For example, a new bakery might see the warmth of its fresh bread as its greatest brand-building asset. Keep your message simple and consistent so people get the same message every time they see your name and logo.

- **Be consistent.** Filter every business proposition through a branding filter. How does this opportunity help build the company's brand? How does this opportunity fit our branding strategy? These questions will keep you focused and put you in front of people who fit your product or service.

- **Shed the dead weight.** Good businesses are willing to change their brands but are careful not to lose sight of their original customer base and branding message. Consider Starbucks, which changed the way it made lattes to speed up the process. "You have to give up something to build a brand," Ries says. "Good brands constantly get rid of things that don't work."

ONLINE TOOLS

Luckily, there are some great blogs and online content sites that can help you understand how a good brand will make your new business more successful. Remember that building a brand will take time—you won't build a brand in three weeks. But what you can do in three weeks is build a foundation for your brand that will stay with your business forever.

Duct Tape Marketing: John Jantsch writes a great, easy-to-understand blog with great, easy-to-implement ideas for marketing and branding your new business

- ducttapemarketing.com

The trade magazine *Brandweek* is a good source of news and information about branding trends. They have a great web site with a lot of content:

- brandweek.com

Business Week Online has a Brand Equity section:

- businessweek.com/innovate/brandequity

Brand New: A great blog on branding and what big companies are doing to their brands:

- underconsideration.com/brandnew

The Origin of Brands Blog: Laura Ries, co-author of *The 22 Immutable Laws of Branding,* writes a great blog with a focus on branding:

- ries.typepad.com

CHAPTER 11

SPIN THE WEB

Your website is up, and you have promoted it on everything from business cards to T-shirts. Your shopping cart program is primed for action. There's only one problem. Nobody shows up.

The net is littered with tens of thousands of dead sites, abandoned because no one visited. You can always tell a dead site—it was last updated on its launch date. So how can you make yours successful?

Throw some money at it—judiciously. No matter if you do business in your town or around the world, the internet has become an essential small business marketing tool! Websites have become an essential marketing tool no matter the size or purpose of your business.

Local shoppers are using the internet to find local businesses in every city in America," says John Jantsch, best-selling author of *Duct Tape Marketing*. If you are starting a business today you need a website. This chapter aims to give you some basic information to get you started quickly. As you get more proficient online, and your business becomes more sophisticated, you will want to make sure that you are keeping up with the current trends in online marketing.

RED TAPE ALERT!

You could be infringing on someone's trade mark by simply registering a domain for your business's new website. It is always smart to talk to a lawyer about not just the name of your legal entitiy, but also the domain name that you will be using to market your business. The last thing you want is a law suit on your hand when you start marketing you business online.

What was true yesterday won't be true next year. This is a technology where significant changes occur in very short periods. In order to succeed in internet marketing you will want make sure that you keep up with the current trends, and apply them to your business. In the Online Tools section at the end of this chapter, you will find listings of some good industry websites to keep on your radar in order to keep your online marketing tactics current.

Get Started: Build Your Site

We have established that you do indeed need a website for your new business. So how do you get it started? Here are a few suggestions, depending on how much you want to pay, and how much you want to do on your own:

- You should be able to find a web development shop to build a suitable company website for thousands or even just hundreds of dollars, depending on your needs. Elance.com and craigslist.org are good places to start your search, or just Google web developers in your area.

- Another option is to build your website yourself. You should have someone involved with solid design and copywriting skills, but technical skills are not necessarily required. You can create a surprisingly robust custom website on your own using simple step-by-step tools on free or low-cost services like homestead.com, weebly.com, or freewebs.com.

- Or you might consider using a news-oriented blog as the core of your website, the way that ducttapemarketing.com and techcrunch.com do. Setting up and customizing a free blog site is easy. Just visit wordpress.com, typepad.com, or blogger.com for details.

The key to getting your website up and running at the beginning of your business is just that: Get it up and running. Use whatever tools are easiest, and cheapest for you, keeping in mind your website goals. Here are some additional questions you will want to answer, before you choose your website design and structure:

1. **Is your website going to sell anything?** If so, make sure you choose a website design or service that will allow you to easily add on a commerce engine. Services like homestead.com give you some easy options. Or you can always use a service like Yahoo! Shopping, and link it into your website.

2. **Is your website something that needs to have frequent updates?** Some websites need to be updated monthly, but sometimes a business owner will want to update his or her website daily. Think about your needs. If you are a restaurant you might want to update your special menu weekly. If you are selling consulting services, writing short blog posts every day in your area of expertise might help prove your expertise to potential clients.

> **TAKE NOTES!**
>
> If you pay for someone to design your website, make sure that you talk to them about "SEO." If they don't know what SEO (Search Engine Optimization) means, find another website designer.

3. **Is your website a "business card" website,** or a website that needs potential clients to be able to interact with it? Many small businesses just need a website with a simple design that contains basic information—it is just there so that when someone searches for your type of business in your location, they find out about you. Nothing more. Sometimes, though, a

website needs to be interactive, allowing a customer to buy something, book a reservation, request a bid, or request more information.

When you start out, it's important to understand that simple is best. You don't need your website to do everything day one. But if you know that eventually you want to sell products online, make the right choices when you start your website so you can add-on to it later, without having to start all over.

TAKE NOTES!

If you have competitors that have been in the business longer, and you know are successful, visit their websites. A little competitive snooping can do nothing but help you understand what you need to do to build your own website.

A Marketing Tool

Think of your website as a marketing tool like the others you use to promote your business. The great thing about it is that there are lots of free and easy-to-use tools that will help you understand how many people visit your site, how long they stay, if they come back, and most importantly if you sell online, how much money you make from your website visitors. The key to your success will be to understand your customers, build a website that gives them what they want, and then measure the results. You will then be able to make small changes, measure some more, and improve the return on your investment.

Savvy marketers master permission marketing, which provides incentives for customers to learn more about your product or service. Let's say you run the Clicks and Bricks Bed and Breakfast in Vermont. Spring is your off-season, and you'd like to reach out to former visitors and those who have sent e-mails inquiring about the Clicks and Bricks B&B.

Using the principles of permission marketing, you can:

- Use your database of customer and prospect e-mails to build an audience for a promotional campaign.

- Recognize that those consumers have indicated a willingness to talk to you. So find something to say to them. You could offer them a "three nights for the price of two" promotion or run a contest for a free two-night midweek stay. Its offers like these that keep customers and prospects engaged.

- Encourage a learning relationship with your customers. Send e-mails about upcoming local events such as the annual Fuzzy Worm Festival, or offer two-for-one coupons for an upcoming art show. Remind them of Vermont's allure in the spring.

- Deepen your communication as site visitors become customers and first-timers become return visitors. Send birthday or anniversary cards. Reward them with a glossy national B&B directory. Show them that you value their patronage.

- Track the results from your different promotions to find out which promotions work best for different kind of customers. Some possibilities include:

  - Build a list of customers that are interested in art shows. Then you can send out special promotions when big art shows are in the area.

  - Keep a list of customers who enjoy nature hikes with a park ranger at the nearby state park. Arrange special day hikes with the state park and e-mail your customers with promotions that include those day hikes.

  - Send out two separate promotions to two subsets of nature-loving customers. You can then compare the results for future promotions.

> **TAKE NOTES!**
>
> WEEK 2
>
> If you are writing a blog on your website, think about sending out a regular e-mail newsletter to your customers or clients and include links to your blog posts. This is a great way to drive traffic to your site, and let people know about your expertise.

The most important aspect to remember about your website, as you use it for marketing, is that it is a dynamic medium. It is meant to be changed, adjusted, and tweaked. It is supposed to be something that evolves as your business evolves. Don't be afraid to use technology tools to help you manage the information, and learn from your customers to better serve them in the future. The Online Tools section at the end of this chapter has additional tools, content, and services you might want to take a look at.

Attracting Visitors to Your Site

Getting visitors to your site is a maddening challenge, especially since the number of websites is over the billion mark. Your strategies for doing so may include search engines, paid search services, and marketing efforts. Let's consider them one at a time.

Search Engines

Search engines, such as Google, Yahoo, and MSN, are web pages that people use to find other web pages by typing a search term into a box and getting search results. Search engine optimization is the process of making sure that when people search for any word or phrase related to your business, they will find your site among the thousands of websites that come up in the search, and that your site appears as close as possible to the beginning of the list. How close depends on how "optimized" your site is; how well you set up your site to accommodate the search engines, such as making sure the right key words appear on your site. The rules for search engines change often, so search engine optimization also means following changes and trends, and modifying your site to accommodate them.

TAKE NOTES!

Want to know more about search engines? The site Searchenginewatch.com can answer your questions. It compares the major search engines and tells you how to get listed. It also provides tips for searchers so you can learn to think like your customers and make it easier for them to find you. Plus, you can get a free newsletter.

Search engines have become a ubiquitous part of American culture. Every day millions of Americans go online to search the internet or Google something or someone. According to the Pew Internet & American Life project,

75 percent of all adults use the internet. Of those users, more than 90 percent use a search engine to find information. (You can check out the latest statistics at pewinternet.org.) Lee Rainie, director of the Pew Internet & American Life Project, states:

> Most people think of the internet as a vast library, and they increasingly depend on search engines to help them find everything from information about the people who interest them to transactions they want to conduct, organizations they need to deal with, and interesting factoids that help them settle bar bets and backyard arguments.

The first thing you will want to do when considering search engines, is to make sure that your website is "search engine optimized." Whoa, you say. This is getting way too technical for me. While some of the ideas in this chapter may sound technical, and may be hard to get your mind around, there are services that are cheap and easy to use so that you don't have to do everything or even anything on your own. What you do need to do, though, is make sure that the popular search engines list your website. Rather than list out specifics here that in six months will be outdated (remember how fast the internet changes), I recommend the following:

1. Make sure your website has some basic SEO (search engine optimization). The easiest way to do this is to search for SEO or SEO tools in Google. You will find thousands of results for these searches. Focus on first reading a few informational articles, and then look at some cheap and fast tools to help do some initial optimization of your website. DO NOT get ahead of yourself and engage an SEO consultant just yet. You are just getting started and you should stick to some basic free or very cheap tools in order to just get your website up and running and listed as soon as possible.

2. Once you have done the few things necessary to optimize your website for search engines, do another search on Google for "get listed in search engines." You will see many results. What you want to do is click around and look at informational articles. Once you read a few articles, then start

looking at some tools that can easily and cheaply help you get listed in multiple search engines.

3. Now that you have done the basic SEO and listing tasks, you might want to explore options for boosting your traffic. There are many, many services that promise too much in this area. Check out some of the links in our Online Tools section, and beware of people trying to charge you for services that won't do much.

Now that your website is search engine optimized, and listed on engines, you will want to think about additional ways to drive traffic to your website. As you read about different strategies and tactics in the rest of this chapter, please make sure that you keep your specific website objectives front and center. If you are starting a convenience store, your objectives online may be to just make sure people know where you are. If you are starting an online ski shop, you will want to make sure you are marketing and reaching all the skiers buying equipment online. Every business has different objectives, so keep yours front and center as you market your website. There is unfortunately no "one size fits all" when putting your business online.

TAKE NOTES!

WEEK 2

People often want to create affiliate programs or join affiliate programs. One of the first and probably most well known affiliate programs was created by Amazon.com. You can join and be an affiliate and receive a commission every time you refer a paying customer to Amazon.com.

One caveat if you are thinking about creating a program or joining a program: The top 10 percent of any program's affiliates will bring in more than 90 percent of the revenue. This means that if you join a program to sell other people goods, don't plan on it making you tons and tons of money. If you start a program to have other people join, know that very few affiliates will be the majority of your affiliate income.

Paid Search Services

We call search results that the search engines produce as part of their normal function and that aren't influenced by ads or payments, "organic" search results. Beyond organic results are paid search results. After optimizing your website for organic search traffic, you may want to experiment with pay-per-click (PPC) advertising. PPC ads run alongside the organic results on search engine results pages, often with the headline "Sponsored Results." You can choose how much you spend to have your ads appear for specific keywords related to your business; you only pay when people actually click on your ads.

If you are going to spend time and money buying PPC advertising online, your MUST make sure you are using a web analytics package to track your results. There is no point in spending money if you do not know what the money is doing for you. The beauty of the web vs. traditional media for advertising is that the web actually lets you track every click and every visitor, and see whether your campaigns are actually bringing in money. There are companies that have a policy that they have to make $2 for every $1 they spend in PPC advertising. This is a great way to make sure that you are never spending more than you make. But the only way that you can make this work is to track your campaigns and understand the analytics behind them. How can you figure this all out? Here are some pointers:

> **TAKE NOTES!**
>
> WEEK 2
>
> Want to know which keywords your should buy for a PPC campaign? Type in different keywords and see whether competitors have PPC advertising. The more familiar you are with where and how your compeitiors are using PPC advertising, the more knowledge you will have for your campaigns.

- Make sure that your website is connected to analytic software. Some hosting services provide this as one of the features, some do not. Ask. If not, use the free Google Analytics tool.

- If someone is designing your website, they should know about tracking software and how to set your website up so you can use it. If they don't, hire someone else.

- If you are still clueless, use a service like elance.com to find a consultant who can help you, or type "web analytics" into Google and peruse the results.

Keeping Visitors at Your Site

A good website design and strategy for attracting visitors takes you three-quarters of the way to success. The final step is getting people to try your offerings and to come back for more, and the best way to do that is to serve customers what they want. If you are selling snowboards, don't try and attract skiers to your website. If you are focusing on being a specialty tea shop online, don't spend PPC money on bringing coffee drinkers to your website. People have very little patience these days and will be gone from your website in milliseconds if they get there and don't find what they were looking for. The best way to keep visitors at your website is to bring the right visitors in. Use SEO and PPC tactics to bring in the visitors, and then use analytic tools to analyze what they do once they get there. Once you understand the big picture, it will be easier for your provide information, products, and services that keep people on your website longer, get them to buy things from you, and in the best cases, have them coming back to you later.

How many people will buy your products after seeing, say, a print ad that you ran in a targeted trade journal? The sad truth is, you will probably never know. But with internet marketing activities, that sort of return-on-investment information is easily available. As we have mentioned above, you should add an analytics package to your website. Google Analytics (google.com/analytics) is a good option; it's easy to install and free to use. Within hours of going live, you can see how many people are coming to their site, what they are clicking on, how many visitors are "converting" to sales or other goals that you configure, how many are exiting your site and at what points, and much more.

Once you get the basics down, it is surprisingly easy to take your analytics and site optimization to the next level. Use a free heat-map analytics tool like CrazyEgg (crazyegg.com) to see where exactly visitors are clicking on your key pages. The heat map technique gives you a visual representation of how many people have clicked on each of the links on a page.

Use split-testing tools like the free Google Optimizer to serve different versions of your key pages in head-to-head tests to see which ones perform the best (Google.com/websiteoptimizer). To learn more about site tuning and the surprising gains it can produce, check out Tim Ash's book *Landing Page Optimization*.

Once you get people to your site, and understand why they are there, you can start to implement some more marketing programs to continue to drive traffic and revenue. Try some of the following:

- **Be helpful.** When a customer always reorders the same item, make it easy for them to reorder by sending reminder e-mails.

- **Stay in touch.** Send an e-mail with a new promotion a few weeks or months after a customer makes a purchase.

- **Have fun.** People who surf the internet are looking for fun. You don't have to be wild and wacky (unless you want to). Just make sure you offer original content presented in an entertaining way.

- **Add value.** Offering something useful that customers can do adds tremendous value to your site. For example, customers can track their own packages at the FedEx site or concoct a recipe for a new drink at the Stolichnaya vodka site. While it doesn't have to be quite so elaborate, offering users the ability to download forms or find useful information that relates to their particular situation will keep them coming back.

- **Keep it simple.** Don't build a site that's more than three or four levels deep. Internet users love to surf, but they get bored when they have to sift through loads of information to find what they're looking for.

- **Make payment a snap.** If you're setting up an online storefront, give customers an easy way to pay you. Consider including a toll-free ordering number or fax line for those customers who are not as internet savvy.

The biggest problem you can have with your website is keeping it up to date—you are almost better off not having one if you are not going to keep it updated. How many times have you been to a website that has clearly not been updated in years and wonder whether the business is even still alive? You can implement all the cool tactics we discuss in this chapter, but don't do it if it is too much for you to keep fresh. You want a website that sells your products or services and nothing sells if it is out of date and old. Do just enough to look professional and to keep customers informed and happy—if you can't do anything else. As your business grows, you can then think about hiring someone to help you out. The key to success online is to keep up with the internet and be relevant and fresh. I hope we have provided enough information for anyone to do that quickly and easily as they get their business online.

ONLINE TOOLS

Learn the basics about online marketing:

- entrepreneur.com/marketing/onlinemarketing
- ducttapemarketing.com
- Seth Godin's marketing blog: sethgodin.typepad.com
- Seth Godin's guide to building a website that works: sethgodin.typepad.com/seths_blog/files/knockknock.pdf

Easy website building tools:

- homestead.com
- weebly.com
- freewebs.com
- Type "create a website" into Google

Blog sites:

- typepad.com
- wordpress.com
- blogger.com

Find a web designer:
- elance.com
- Craig's List: craigslist.com

Learn about search engines and SEO:
- searchenginewatch.com
- searchengineguide.com
- seo.com
- seobook.com/blog

Tools and content for analyzing and improving your SEO and online marketing:
- analytics.google.com
- google.com/webmastertools
- webmasterworld.com
- crazyegg.com

PPC advertising:
- adwords.google.com
- searchmarketing.yahoo.com
- adcenter.microsoft.com
- keyworddiscovery.com

Sites that offer quality programs:
- linkshare.com
- Commission Junction: cj.com

Directories of affiliate programs:
- clickslink.com
- affiliatescout.com
- affiliateprograms.com

CHAPTER 12

SPREAD THE WORD

Paid advertising isn't the only way to spread the word about your business. In fact, one of the best ways to get your business noticed does not have to cost you a dime. We are talking about public relations.

Public relations is a broad category, spanning everything from press releases and networking at chamber of commerce meetings to sponsoring contests or holding gala special events. This chapter will show you the basics of public relations and give you plenty of ideas to get started. These ideas will get you on the right track and help you through the life of your business. And ideas are what it's all about, because when it comes to public relations, you are limited only by your own imagination.

Remember, this information is intended to help you learn and understand how to be most effective with your PR strategy. Although you won't be able to accomplish most of this in three weeks, you will be able to at least do the research and get everything organized so that you can take advantage of appropriate opportunities as they come along.

Getting Publicity

Just what is public relations, or PR? And how does it differ from advertising? PR is the opposite of advertising. In advertising, you pay to have your message placed in a newspaper, TV, or radio spot. In public relations, the article that features your company is not paid for. The reporter, whether broadcast or print, writes about or films your company as a result of information he or she received and researched.

Publicity is more effective than advertising, for several reasons. First, publicity is far more cost-effective than advertising. Even if it is not entirely free, your expenses are generally limited to the cost of phone calls and mailings to the media. Second, publicity has greater longevity than advertising. An article about your business will be remembered far longer than an ad. Publicity also reaches a far wider audience than advertising generally does. Sometimes your story might even be picked up by the national media, spreading the word about your business all over the country. Finally, and most importantly, publicity has greater credibility with the public than does advertising. Readers feel that if an objective third party—a magazine, newspaper, or radio reporter—is featuring your company, you must be doing something worthwhile.

Why do some companies succeed in generating publicity while others don't? It's been proven time and time again that no matter how large or small your business is, the key to securing publicity is identifying your target market and developing a well-thought-out public relations campaign. To get your company noticed, follow these seven steps.

1. **Write your positioning statement.** This sums up in a few sentences what makes your business different from the competition.

2. **List your objectives.** What do you hope to achieve for your company through the publicity plan you put into action? List your top five goals in order of priority. Be specific, and always set deadlines. Using a clothing boutique as an example, some goals may be to increase your store traffic, which will translate into increased sales, or to create a high profile for your store within the community.

3. **Identify your target customers.** Are they male or female? What age range? What are their lifestyles, incomes, and buying habits? Where do they live?

4. **Identify your target media.** List the newspapers, print, and online publications and TV and radio programs in your area that would be appropriate outlets. Make a complete list of the media you want to target, then call them and ask whom you should contact regarding your area of business. Identify the specific reporter or producer who covers your area so you can contact them directly. Make your own media directory, listing names, e-mail addresses, physical addresses, and telephone and fax numbers. Separate TV, radio, online, and print sources. Know the "beats" covered by different reporters so you can be sure you are pitching your ideas to the appropriate person.

5. **Develop story angles.** Keeping in mind the media you're approaching, make a list of story ideas you can pitch to them. Develop story angles you would want to read about or see on TV. Plan a 45-minute brainstorming session with your spouse, a business associate, or your employees to come up with fresh ideas.

If you own a toy store, for example, one angle could be to donate toys to the local hospital's pediatric wing. If you own a clothing store, you could alert the local media to a fashion trend in your area. What's flying out of your store so fast you can't keep it in stock? If it's shirts featuring the American flag, you could talk to the media about the return of patriotism. Arrange for a reporter to speak with some of your customers about why they purchased that particular shirt. Suggest the newspaper send a photographer to take pictures of your customers wearing the shirts.

6. **Make the pitch.** Put your thoughts down, and send them to the journalist in a "pitch e-mail." Start with a question or an interesting fact that relates your business to the target medium's audience. For instance, if you were writing for a magazine aimed at older people, you could start off "Did you know that more than half of all women over 50 have not begun saving for retirement?" Then lead into your pitch: "As a Certified Financial Planner, I can offer your readers 10 tips to start them on the road to a financially comfortable retirement…" Make your e-mail no longer than two paragraphs; include your telephone number so the reporter can contact you.

   If appropriate, include a press release with your e-mail. Be sure to include a positioning statement in any correspondence or press releases you send.

7. **Follow up.** Following up is the key to securing coverage. Wait four to six days after you've sent the information, then follow up your pitch e-mail with a telephone call. If you leave a message on voice mail and the journalist does not call you back, call again until you get him or her on the phone. Do not leave a second message within five days of the first. If the reporter requests additional information, send it immediately and follow up to confirm receipt.

Talking to the Media

Once you reach the journalist on the telephone, remember that he or she is probably on deadline. Be courteous, and ask if he or she has time to talk. If not, offer to call back at a more convenient time. If the journalist can talk to you, keep your initial pitch to 20 seconds; offer to e-mail additional information to support your story ideas.

The following tips will boost your chances of success:

- **Don't stop when you hear "No."** If a journalist rejects your idea, ask if he or she can recommend someone else who might be interested.

- **Know exactly what you're going to say.** Have it written down in front of you before you telephone the journalist—you'll feel more confident.

3 WEEKS TO STARTUP

- **Everyone likes a compliment.** If you've read a story you particularly enjoyed by the reporter you're contacting, let him or her know. This will also show that you're familiar with that journalist's work.

- **Be persistent.** Remember, not everyone will be interested. If your story idea is turned down, try to find out why and use that information to improve your next pitch. Just keep going, and don't give up. You will succeed eventually, but it may take time to get the pitch right and to pitch it to the right person at the right time.

- **Don't be a pest.** You can be persistent without being annoying. Use your instincts; if the journalist sounds rushed, offer to call back.

- **Be helpful.** Become a resource by providing journalists with information. Remember, they need your story ideas. There are only so many they can come up with on their own.

- **Be nice to everyone you speak with.** Always remember that assistants get promoted, no matter how low they are on the totem pole. After you establish a connection, keep in touch; you never know where people will end up.

> **WEEK 2**
>
> **TAKES NOTES!**
>
> Does your business use recycled paper products or donate to a homeless shelter? Today, many consumers consider such factors when deciding whether to patronize your business. A business's "social responsibility" quotient can make a difference in its bottom line. Think of unique differentiators that your business brings to the table, and capitalize on them. Make sure you always mention these unique aspects of your business in press releases, on your website, in your blog, on advertising, etc. If there is a cause that you truly believe in, and fits into your company's brand, take the step s to have your new company support this cause with time and money. People will notice, and your customers will feel better about buying goods and services from you.

- **Say thank you.** When you succeed in getting publicity for your business, always write a thank-you note to the journalist who worked on it with you. You'd be surprised how much a note means.

Plan your publicity efforts just as carefully as you plan the rest of your business. You'll be glad you made the effort when you see your company featured in the news—and when you see the results in your bottom line.

Meet the Press

Think of a press release as a ticket to publicity—one that can get your company coverage in all kinds of publications. Editors and reporters get hundreds of press releases a day. How do you make yours stand out?

First, be sure you have a good reason for sending a press release. A grand opening, a new product, a record-setting sales year, a new location, or a special event are all good reasons.

Second, make sure your press release is appropriately targeted for the publication or broadcast you're sending it to. The editor of *Road & Track* is not going to be interested in the new baby pacifier you've invented. It sounds obvious, but many entrepreneurs make the mistake of sending press releases at random without considering a publication's audience.

To ensure readability, your press release should follow the standard format. Use a wire service to distribute your release and use their guidelines for submission to craft your press release template.

Limit your press release to one or two pages at most. It should be just long enough to cover the six basic elements: who, what, when, where, why, and how. The answers to these six questions should be mentioned in order of their importance to the story to save the editor time and space.

Don't embellish or hype the information. Remember, you are not writing the article; you are merely presenting the information and showing why it is relevant to that publication in hopes that they will write about it. Pay close attention to grammar and spelling. Competition for publicity is intense, and a press release full of typos or errors is more likely to get tossed aside.

Some business owners use attention-getting gimmicks to get their press releases noticed. In most cases, this is a waste of money. If your release is well written and relevant, you don't need singing telegrams or a bouquet of flowers to get your message across.

Make sure that you make your press release "web ready." Refer to our Online Tools section to find resources that will help you write a web-ready release. If you write it correctly, when your release is distributed on "the wire" and it appears on Yahoo! News or Google News (they publish millions of releases that are sent through an online wire service), it links directly to the relevant places on your website.

If you have the money to invest, you may want to try sending out a press kit. This consists of a folder containing a cover letter, a press release, your business card, and photos of your product or location. You can also include any other information that will convince reporters your business is newsworthy: reprints of articles other publications

> **TAKE NOTES!**
>
> **WEEK 2**
>
> Most magazines publish their editorial calendars online. Research the publications in which you would love to be included, find an interesting angle, and send in appropriate story ideas. If you keep on top of editorial calendars and pitch ideas at the right time, one of them will eventually make it into a publication.

have written about your business, product reviews, or background information on the company and its principals. If you do send out a press kit, make sure it is sharp and professional-looking and that all graphic elements tie in with your company's logo and image. If you don't have the money to spend on making your press kit look good and high-end, DON'T send one out. You are better off sending only a press release then a cheap looking press kit.

Image Power

Throughout this book, we've touched on the various aspects of developing a corporate image. Your business cards, logo, signage, and letterhead all tie into that image. So do your marketing materials and ads. It's equally important to keep your image in mind when planning a publicity campaign.

Any events or causes you participate in should be in keeping with your business image. If your company is in a fun, creative industry like the toy business, you can get zany and silly with special events like a balloon-popping race or pot-bellied pig races. On the other hand, if you're in a serious industry like medical transcription or accounting, it's better to take part in more serious events like a 10K walk or a blood drive.

The publications and broadcast stations you target with your publicity must fit your image, too. A company that makes clothes targeted at teenage skateboarders would prefer publicity in a cutting-edge lifestyle magazine rather than in a mainstream publication aimed at middle-aged moms. Think about how the publication or broadcast will affect your image, and make sure the results will be positive. Remember though, any press mention is usually better than no press mention.

Don't forget the most important parts of your public image: yourself and your employees. Your marketing materials and corporate sponsorships can tout your socially responsible, kind-hearted company but if your employees are rude and uncaring toward customers, all your efforts to promote that image will be in vain.

Make sure your employees understand the image you are trying to convey to customers and how they contribute to creating that image. Show them by example how you want them to behave whenever they're in the public eye.

Special Events

Ever since the 19th century, when travelling shows were staged to sell "Doctor Winthrop's Miracle Elixir" and other patent medicines, business people have understood the value of promotional events. Even the most obscure product or service takes on new cachet when accompanied by a dash of showmanship. From "fun runs" to fashion shows, contests to concerts, businesses have learned it pays to be associated with special events.

In fact, special events are one of the fastest-growing areas of marketing today. And while large corporations shell out billions each year to host events, small companies, too, can use promotions to reach their market in a way no conventional method could.

No matter how spectacular an event is, however, it can't stand alone. You can use advertising or public relations without doing a special event, but you need both advertising and public relations to make your event work. How do you put together the right mix to make your event successful?

First, you must know what you want to accomplish. The desired outcome of event marketing is no different from that of any other marketing effort: You want to draw attention to your product or service, create greater awareness of it and increase sales.

While the number of special event ideas is infinite, some general categories exist. Following are some of the most popular.

Grand Openings

You're excited about opening your new business. Everyone else will be, too... right? Wrong. You have to create the excitement, and a knockout grand opening celebration is the way to do it. From start to finish, your event has to

TAKE NOTES!

When appropriate, capitalize on old-fashioned publicity stunts. No, you don't have to swallow goldfish or sit atop a telephone pole, but consider the landscaping company whose precision lawn-mowing team shows off its fancy footwork marching in local parades.

WEEK 2

scream, "We're here. We're open. We're ready to go. We're better than, different from, and more eager to serve you than our competitors. We want to get to know you and have you do business with us." Make sure your grand opening fits with the brand that you have created for your company.

A grand opening is one of the best reasons to stage a special event. No one thinks twice about why you're blowing your own horn. What you want people to think about is what a great time they had at your event. And this means more than a run-of-the-mill, garden-variety ribbon cutting. Be original! If you own an electronics store, open your doors via remote control. If you are opening a yarn store, unravel a huge knitted ribbon. If you sell sporting goods, reel in both ends of an enormous bow until the ribbon is untied. Whatever your specialty, do something unusual, entertaining, and memorable.

Give thought to what other activities go along with your grand opening. Design a terrific invitation, do plenty of publicizing, provide quality refreshments and entertainment, select a giveaway that promotes your business (and draws people into the store to get it), and incorporate some way of tracking who attended your event (contest entry forms, coupons, free newsletter subscriptions, birthday club sign-ups, and so on).

Entertainment and Novelty Attractions

Time, space, and popular appeal are three things to consider if you host or sponsor a one-time special attraction. If a beach motif fits your business, and space permits, having a huge sand castle built in your parking lot might draw attention and business for the entire time it takes to construct it. Just keep in mind that the novelties and entertainment shouldn't last so long or be so distracting that no one finds the time or inclination to do business with you. Think of these events as the appetizer, with your product or service as the main course.

RED TAPE ALERT!

Before sponsoring a contest or giving away a prize, make sure you do a little searching on Google about laws regarding sweepstakes, contest and giveaways in your state. Most states have rules that allow you to run almost any type of contest you want without a lot of hassle, as long as you keep the prizes below a certain $ amount.

Holidays and Seasonal Events

Some of the most common and easily developed special events are based on holidays or times of year. For example, during the Christmas season, Santa's Workshop can be found in thousands of communities, not just the North Pole. Or kick off the summer season with a Beach Boys music marathon.

Again, when planning an event tied to a holiday or season, make originality your motto. If the average December temperature in your city is a balmy 76 degrees, then don't dredge up icicles and fake snow for the store. Take a cue from your locale: Put antlers on pink flamingos and dress Santa in shorts and sunglasses.

Co-sponsoring

You can partner with complementary businesses to host an event, or you can take part as a sponsor of an established charity or public cause. Sporting events, fairs, and festivals have proved to be popular choices with good track records for achieving marketing goals. Keep in mind, not every event is right for every business. As with any marketing strategy, your event must be suited to your customers' needs.

Think about how your company can benefit any event. If you are a florist, for instance, you could provide flowers for a wide range of charity luncheons or galas. A health-food retailer could provide free energy bars to participants in a local 10K race. Whatever you do, be sure to promote it with press releases, a sign in your window, or a mention in the event's program.

Games and Contests

From naming a mascot to guessing the number of jellybeans in a jar, contests are a proven means of attracting attention. But they pay off big only when they're properly promoted and ethically managed. Be sure your prizes are first-rate and that you get the word out in a timely and professional manner. Let people know how and when they can participate. Think through all the ramifications of judging contestants, selecting winners, and awarding prizes. Check out the need for special permits or licenses well before staging any contest (it never hurts to get a legal opinion just to be on the safe side). Above all, deliver on your promises.

Networking

The ability to network is one of the most crucial skills any startup entrepreneur can have. How else will you meet the clients and contacts necessary to grow your business?

But many people are put off by the idea of networking, thinking it requires a phony, glad-handing personality that oozes insincerity. Nothing could be further from the truth.

Think a moment. What does a good networker do? How does he or she act? What is his or her basic attitude? You'll probably be surprised at how

> **TAKE NOTES!**
>
> WEEK 2
>
> Whenever possible, tie your business to a current event or trend. Does your product or service somehow relate to the Olympics, the presidential election, the environment, or the hot movie of the moment? Whether you're planning a special event or just sending out a press release, you can gain publicity by association.

much you instinctively know about the subject. You may decide, for example, that a good networker should be outgoing, sincere, friendly, supportive, a good listener, or someone who follows up and stays in touch. To determine other skills an effective networker needs, simply ask yourself "How do I like to be treated? What kinds of people do I trust and consider good friends?"

Now that you have an idea of what attributes a good networker must have, take an objective look at your own interactive abilities. Do you consider yourself shy and regard networking groups as threatening? Do you tend to do all the talking in a conversation? Do you give other people referrals and ideas without a thought to your own personal gain? Can people count on your word?

Many people go to networking events, but very few know how to network effectively. Networking is more than just getting out and meeting people. Networking is a structured plan to get to know people who will do business with you or introduce you to those who will.

The best way to succeed at networking is to make a plan, commit to it, learn networking skills, and execute your plan. To make the best plan, ask yourself: What do I want to achieve? How many leads (prospects) do I want per month? Where do my customers and prospects go to network? What business organizations would benefit my business? How can I build my image and my business's image? What would I like to volunteer to do in the community?

Make a five-year networking plan listing your five best customers, five targeted prime prospects, and five targeted organizations. Next, set goals for involvement in each organization, determine how much time you will need to commit to each organization and prospect, and decide what kinds of results you expect.

Now that you have a plan, get committed. Tell yourself that you will devote enough time and effort to make it work. Half the battle of networking is getting out there and in the swim.

The other half of the battle is learning to network effectively. Typically, ineffective networkers attend several networking groups but visit with the same friends each time. Obviously, this behavior defeats the entire purpose of networking. If you stick with familiar faces, you never meet anyone new. And since most people stay within their circle of friends, newcomers view the organization as a group of cliques. This is one reason people fear going to new organizations by themselves— they're afraid no one will notice them.

The trick with networking is to become proactive. This means taking control of the situation instead of just reacting to it. Networking requires going beyond your comfort zone and challenging yourself. Try these tips:

> **TAKE NOTES!**
>
> **WEEK 2**
>
> For networking purposes, always have your quick two-minute "elevator pitch" ready to give when someone asks you what you do. An elevator pitch is exactly what it sounds like: pretend you are riding up in an elevator with Donald Trump. What would you tell him about your business to get him and keep him interested?
>
> Not sure what a pitch is? Check out Guy Kawasaki's blog: blog.guykawasaki.com. Type "pitch" into the search box to see what Guy has to say about perfecting your pitch.

- **Set a goal to meet five or more new people at each event.** Whenever you attend a group, whether a party, a mixer, or an industry luncheon, make a point of heading straight for people you don't know. Greet the newcomers—they will love you for it! If you don't make this goal a habit, you'll naturally gravitate toward the same old acquaintances.

- **Try one or two new groups per month.** You can attend almost any organization's meetings a few times before you must join. This is another way to stretch yourself and make a new set of contacts. Determine what business organizations and activities you would best fit into. It may be the chamber of commerce, the arts council, a museum society, a civic organization, a baseball league, a computer club, or the PTA. Attend every function you can that synergizes your goals and customer/prospect interaction.

- **Carry your business cards with you everywhere.** After all, you never know when you might meet a key contact, and if you don't have your

cards with you, you lose out. Take your cards to church, the gym, parties, the grocery store—even on walks with the dog.

- **Don't make a beeline for your seat.** Frequently, you'll see people at
networking groups sitting at the dinner table staring into space—half
an hour before the meal is due to start. Why are they sitting alone?
Take full advantage of the valuable networking time before you have
to sit down. Once the meeting starts, you won't be able to mingle.

- **Don't sit by people you know.** Mealtime is a prime time for meeting
new people. You may be in that seat for several hours, so don't limit
your opportunities by sitting with your friends. This is a wonderful
chance to get to know new people on either side of you. Sure, it's more
comfortable to hobnob with familiar faces. But remember, you are
spending precious time and money to attend this event. Get your
money's worth; you can talk to your friends some other time.

- **Get active.** People remember and do business with leaders. Don't just
warm a chair—get involved and join a committee or become a board
member. If you don't have time, volunteer to help with hospitality at
the door or checking people in. This gives you a reason to talk to others,
gets you involved in the inner workings of the group, and provides
more visibility.

- **Be friendly and approachable.** Pretend you are hosting the event.
Make people feel welcome. Find out what brought them there, and see
if there's any way you can help them. Introduce them to others, make
business suggestions or give them a referral. Not only will you probably make a friend, but also putting others at ease eliminates self-con-
sciousness. A side benefit: What goes around comes around. If you
make the effort to help others, you'll soon find people helping you.

- **Set a goal for what you expect from each meeting.** Your goals can
vary from meeting to meeting. Some examples might be: learning from
the speaker's topic, discovering industry trends, looking for new
prospects, or connecting with peers. If you work out of your home,

you may find your purpose is simply to get out and talk to people face to face. Focusing your mind on your goal before you even walk into the event keeps you on target.

- **Be willing to give to receive.** Networking is a two-way street. Don't expect new contacts to shower you with referrals and business unless you are equally generous. Follow up on your contacts; keep in touch; always share information or leads that might benefit them. You'll be paid back tenfold for your thoughtfulness.

You're the Expert

As an entrepreneur, it's your responsibility to get your business noticed—which means you've got to toot your own horn. You need to do whatever it takes to let others know you exist and that you are an expert source of information or advice about your industry.

Being regarded as an industry expert can do wonders for your business. How can you get your expertise known?

- Make sure you know everything you can about your business, product and industry.

- Contact experts in the field and ask them how they became experts.

- Talk to as many groups as possible. (If public speaking strikes fear in your heart, you'd better find a way to get over it. This is one skill you're going to need as an entrepreneur.) Volunteer to talk to key organizations, service clubs, business groups—whoever might be interested in what you have to say. Do it free of charge, of course, and keep it fun, interesting, and timely.

- Contact industry trade publications and volunteer to write articles, opinion pieces, or columns. These days everyone has blogs and blogs need fresh content to be interesting. If you position yourself as a reliable resource with credible information on a topic, you can most likely be a contributor to a blog in your area of expertise.

- Get that blog started. You can use free blogging tools like Typepad.com or Wordpress.com that make blogging easy. The biggest hurdle in blogging is making the time to write consistently on interesting relevant topics.

- Offer seminars or demonstrations related to your business (a caterer could explain how to cook Thai food, for instance).

- Host (or be a guest on) a local or web radio or TV talk show.

- Conduct free webinars online and invite anyone and everyone who might be interested. There are plenty of cheap and easy to use "webinar" technology providers like Webex and GoToWebinar that allow you to essentially conduct a live online class over the phone and over the internet.

- Do all this, and by the time you contact media people and present yourself as an expert, you'll have plenty of credentials.

Social Media

As you become an expert in your field, you will find that it is easier to begin to engage in the latest of PR: social media. The most important aspect of marketing using the social media platform is first finding the platform best suited for your business, and secondly, the platform you are most likely to find your customers using. Social media is a new way of publicizing and advertising your business. It is a medium that is changing rapidly, day by day and week by week. Social media is very likely to become an integral part of any company's PR strategy, but today the problem is that it is so new and so technology dependent that it is hard to write about, hard to describe, hard to pin down. So what can you do to get in on the game?

First, you have to take a little time and do your research. Look for conversations about your company or product that are already happening online. Where are these conversations happening? On blogs? On community forums? On YouTube? On Facebook? Where are your competitors?

Where aren't they? Finding out all of this information will help you pinpoint what you can do to develop a social media strategy. If you are utterly confused, there are a few websites that explain social media and what it can do for your business. Check out the Online Tools section at the end of this chapter for a list of them.

If you have been on YouTube, then you have probably seen some kooky yet fun videos that companies have used to promote their products and services. Search for a few common products on YouTube.com if you haven't seen any to get an idea of what is out there. The major thing to remember, when you are trying to craft your social media strategy, is that this is a rapidly changing space. In a few months, YouTube could be obsolete and there could be something new that everyone is using. Facebook could get bought by someone and turned into something else. What is important is to get the basic ideas of what you can do today, and then research and find out what is being done while you start your business.

The biggest reason to engage in social media isn't to replace a traditional advertising/marketing campaign, but to enhance it with nontraditional ideas and platforms. If your customers are talking about your product and company online, then go to where they are and JOIN the conversation. Create a platform where you can direct the conversation and engage your customers. People are getting more and more used to the idea of being able to contribute thoughts, feedback, and opinions to companies of products and services that they use. Social media is another way to engage with your customers, reinforce your company brand, and let customers reach you to give you their feedback as often as they want.

ONLINE TOOLS

Because we want you to be able to get your PR strategy started quickly, and to give you tools and ideas that will help you do that, we have put together some places you can go online to get help quickly. Check out the links below and get going on your PR strategy for your new business.

Great information on building a PR strategy can be found at

- Entrepreneur.com (click into the "Marketing " channel, and then click through into the Public Relations area)

Online wire services for press releases:

- Businesswire.com
- prndirect.prnewswire.com
- prweb.com

Good information on PR for a start-up:

- prtoolkit.prnewswire.com

This site lets you subscribe to a service to receive editorial calendars from thousands of publications:

- myedcals.com

Another subscription based service for editorial calendars:

- mediacalendars.com

Good social media blog sites:

- r2integrated.com/social
- socialmedia.biz
- socialmediatoday.com
- socialmediaclub.org

A directory of top social media sites:

- socialmedia.alltop.com

Here are a few fast-and-easy social media solutions. Check out these websites, browse the content, search for your competitors, and become comfortable with the media. You will notice that some of the more low-budget, home-grown video solutions are some of the more entertaining and effective. Check out these sites for more information on what people are doing and explore uploading one or two videos featuring one of your customers:

- video.google.com
- photobucket.com
- dailymotion.com
- brightcove.com
- youtube.com
- vimeo.com

WEEK 2 CHECKLIST

At this point, we'd like to pause and suggest taking stock of where you should be in our three-week timeframe.

	YES	NO
You understand your **marketing strategy** and main points of implementation, as explained in Chapter 12.		
You understand your underlying **branding strategy** as explained in Chapter 10. You have a logo ready or the work contracted.		
You've read Chapter 11 and made decisions about a **website**. You either know that you don't need or even want one, or, if you do need and want a website, you're started on it. You've defined its business objectives. You've selected a hosting strategy and you know who's going to build the initial site, and you have an estimate of initial costs.		
You either don't need a **credit card merchant account**, as explained in Chapter 6, or, if you do, you've reviewed options, chosen a vendor, and, if necessary, applied for the account.		
You've read through the **insurance** advice in Chapter 7, talked to a broker if necessary, priced polices and purchased the insurance you've decided you'll need.		
You have job descriptions of startup **employees** finished and the recruiting process started, as explained in Chapter 8.		

WEEK 3:
LAUNCH IT!

CHAPTER 13

SELL IT!

Some startups depend on making the first sale before they actually start up. Most, however, either understand selling instinctively, or sell despite themselves, or need to look at sales techniques almost as soon as they get going. This chapter is one of those you'll probably need almost as soon as you get going, but maybe not during those first three weeks.

No matter what business you're in, if you're an entrepreneur, you're in sales. "But I hate to sell," you groan. You're not alone. Many people are intimidated by selling—either because they're not sure how to proceed or they think they don't have the right personality to sell.

Well, guess what? Anyone can sell—anyone, that is, who can learn to connect with the customer, listen to his or her needs, and offer the right solutions. In fact, as your business's founder, you're better positioned than anyone else to sell your products and services. Even if you have a team of experienced salespeople, there's no one else who has the same passion for, understanding of, and enthusiasm about your product as you do. And once you finish reading this chapter, you'll have the tools you need to start impacting sales immediately.

Understanding Your Unique Selling Proposition

Before you can begin to sell your product or service to anyone else, you have to sell yourself on it. This is especially important when your product or service is similar to those around you. Very few businesses are one-of-a-kind. Just look around: How many clothing retailers, hardware stores, air conditioning installers, and electricians are truly unique?

The key to effective selling in this situation is what advertising and marketing professionals call a "unique selling proposition" (USP). Unless you can pinpoint what makes your business unique in a world of homogeneous competitors, you cannot target your sales efforts successfully.

Pinpointing your USP requires some hard soul-searching and creativity. One way to start is to analyze how other companies use their USPs to their advantage. This requires careful analysis of other companies' ads and marketing messages. If you analyze what they say they sell, not just their product or service characteristics, you can learn a great deal about how companies distinguish themselves from competitors.

> **WEEK 3**
>
> ### TAKE NOTES!
>
> Sell benefits, not features. The biggest mistake entrepreneurs make is focusing on what their product or service is (its features). Rather, it's what it does (its benefits) that's important. A health-food product contains nutrients that are good for the body. That's what it is. What the product does is make the customer thinner, more energetic, and able to do more with less sleep.

For example, Charles Revson, founder of Revlon, always used to say he sold hope, not makeup. Some airlines sell friendly service, while others sell on-time service. Neiman Marcus sells luxury, while Wal-Mart sells bargains.

Each of these is an example of a company that has found a USP "peg" on which to hang its marketing strategy. A business can peg its USP on product characteristics, price structure, placement strategy (location and distribution), or promotional strategy. These are what marketers call the "four P's" of marketing. They are manipulated to give a business a market position that sets it apart from the competition.

> **TAKE NOTES!**
>
> WEEK 3
>
> Want to boost sales? Offer a 100 percent guarantee. This minimizes customer objections and shows you believe in your product or service. Product guarantees should be unconditional, with no hidden clauses like "guaranteed for 30 days." Use guarantees for services, too: "Satisfaction guaranteed. You'll be thrilled with our service, or we'll redo it at our expense."

Sometimes a company focuses on one particular "peg," which also drives the strategy in other areas. A classic example is Hanes L'Eggs hosiery. Back in an era when hosiery was sold primarily in department stores, Hanes opened a new distribution channel for hosiery sales. The idea: Since hosiery was a consumer staple, why not sell it where other staples were sold—in grocery stores?

That placement strategy then drove the company's selection of product packaging (a plastic egg) so the pantyhose did not seem incongruent in the supermarket. And because the product did not have to be pressed and wrapped in tissue and boxes, it could be priced lower than other brands.

Uncover Your USP

The best way to uncover your USP and use it to power up your sales is to put yourself in your customer's shoes. Too often, entrepreneurs fall in love with their product or service and forget that it is the customer's needs, not their own, that they must satisfy. Step back from your daily operations and carefully scrutinize what your customers really want. Suppose you own a pizza parlor. Sure, customers come into your pizza place for food. But is food all they want? What could make them come back again and again and ignore your competition? The answer might be quality, convenience, reliability, friendliness, cleanliness, courtesy, or customer service.

Remember, price is never the only reason people buy. If your competition is beating you on pricing because they are larger, you have to find another sales feature that addresses the customer's needs and then build your sales and promotional efforts around that feature.

> **WEEK 3**
>
> **TAKE NOTES!**
>
> Condition prospects to say yes by asking questions they will agree with. "It's a great day, isn't it?" or "You got an early start today, didn't you?" Little questions like these help start customers on a momentum that builds trust. Subconsciously, because they are agreeing with you, they begin to trust you.

Also, know what motivates your customers' behavior and buying decisions. Effective marketing requires you to be an amateur psychologist. You need to know what drives and motivates customers. Go beyond the traditional customer demographics, such as age, gender, race, income, and geographic location, that most businesses collect to analyze their sales trends. For our pizza shop example, it is not enough to know that 75 percent of your customers are in the 18-to-25 age range. You need to look at their motives for buying pizza—taste, peer pressure, convenience, and so on. Cosmetics and liquor companies are great examples of industries that know the value of psychologically oriented promotion. People buy these products based on their desires (for pretty women, luxury, glamour and so on), not on their needs.

> **WEEK 3**
>
> **TAKE NOTES!**
>
> What's the best way to reach a prospect? Send an email and follow it up with a phone call. Next best is a referral. Then comes a cold call, then a personal visit. Least effective is a direct-mail piece.

Finally, uncover the real reasons customers buy your product instead of a competitor's. As your business grows, you'll be able to ask your best source of information: your customers. For example, the pizza entrepreneur could ask them why they like his pizza over others, plus ask them to rate the importance of the features he offers, such as taste, size, ingredients, atmosphere, and service. You will be surprised how honest people are when you ask how you can improve your service.

Since your business is just starting out, you won't have a lot of customers to ask yet, so "shop" your competition instead. Many retailers routinely drop into their competitors' stores to see what and how they are selling. If you are really brave, try asking a few of the customers after they leave the premises what they like and dislike about the competitors' products and services.

RED TAPE ALERT!

WEEK **3**

If you choose to buy potential customer lists to use as leads, make sure you buy them from a reputable source. There are laws in place to protect consumers from spamming and cold calling, and while we all know they are not entirely effective, your business can suffer if reported to certain agencies. Online, you can be black-listed by an ISPS, which will prevent you from sending any e-mails to anyone using that ISP. Getting un-blacklisted can take a lot of time and be a very big pain for your business.

Once you have gone through this market intelligence process, you need to take the next—and hardest—step: clearing your mind of any preconceived ideas about your product or service and being brutally honest. What features of your business jump out at you as something that sets you apart? What can you promote that will make customers want to patronize your business? How can you position your business to highlight your USP?

Do not get discouraged. Successful business ownership is not about having a unique product or service; it's about making your product stand out—even in a market filled with similar items.

Cold-Calling

The aspect of selling that strikes the greatest fear in people's hearts is usually cold calls. A good way to make cold calls more appealing is to stop thinking of them as "cold" calls. Try thinking of them as "introductory" calls instead. All you are trying to do is introduce yourself and your business to the prospect.

It's important to understand the purpose of introductory calls so you have a realistic attitude about this business development activity. Phone prospecting takes longer to pay off than other types of marketing efforts, so go into it knowing you're exploring a new frontier, and it's going to take some time to get results.

TAKE NOTES!

Sell to the people most likely to buy. Your best prospects have a keen interest in your product or service and the money to purchase it. If you're selling fax machines, don't try to sell to people who have never bought one. Sell to those who already have one or those you know are interested in buying one. Show them how yours is superior.

Just as with any marketing method, you should never make introductory calls without a plan. First, always use a targeted list of prospects when making your calls. If your product is household cleaning services, why call a random neighborhood if you have no knowledge of income levels, number of household wage earners, or number of children? If you sell nutritional products to hospitals, why call nurses or doctors if a third-party pharmacy makes all the buying decisions? Get the right list of prospects.

TAKE NOTES!

Got cold-call phobia? Psych yourself up with a numbers game: If every sale brings you $200 profit and it takes an average of 10 calls to make one sale, then each "no" is worth $20. Or try the "immersion" technique: Make 100 cold calls without worrying about the results. When it's over, you'll have learned a great deal about selling...and your fear of cold calls will be history.

You can obtain information about prospects from the list broker who provides you with the list; if you are working from your house list, you should already have the information. If for some reason you don't, try an introductory call like the following: "We provide mobile pet grooming for dogs and cats. Would that be a service your customers would want to know about, Dr. Veterinarian?"

3 WEEKS TO STARTUP

Second, determine the best time frames for calling. If you are selling financial services to upper-income CEOs or entrepreneurs, wouldn't it be nice to know when their corporate fiscal years end? Perhaps most of their investment purchases are made two to four weeks prior to that year-end close-out. That's when they know how much extra income needs to be sheltered in a pension plan.

Sometimes timing is your ace in the hole. Granted, follow-up calls throughout the year may make that one important sale possible, but knowing when to instigate the first call is a priceless piece of information.

Third, plan by preparing a "sales script" ahead of time. Write down what you are going to say, what responses the prospect is likely to have,

> ### TAKE NOTES!
>
> **WEEK 3**
>
> Tips for better cold calls: Stand up when you talk on the phone. It puts power and confidence in your voice. Smile when you say hello. It makes you sound relaxed and confident. Prospects can't see these telephone tricks, but they'll hear and feel the difference in your tone—and in your persuasive powers.

and how you will reply to them. No, you're not going to follow this word for word, but if you're nervous about making calls, it helps to have something in front of you. Chances are, after you get beyond the opening sentences, you'll be able to "wing it" just fine.

If preparation for cold-calling is easy but actually making calls is painful for you, here are seven easy steps to get you on the phone fast.

1. **Personalize each call by preparing mentally.** Your mind-set needs to be aligned with your language, or the conversation will not ring true. You need to work on developing a warm but not sugarcoated telephone voice that has that "Don't I know you?" or "Gee, you sound familiar" ring to it.

2. **Perfect your phone style alone before making any calls.** If you are self-conscious about calling, you need to feel safe to act uninhibited. Try this: Gather a mirror, a sales journal of incoming and outgoing phone scripts, a pen, and a legal-sized pad. Either write or select a favorite phone dialogue; then talk to yourself in the mirror. Do you look relaxed, or are your

facial expressions rigid? Our exteriors reflect our inner selves. If you look like you're in knots, your voice will sound strained as well.

TAKE NOTES!

Want to know the best way to talk yourself out of a sale? Overselling—pushing your features and benefits too hard—is a common problem for salespeople. The problem is when you are doing that, you aren't hearing the customer's needs. Shut up and listen. Then start asking questions. Keep asking questions until you can explain how your product or service meets the customer's needs.

Push the "record" button on your tape recorder, and pretend you're talking to a new prospect. Play back the tape, and listen to your conversation. Ask yourself how you could improve your delivery. If your voice seems unnatural and the dialogue contrived, do not despair. As you practice and participate in real phone experiences, you will improve. Mastering the art of cold-calling is no different than improving your golf swing or skiing technique.

3. **Attitude is everything.** Make sure you are making calls when you are feeling motivated and excited. Calling someone when you are having a bad day will likely show through to your prospect.

4. **Use your imagination.** Pretend you are a prospective customer calling a bookstore to see if they have a book in stock. It's always easier to imagine you're a customer in need of information than a salesperson trying to force your way into the customer's time. The inquiry call is good practice because the tone of the conversation is "Can you help me?" or "I need some information." Try to convey that same attitude when you use the phone to contact future customers.

5. **Watch your tone of voice.** You do not want to sound sheepish and embarrassed, nor do you want to be arrogant. The ideal tone is warm, businesslike, curious, and straight to the point. A good option is a question or a cut-to-the-chase statement such as: "I've got fun news. We are offering a two-for-one special during the next 30 days on all our coffee drinks, just to get people into the store. I need to know if you have ever stopped

in while shopping at the mall, and, if not, why not? We have the greatest ice-blended mochas in town."

6. **Make your goal a fast "50 in 150"**—that is, 50 calls in 150 minutes. Three minutes per call is all you need. With so many voice-mail systems intercepting calls today, this should be easy. Never give people the impression you have time to chat. Chatting is not prospecting. You're on a mission. Get to the point, then move to the next prospect.

TAKE NOTES!

Star Power

You can find salespeople of all ranges, temperaments and styles of selling. Some are more aggressive than others. Some are more consultative. Some are highly educated, some not so. But they're all champs because they're the ones who consistently build the business, keep the territory and retain their customers. And they share these three traits:

1. **Attitude**. Attitude makes all the difference. Sales champs set priorities and keep things moving forward, ending each day with a sense of accomplishment. Sales champs don't let losing a deal get them down. If they can't change a situation, they change their attitude about it. In sales, you've got to make things happen for your business—and the best salespeople can't wait to get started every day.

2. **Tenacity.** When sales champs know they have something of value for a prospect or client, they don't give up. They learn more about the situation, the potential customer and the customer's company. They study what went wrong and improve their approach for the next time so they can come back with new ideas. They are not easily defeated. However, sales champs understand when they're wasting time and when it's best to move on to the next tactic or even the next sale. If you get smarter each time you come back, you will succeed. When prospects see how much you believe in your vision and in their goals they, too, will be enthusiastic about what you have to offer.

3. **Follow-through.** A broken promise makes it extremely difficult to regain a customer's trust. Sales champs don't make promises they can't keep. They don't try to be everything to everybody. But once they give their word, they stick to it.

A sales champ doesn't exhibit all these traits all the time. Sales champs have the same flaws as everyone else. But they know that in the end, the harder they work at sharpening these traits, the better these traits will work for them.

WEEK
3

7. **Take five after 15.** After 15 calls, take a five-minute break—stretch, eat, sip a soda, turn on some tunes, and pat yourself on the back because you're making it happen. Then grab the phone for 15 more calls.

Following Up

Your initial cold call typically will not result in a sale, or even in an appointment to make a sales presentation. One study shows it takes an average of seven contacts, impressions, or follow-ups to make a sale.

Think of each follow-up contact as a chance to get closer to the prospect and change his or her mind about meeting with you. Plan your follow-up contacts carefully, and be flexible and creative.

How do you start the follow-up call? Here are some lead-in lines:

- "I thought of a few things that might help you decide…"

- "I have some new information that I thought you might want to know about…"

- "There has been a change in the status of…"

- "I just was thinking about you recently and I wanted to tell you about…"

Here are other sales tools you can use in follow-up situations:

- An endorsement from a mutual friend: A friend is far more influential than you are.

- An article about your company: Something in print can work wonders. You can even send articles about the prospect's company or, better yet, about a personal interest of the prospect. "Thought you might be interested in…"

- An invitation to visit your facility: Bring the prospect to your home turf.

- A meal: Meetings in a nonbusiness environment are powerful and help you build personal relationships that lead to sales.

Making Sales Presentations

Your cold calls and follow-up efforts have paid off, and you have made an appointment to visit a prospect in person and make a sales presentation. How can you make sure it's a success? Four elements determine whether a sale will be made or not:

1. **Rapport:** Putting yourself on the same side of the fence as the prospect

2. **Need:** Determining what factors will motivate the prospect to listen with the intent to purchase

3. **Importance:** The weight the prospect assigns to a product, feature, benefit, price, or time frame

4. **Confidence:** Your ability to project credibility, to remove doubt, and to gain the prospect's belief that the risk of purchase will be less than the reward of ownership

---

TAKE NOTES!

Presentation Perfect

Want to improve your sales presentation skills? Use these strategies to hone your speaking abilities:

- **Tag-team-sell for evaluation purposes.** Have a colleague go on sales calls with you once a week to listen to your presentation. Create a review form for them to fill out immediately after your performance. (Include your strengths as well as your weaknesses.) Read it right away, and talk about what you can do to improve.

- **Record your telephone sales conversations.** Use them as a self-monitor of your ability to present a clear and confident message. Play them back. If you can't stand your voice, change your pitch.

- **Videotape the first five minutes of your sales presentation.** Ask a friend or colleague to be the prospect. Watch the video together, and rate your performance. Repeat the process once a week for two months. Work to eliminate your two worst habits; at the same time, work to enhance your two best strengths.

- **Above all, be yourself.** Don't put on an act. Your personality will shine if you believe in what you are saying. Being genuine will win the prospect's confidence—and the sale.

WEEK
3

Here is a closer look at the steps you can take to make your sales presentation a success.

Before the Presentation

Once you have a presentation scheduled, learn about your customer's business. Potential clients expect you to know their business, customers, and competition as well as you know your own product or service. Study your customer's industry. Know its problems and trends. Find out who the company's biggest competitors are. Some research tools include the company's annual report, brochures, catalogs, and newsletters; trade publications; chamber of commerce directories; and the internet.

Write out your sales presentation. Making a sales presentation isn't something you do on the fly. Always use a written presentation. The basic

TAKE NOTES!

Pass it On

Referrals are among a salesperson's best weapons. Yet many salespeople fail to take advantage of this powerful marketing tool. Here are secrets to getting and making the most of referrals:

- Ask for specific referrals. Many salespeople ask for referrals by saying "Do you know anyone else who might be interested in my product?" The prospect replies "Not off the top of my head, but I'll let you know if I think of anyone." And that's where it ends. More effective is to ask for a specific referral that deals with a need your business addresses. For instance, ask "Steve, at your last Rotary Club meeting, did you talk to anyone who was thinking about moving or selling a home?"
- Gather as much information about the referral as possible. Use this to prepare for the cold call.
- Ask your customer for permission to use his or her name when contacting the referral.
- Contact the referral as soon as possible.
- Inform your customer about the outcome of the referral. People like to know when they have been of help.
- Prospect for referrals just as you would for sales leads.

structure of any sales presentation includes five key points: Build rapport with your prospect, introduce the business topic, ask questions to better understand your prospect's needs, summarize your key selling points, and close the sale. Think about the three major selling points of your product or service. Develop leading questions to probe your customer's reactions and needs.

> **TAKE NOTES!**
>
> **WEEK 3**
>
> Offer a first-time incentive to help clinch the sale. If prospects like your product or service, they'll be inclined to make a decision now rather than wait a few days or put off the decision indefinitely. First-time incentives might include "10 percent off with your purchase today" or "With today's purchase, you'll receive one free hour of consultation."

Make sure you are presenting to the decision maker. This seems elementary, but many salespeople neglect to do it. Then, at the last minute, the buyer wriggles off the hook by saying he or she needs a boss's, spouse's or partner's approval. When you are setting the appointment, always ask "Are you the one I should be talking to, or are there others who will be making the buying decision?"

In the Customer's Office

- **Build rapport.** Before you start discussing business, build rapport with your prospect. To accomplish this, do some homework. Find out if you have a colleague in common. Has the prospect's company been in the news lately? Is he or she interested in sports? People generally like to talk about themselves, and this will make the prospect more comfortable with you. Get a little insight into the company and the individual so you can make the rapport genuine.

- **Ask questions.** Don't jump into a canned sales spiel. The most effective way to sell is to ask the prospect questions and see where he or she leads you. Of course, your questions are carefully structured to elicit the prospect's needs—ones that your product just happens to be able to fill.

- **Direct your questions.** Ask questions that require more than a yes or no response, and that deal with more than just costs, price, procedures and the technical aspects of the prospect's business. Most important, ask questions that will reveal the prospect's motivation to purchase, his or her problems and needs, and the prospect's decision-making processes. Don't be afraid to ask a client why he or she feels a certain way. That's how you'll get to understand your customers.

- **Take notes.** Don't rely on your memory to remind you of what's important to your prospect. Ask upfront if it's all right for you to take notes during your sales presentation. (Prospects will be flattered.) Write down key points you can refer to later during your presentation.

- **Be sure to write down objections.** This shows your prospect you are truly listening to what he or she is saying. In this way, you can specifically answer objections by showing how the customer will benefit from your product or service. It could be, for instance, by saving money, raising productivity, increasing employee motivation, or increasing his or her company's name recognition.

- **Learn to listen.** Salespeople who do all the talking during a presentation not only bore the prospect, but also generally lose the sale. A good rule of thumb is to listen 70 percent of the time and talk 30 percent of the time. Don't interrupt. It's tempting to step in and tell the prospect something you think is vitally important. Before you speak, ask yourself if what you're about to say is really necessary.

- **When you do speak, focus on asking questions.** Pretend you are Barbara Walters interviewing a movie star: Ask questions; then listen. You can improve your listening skills by taking notes and observing your prospect's body language, not jumping to conclusions.

- **Answer objections with "feel," "felt" and "found."** Don't argue when a prospect says "I'm not interested," "I just bought one," or "I don't have time right now." Simply say "I understand how you feel. A lot of my present customers felt the same way. But when they found out how much time they saved by using our product, they were amazed." Then ask for an appointment. Prospects like to hear about other people who have been in a similar situation.

- **Probe deeper.** If a prospect tells you "We're looking for cost savings and efficiency," will you immediately tell him how your product meets his need for cost savings and efficiency? A really smart salesperson won't—he or she will ask more questions and probe deeper: "I understand why that is important. Can you give me a specific example?" Asking for more information—and listening to the answers—enables you to better position your product and show you understand the client's needs.

- **Find the "hot button."** A customer may have a long list of needs, but there is usually one "hot button" that will get the person to buy. The key to the hot button is that it is an emotional, not practical, need—a need for recognition, love, or reinforcement. Suppose you are selling health-club memberships. For a prospect who is planning a trip to

TAKE NOTES!
The Price Isn't Right

WEEK 3

How do you overcome that most common objection, "Your price is too high"? Lawrence L. Steinmetz, author of *How to Sell at Prices Higher Than Your Competitors,* says you need to learn how to acknowledge that your price is higher than competitors' and use that as a selling tool.

Showing that customers get more services, better warranties, or higher-quality products for the extra cost makes the higher price seem less imposing. Telling them why the competition's services or products don't measure up differentiates you from the competition and convinces customers you're worth the extra money.

Whatever you do, don't be too willing to negotiate or slash prices. "When you ask a customer 'Is that too much?' you are encouraging him or her to beat you up," says Steinmetz.

With the right ammunition, you can turn price problems into selling points.

Hawaii in two months, the hot button is likely to be losing a few pounds and looking good in a swim suit. For a prospect who just found out he has high blood pressure, the hot button could be the health benefits of exercise. For a busy young mother, the hot button may be the chance to get away from the kids for a few hours a week and reduce stress.

- **Eliminate objections.** When a prospect raises an objection, don't immediately jump in with a response. Instead, show empathy by saying "Let's explore your concerns." Ask for more details about the objection. You need to isolate the true objection so you can handle it. Here are some ways to do that:

  - Offer a choice. "Is it the delivery time or the financing you are concerned about?"

  - Get to the heart of the matter. "When you say you want to think about it, what specifically did you want to think about?"

  - Work toward a solution. Every sale should be a win-win deal, so you may need to compromise to close the deal: "I'll waive the delivery charge if you agree to the purchase today."

  As you get more experience making sales calls, you'll become familiar with different objections. Maintain a list of common objections and ways you have successfully dealt with them.

- **Close the sale.** There is no magic to closing the sale. If you have followed all the previous steps, all you should have to do is ask for the customer's order. However, some salespeople make the mistake of simply not asking for the final decision. It's as if they forget what their goal is!

  For some, "closing" sounds too negative. If you're one of them, try changing your thinking to something more positive, such as "deciding." As you talk with the customer, build in the close by having fun with it. Say something like "So how many do you want? We have it in a rainbow of colors; do you want them all?" Make sure to ask them several times in a fun, nonthreatening way; you're leading them to make the decision.

After the Sale

Once you've made the sale, begin immediately to work on keeping that customer happy and building repeat business.

- **Follow up.** What you do after the sale is as crucial as what you do to get it. "Nearly 85 percent of all sales are produced by word-of-mouth referrals," says sales guru Brian Tracy. "In other words, they're the result of someone telling a friend or associate to buy a product or service because the customer was satisfied." Concentrate on developing future and referral business with each satisfied customer. Write thank-you notes, call the customer after the sale to make sure he or she is satisfied, and

TAKE NOTES!

The right sales team—whether they are in-house employees or outside sales representatives—makes a big difference in how quickly your company grows. How to make sure you're hiring the right people? Try these tips:

- Don't rely solely on resumes. Good salespeople sell themselves so well, they don't even need resumes.

- In the first phone contact, if the applicant doesn't ask for an appointment, stop right there. If the person doesn't ask for an interview now, he or she won't ask for orders later.

- Does the person sound like someone you want to spend time with? If you don't want to, neither will your customers.

- Does the applicant listen? If they're too busy talking, they'll be too busy to listen to your customers.

- At the end of the call, say you plan to talk to several candidates and will get back to them. If someone says "You don't need to talk to more people. I'm the one you want." That's a sign they might be the person you need.

---

maintain a schedule of future communications. Remind the client you are out there, and always show attention and responsiveness.

- **Ask for feedback.** Ask customers what you need to do to maintain and increase their business. Many customers have minor complaints but will never say anything. They just won't buy from you again. If you ask their opinions, on the other hand, they'll be glad to tell you— and, in most cases, will give you a chance to solve the problem. You may find that some complaints will even lead to a making a valuable change to your product, service, or sales process that will result in more sales.

Speaking Effectively

The difference between good and great salespeople is the way they deliver their messages. You can have the greatest sales pitch in the world, but if you deliver it with no enthusiasm, sincerity, or credibility, you will lose the sale.

Here are some suggestions to improve your speaking skills and power up your presentations:

- **Speak clearly and slowly.** Many people tend to speak more quickly when they are nervous. If the prospect doesn't understand you, you won't get the sale.

- **Lean forward.** Leaning into the presentation gives the prospect a sense of urgency.

- **Don't fidget.** Knuckle-cracking, hair-twirling, and similar nervous habits detract from your presentation.

- **Don't say "um," "ah," or "er."** These vocal tics are so irritating, they make the prospect focus on the flaws rather than the message. Best cure? Practice, practice, practice.

- **Be animated.** Act as if the best thing in the world just happened to you.

- **Vary your voice.** Don't drone on in a monotone. Punch the critical words. Go from high to low tones.

- **Look prospects in the eye.** Eye contact signals credibility and trust-worthiness.

- **Follow the prospect's lead.** Keep your tone similar to his or her tone. If the prospect is conservative, do not get too wild.

- **Relax.** High anxiety makes prospects nervous. Why do salespeople get nervous? Either they are unprepared or they need the money from the sale. Calm down. Never let them see you sweat.

ONLINE TOOLS

Lead Generation and Lead Scrubbing Resources

When a lead comes in, it is important to understand your potential new customer's background and objectives. If they are a business organization, get to know their business and the team involved in the sales process. Understand clearly who your key decision makers are and understand the influencers and stakeholders related to the purchase process for your product or service. For example, if your product or service is big ticket item that is technical in nature, it will probably be best to go to the CTO, COO and/or the IT Manager/MIS. However, the financial decision and pricing negotiations will likely involve the CFO.

Get information about private and public companies based on Dunn and Bradstreet's research:

- hoovers.com/free

A community-driven source to get contact information
- jigsaw.com

Sales Genius is a powerful way to track lead generation activity from contact to close with a focus on best practices, deliverability, usability and measurable statistics:

- genius.com

Online Meeting Tools

Web-Touch selling enhances the traditional face-to-face approach and augments telesales with a more personal approach. Online meetings allow your sales force to be present anywhere in the world through video conferenceing, screen sharing, and file sharing via the Internet.

- Web Touch Selling free Webinar: webex.com/web-seminars/view_recording 668063875

- WebEx MeetMeNow: meetmenow.webex.com

- GoTo Meeting by Citrix Online: gotomeeting.com

- iLinc: ilinc.com

- Intercall (formerly Raindance): intercall.com

- MS LiveMeeting: office.microsoft.com/en-us/livemeeting

- Mega Meeting: megameeting.com

- Adobe Connect: adobe.com/products/connect

CRM/SFA/Contact Management

Contact management, customer relationship management, and sales force automation are the ties that bind the process of taking a new lead from initial interest to becoming a new customer and then tracking communications related to ongoing service and support. There are free services available online that will help you start on the right foot to ensure a clear understanding of who your potential customers are, how well your sales process converts opportunities into paying customers, and how well you are retaining customers to generate ongoing revenue.

We start with emailcenterpro. It is an ideal system for managing shared business e-mails, developed by and supported by the authors' company (Palo Alto Software):

- emailcenterpro.com

- Outlook Contact Manager: office.microsoft.com/en-us/contactmanager
- highrisehq.com
- xrms.sourceforge.net
- sugarCRM.com
- freeCRM.com

Training

Sales training is a cornerstone of any successful sales strategy. Sales training helps establish an effective sales culture and develops procedures to maximize your close ratios and return on investment in personnel. Sales training resources come in many forms including live online training, 24/7 on-demand video, reading resources, daily or weekly tips, best practices in the form of white papers and articles, and case studies to focus on specific industries and problems that your product or service helps solve.

- Miller Heiman is one of the world's leading training organizations focused on complex sales engagements: millerheiman.com/knowledge_center
- Sales Performance International has a solutions selling technique: spisales.com
- SellingPower.com: a website specializing in sales management, motivation, and resources: sellingpower.com
- Skip Miller's M3 Learning Corporation, another well-known sales training organization: m3learning.com

CHAPTER 14

SUPERIOR CUSTOMER SERVICE

To the ordinary entrepreneur, closing and finalizing the sale is the completion of serving the customer's needs. But for the pro, this is only the beginning. Closing the sale sets the stage for a relationship that, if properly managed by you, the entrepreneur, can be mutually profitable for years to come.

In this chapter, we're looking at a long-term frame of mind that will help you keep customers and build repeat business and establish a reputation that will help your new company grow. Although this is another chapter that is not strictly tied to the first three weeks, we suggest you read it now so you keep it in mind as you build that business.

Ever heard of the "80-20 rule?" This rule states that 80 percent of your business comes from 20 percent of your customers. Repeat customers are the backbone of every successful business. So now that you know how to land customers, it is time to learn how to keep them.

Building Customer Relationships

It's tempting to concentrate on making new sales or pursuing bigger accounts. But paying attention to your existing customers, no matter how small they are, is essential to keeping your business thriving. The secret to repeat business is following up in a way that has a positive effect on the customer.

> **WEEK 3**
>
> ### TAKE NOTES!
>
> Make it easy for customers to contact you—by phone, e-mail, or real-time chat—to share ideas, frustrations, and suggestions.

Effective follow-up begins immediately after the sale, when you call the customer to say "thank you" and find out if he or she is pleased with your product or service. Beyond this, there are several effective ways to follow up that ensure your business is always in the customer's mind.

- **Let customers know what you are doing for them.** This can be in the form of a newsletter mailed to existing customers, or it can be more informal, such as a phone call. Whichever method you use, the key is to dramatically point out to customers what excellent service you are giving them. If you never mention all the things you're doing for them, customers may not notice. You are not being boastful when you talk to customers about all the work you have done to please them. Just make a phone call and let them know they don't have to worry because you handled the paperwork, called the attorney, or double-checked on the shipment—one less thing they have to do.

- **Write existing customers personal messages frequently.** "I was just sitting at my desk, and your name popped into my head. Are you still having a great time flying all over the country? Let me know if you need another set of luggage. I can stop by with our latest models anytime." Or, if you run into an old customer at an event, follow up with a note: "It was great seeing you at the CDC party. I will call you early in the new year to schedule a lunch."

- **Keep it personal.** Voice mail makes it easy to communicate, but the personal touch is lost. Don't count leaving phone messages as a legitimate follow-up. If you're having trouble getting through, leave a voice-mail message that you want to talk to the person directly or will stop by her office at a designated time.

RED TAPE ALERT!

WEEK 3

Be aware of the channels a customer might go through to report you if they feel that you have not addressed what they feel is a legitimate concern. Most of the times it is better to figure out a solution with an angry customer rather than having to deal with disputes from the Better Business Bureau or a local government agency. If your customer claims he found a hair in his soup, don't argue —apologize and comp his meal. The last thing you need is to lose your restaurant license due to a complaint.

- **Remember special occasions.** Send regular customers birthday cards, anniversary cards, holiday cards... you name it. Gifts are excellent follow-up tools, too. You don't have to spend a fortune to show you care; use your creativity to come up with interesting gift ideas that tie into your business, the customer's business, or his or her recent purchase.

- **Pass on information.** If you read an article, see a new book, or hear about an organization that a customer might be interested in, drop a note or make a quick call to let them know.

- **Consider follow-up calls business development calls.** When you talk to or visit old clients or customers, you'll often find they have referrals to give you, which can lead to new business.

- **Stay in touch.** With all that your existing customers can do for you, there's simply no reason not to stay in regular contact with them. Use your imagination, and you'll think of plenty of other ideas that can help you develop a lasting relationship.

Customer Service

There are plenty of things you, the entrepreneur, can do to ensure good customer service. And when you're a one-person business, it's easy to stay on top of what your customers want. But as you add employees, whether it's one person or 100, you are adding more links to the customer service chain—and creating more potential for poor service along the way.

TAKE NOTES!

When customers are happy with your service, ask them for a testimonial. Get permission from customers to use quotes on your website, in print ads, and in brochures. Also ask if you can give existing customers' phone numbers to certain qualified prospects so they can get a solid recommendation about your business or product firsthand.

That's why creating a customer service policy and adhering to it is so important. Here are some steps you can take to ensure that your clients receive excellent service every step of the way.

- Put your customer service policy in writing. These principles should come from you, but every employee should know what the rules are and be ready to live up to them.

- Hire smart people. Once they are trained, give them the power to help customers. Don't you hate it when a customer service person tells you there is nothing they can do to help solve your problem? Put your customer service people in a better position and give them some leeway and the power to use their own brain and make judgment calls.

- Establish support systems that give the employees clear instructions for gaining and maintaining service superiority. These systems will help you out-service any competitor by giving more to customers and anticipating problems before they arise.

- Develop a measurement of superb customer service. Then track performance and reward employees who practice it consistently.

- Be certain that your passion for customer service runs rampant throughout your company. Your employees should see how good service relates to your profits and to their future with the company.

- Be genuinely committed to providing more customer service excellence than anyone else in your industry. This commitment must be so powerful that every one of your customers can sense it.

- Share information with people on the front lines. Meet regularly to talk about improving service. Solicit ideas from employees—they are the ones who are dealing with the customers most often.

- Act on the knowledge that customers value attention, competence, promptness, and dependability. They love being treated as individuals and being referred to by name. (Don't you?)

WEEK 3

TAKE NOTES!

Go to the Source

Excellent customer service is more than what you say or do for the customer; it also means giving customers a chance to make their feelings known. Here are some suggestions for finding out what your customers want, need, and care about:

- Attend trade shows and industry events that are important to your customers. You'll find out what the competition is doing and what kinds of products and services customers are looking for.

- Nurture a human bond, as well as a business one, with customers and prospects. Take them out to an event or a meal if it makes sense. In the relaxed atmosphere of socializing, you'll learn the secrets that will allow you to go above and beyond your competition.

- Keep alert for trends; then respond to them. Read industry trade publications; be active in trade organizations; pay attention to what your customers are doing.

- Ask for feedback. Survey your customers regularly to find out how you're doing. Send links to online forms; call them by phone. Ask for suggestions, then fix the trouble areas revealed.

Whatever you do, don't rest on your laurels. Regularly evaluate your product or service to be sure it is still priced, packaged, and delivered right.

- Even as your business grows, find time to jump into customer service at least once a quarter. There's nothing like interacting with customers to make sure that you are indeed providing the best possible service.

Interacting with Customers

Principles of customer service are nice, but you need to put those principles into action with everything you do and say. There are certain "magic words" that customers want to hear from you and your staff. Make sure all your employees understand the importance of these key words:

- **"How can I help?"** Customers want the opportunity to explain in detail what they want and need. Too often, business owners feel the desire or the obligation to guess what customers need rather than carefully listening first. By asking how you can help, you begin the dialogue on a positive note (you are "helping," not "selling"). And by using an open-ended question, you invite discussion.

- **"I can solve that problem."** Most customers, especially B2B customers, are looking to buy solutions. They appreciate direct answers in a language they can understand.

- **"I don't know, but I'll find out."** When confronted with a truly difficult question that requires research on your part, admit it. Few things ruin your credibility faster than trying to answer a question when you are unsure of all the facts. Savvy buyers may test you with a question they know you can't answer, and then just sit quietly while you struggle to fake an answer. An honest reply enhances your integrity.

- **"I will take responsibility."** Tell your customer you realize it's your responsibility to ensure a satisfactory outcome to the transaction. Assure the customer you know what she expects and will deliver the product or service at the agreed-upon price. There will be no unexpected expenses or changes required to solve the problem.

- **"I will keep you updated."** Even if your business is a cash-and-carry operation, you probably still need to coordinate and schedule numerous events. Assure your customers they will be advised of the status of these events. The longer your lead time, the more important this is. The vendors that customers trust the most are those that keep them apprised of the situation, whether the news is good or bad.

- **"I will deliver on time."** A due date that has been agreed upon is a promise that must be kept. "Close" does not count.

- **"Monday means Monday."** The first week in July means the first week in July, even though it contains a national holiday. Your clients are waiting to hear you say "I deliver on time." The supplier who consistently does so is a rarity and well remembered.

TAKE NOTES!
Complaint Department

Studies show that the vast majority of dissatisfied customers will never tell you they're dissatisfied. They simply leave quietly, then tell everyone they know not to do business with you. So when a customer does complain, don't think of it as a nuisance—think of it as a golden opportunity to change that customer's mind and retain his or her business.

Even the best product or service meets with complaints or problems now and then. Here's how to handle them for positive results:

- Let customers vent their feelings. Encourage them to get their frustrations out in the open.
- Never argue with a customer.
- Never tell a customer "You do not have a problem." Those are fighting words.
- Share your point of view as politely as you can.
- Take responsibility for the problem. Don't make excuses. If an employee was sick or a third-party supplier let you down, that's not the customer's concern.
- Immediately take action to remedy the situation. Promising a solution then delaying it only makes matters worse.
- Empower your front-line employees to be flexible in resolving complaints. Give employees some leeway in deciding when to bend the rules. If you don't feel comfortable doing this, make sure they have you or another manager handle the situation.
- Imagine you're the one with the complaint. How would you want the situation to be handled?

- **"It will be just what you ordered."** It will not be "similar to," and it will not be "better than" what was ordered. It will be exactly what was ordered. Even if you believe a substitute would be in the client's best interests, that's a topic for discussion, not something you decide on your own. Your customer may not know (or be at liberty to explain) all the ramifications of the purchase.

WEEK 3

TAKE NOTES!

To ensure you don't drop the ball on follow-up, check out one of the many contact management programs on the market. These little wonders can remind you of everything from a client's birthday to an important sales call.

- **"The job will be complete."** Assure the customer there will be no waiting for a final piece or a last document. Never tell the customer you will be finished "except for…"

- **"I appreciate your business."** This means more than a simple "Thanks for the order." Genuine appreciation involves follow-up calls, offering to answer questions, making sure everything is performing satisfactorily, and ascertaining that the original problem has been solved.

Neglecting any of these steps conveys the impression that you were interested in the person only until the sale was made. This leaves the buyer feeling deceived and used, and creates ill will and negative advertising for your company. Sincerely proving you care about your customers leads to recommendations—and repeat sales.

Going Above and Beyond

These days, simply providing adequate customer service is not enough. You need to go above and beyond the call of duty to provide customer service that truly stands out. How to do this?

Begin by thinking about your own experiences as a customer—what you have liked and disliked in certain situations. Recall the times you were delighted by extra efforts taken to accommodate your needs or outraged by rudeness or negligence. This will give you greater insight into what makes for extraordinary customer service. To put yourself in the customer's shoes, try visiting a wide range of businesses your customers are likely to frequent. This could include your direct competitors, as well as companies that sell related products and services. Observe how customers are treated in addition to the kinds of services that seem to be important to them. Then adapt your business accordingly.

Going above and beyond is especially important when a customer has complained or if there is a problem with a purchase. Suppose an order is delayed. What can you do?

- Call the customer personally with updates on the status of the order and expected arrival time.

- Hand-deliver the merchandise when it arrives.

- Take 20 or 30 percent off the cost. Or maybe credit the shipping cost.

- Send a note apologizing for the delay... tucked inside a gift basket full of goodies.

These are all ways of showing customers you're on their side.

Going above and beyond doesn't always mean offering deep discounts or giving away products. With a little ingenuity and effort, you can show customers they are important at any time. Suppose you've just received the newest samples and colors for your home furnishings line. Why not invite your best customers to a private showing, complete with music, appetizers, and a coupon good for one free hour of consultation?

Emergency orders and last-minute changes should be accommodated when possible, especially for important occasions such as a wedding or a big trade show. Customers remember these events, and they will remember your flexibility and prompt response to their needs, too.

TAKE NOTES!

WEEK 3

Create external incentives to keep customers coming back. Offer customers free merchandise or services after they buy a certain amount. This gets them in the habit of buying again and again.

Being accessible to your customers also wins loyalty. One entrepreneur who runs a computer chip company has installed a customer service line on every employee's telephone, from the mail room clerk on up. This means every caller gets through to a real person who can help him or her, instead of getting lost in a voice-mail maze. We have all had to call large companies and deal with complicated and confusing menu systems.

Customer loyalty is hard to win and easy to lose. But by going above and beyond with your customer service, you'll soon see your sales going above and beyond those of your competitors.

ONLINE TOOLS

CRM/SFA/Contact Management

Manage and in some cases automate your customer follow-up activities with the right contact management solutions to fit your needs. Your follow-up communications might include following up immediately after a sale, driving awareness surrounding changes and new versions of your products and services, sending a monthly newsletter, and generally keeping customers aware of what is happening in the industry and with your company. These types of activities can all be effectively managed using customer relationship databases, not to mention tracking the effectiveness of your customer service and individual and group performance.

Please note that these resources are included in the chapter on sales as well. Why? Because customer service and support are the second half of the customer lifecycle. Moving from initial interest to closing the sale is the focus of sales and marketing. Sharing and understanding what happened during those initial stages and then tracking ongoing communications, service, and support are how you keep customers long-term and generate ongoing revenues from your existing customer base.

We start with Email Center Pro, a web application and software as a service, an ideal system for managing shared business e-mails developed by and supported by the authors' company (Palo Alto Software):

- emailcenterpro.com

- office.microsoft.com/en-us/contactmanager

- highrisehq.com

- xrms.sourceforge.net

- sugarcrm.com

- freecrm.com

Remote Support

In an ideal world, computer-related issues would be resolved by simply pulling up a chair next to your end-user and taking care of the problem hands-on. The reality of geographically dispersed customers and support technicians means that this is rarely an opportunity. Remote support solutions are a well-established alternative, and most even have specific permission levels to put even the most security conscious of users at ease.

- UltraVNC: uvnc.com

- LogMeIn Rescue: secure.logmein.com/home.asp?lang=en

- gotoassist.com

- WebEx Remote Support: webex.com/lpt/remotesupport

- techinline.com/trial

Telephone Systems with Intelligence

Physical phone systems and lines are quickly becoming replaced by Voice over Internet Protocol (VoIP) systems with computer-based menus, call routing, extension management and voice-mail. The lack of hardware means that capabilities that used to only be within the reach of large organizations are available even at the solopreneur level.

- gotvmail.com

- onebox.com

- ringcentral.com

- virtualpbx.com

- vocalocity.com

Engage with Your Community of Customers

Communities sprout up online surrounding products and services every second of every minute of every day. Engaging with your community of customers and participating in the discussion far outweighs trying to police or moderate the information that flows between and from customers and potential customers. Here are tools that help you be part of the community rather than an outsider looking in:

To connect with customers who are talking about your company and provide short, concise, up-to-the-minute updates:

- twitter.com

- socialthing.com

- twhirl.org

- toluu.com

Engage with customers, share relevant content, and welcome comments from the online community by starting a blog. Blogs are free and easy to start without needing a team of engineers:

- wwordpress.com

- ttypepad.com

- blogger.com

Knock down geographical boundaries, provide added value to your customers, and generate new leads for a very low cost per lead by hosting and sponsoring online workshops & webinars:

- WebEx Event Center: webex.com/smb/webinars.html

- Goto Webinar by Citrix Online: gotowebinar.com

- iLinc EventPlus: ilinc.com/products/eventplus

- Intercall (formerly Raindance): intercall.com

- MS LiveMeeting: office.microsoft.com/en-us/livemeeting

- Mega Meeting: megameeting.com

- Adobe Connect: adobe.com/products/connect

- Leverage and generate online referrals using LinkedIn: linkedin.com

- Hoovers, for information about private and public companies based on Dunn and Bradstreet's research: hoovers.com/free

- A community-driven source to get contact information: jigsaw.com

Effective Customer Communication

Rather than spending time managing communications, spend time communicating. There are many technologies available to speed communications and foster the sharing of best practices among your employees internally.

Collaborate as a team to answer e-mail, assign messages to individuals, categorize and tag messages for reporting and easy searches later, and cut your response time down dramatically using a shared e-mail platform like Email Center Pro:

- emailcenterpro.com

Chat in real time with employees internally while on the phone with a customer to provide fast and accurate answers and information without creating extra follow-up steps:

- aimpro.premiumservices.aol.com

- Yahoo Messenger: messenger.Yahoo.com

- Google Talk: google.com/talk

- meebo.com

Provide a method on your website for customers to connect with your employees live to answer questions, make purchases, and provide information about your products and services. This is especially effective for international prospects and customers who wish to avoid low quality and potentially expensive telephone conversations but seek answers in real time.

- boldchat.com
- websitealive.com
- solutions.liveperson.com
- talisma.com

CHAPTER 15

KEEPING TRACK

We don't want to burden

you with lots of administrative problems, but in our times, you really have to make sure the basic bookkeeping is done. The bad news is that not keeping track of the basic records could cost you a lot of money, hassle, penalties, and problems. The good news is that this gets easier every day. There is good software available, some of it amazingly cheap, some of it free. There are also some good web applications available as well.

Simply put, a business's bookkeeping system tracks the money coming in against the money going out. And, ultimately, you won't be able to keep your doors open if you have more dollars going out than coming in.

Aside from every business owner's inherent desire to stay in business, there are two other key reasons to set up a good bookkeeping system:

1. It is legally required.

2. Bookkeeping records are an excellent business management tool.

And there is also the alternative of hiring a bookkeeper to come into your space once every so often to balance the checkbook, record business transactions, and keep the books in shape. For a brand new startup, this could be just a few hours a week, or even just a few hours a month. And don't let this be the old-fashioned hard-copy written records; there are too many better easier alternatives available either online or as packaged software. Frankly, it's silly to not use something better.

> **WEEK 3**
>
> ## TAKE NOTES!
>
> The hardest part of this, and the one that's hardest to get away from, is the data entry. Traditionally, the ease of data entry has been the best factor to use when choosing between various accounting software options.
>
> There is a shortcut, though: Find out what software links automatically to your bank statement.

Our plan for this chapter is to run you through some basic definitions and simple concepts that will help you either do it yourself, manage the software, manage the online application, or, at the very least, understand what's going on enough to stay abreast of your standard bookkeeping, regardless of who does it.

After that, we will review some of the various tools available. We strongly recommend you assume that this information gets stale, so pay special attention to the process of choosing and selecting, and plan to do the search yourself.

Are you going to keep the books? Or are you going to pay somebody an hourly rate to keep the books? Not every startup entrepreneur has to be a bookkeeper, but every startup needs to keep books.

To our mind, it's been getting easier all the time. In the old days, bookkeeping was a skill to be learned, involving debits and credits and books and balancing and lots of extra trouble if you didn't do it.

Bookkeeping Basics

Don't worry. The software does most of the work, and it's not all that complicated anyhow.

The western system of double-entry bookkeeping is an amazing invention. It may not be quite as far-reaching as the invention of the wheel, or the printing press, but it ranks up there for the impact it's had on our civilizations.

Ultimately, every transaction has two equal sides. For every check you write, there's an amount that goes out of your checking account balance, and an amount that goes into some business account that you need to keep track of to stay legal and sane.

You don't technically need to know this, particularly not if you don't do the books but instead have somebody else you trust do the books for you. But it's not that hard. I find that most people are relieved when the mystery of debits and credits is shown for the relatively simple and conventional mechanism that it is.

Let's take some simple examples:

A check for $700 to the landlord is $700 going out of the checking account, and $700 going into your rent expense. You need to know both of these numbers, and you can't really be in business without keeping track of them. If you don't, you run the risk of bouncing checks and not being able to deduct expenses from your taxable income. That's bad stuff.

This is what the famous terminology *debits and credits* is about. Standard bookkeeping credits your bank

---

TAKE NOTES!

WEEK 3

Here's the basic terms:

Bookkeeping is keeping track of all financial transactions: checks, deposits, cash receipts, and so forth. This is almost always done by software, and the best way to decide which software to use is to choose one that your bank statements can link to.

Accounting is done by an accountant, and involves higher-level work, such as tax reports and tax planning.

Bookkeeping goes on all the time. Accounting, for most companies, happens once a year at tax time. All of the software and online options you'll look at will call themselves accounting—even though it's really bookkeeping.

account the $700 and debits your rent expense account the other side of that same $700. It's a standard convention. A check credits the checking balance and debits the expense account.

By convention, or agreement of bookkeepers for centuries if you want to call it that, a standard sales transaction credits sales and debits the account that gets the money. A check from a customer debits the checking account balance (in that case, it's increasing it) and credits sales.

By convention, investment in the company is a credit. So when an investor writes you a check and you deposit it in the bank, the checking account gets debited—so it increases—and the investment account gets credited, so it also increases.

In actual practice, any accounting software or online application you can find will manage this basic bookkeeping function automatically. It won't let you record a check without having you also record the category of expense or cost that's related to it. So the debits and credits are automatic.

TAKE NOTES!

So you make a sale. When you deliver the goods, you record it as a sale. If the customer didn't pay you immediately, you record the accrued amount as **Accounts Receivable.**

You order some goods. When you receive them, you don't pay for them. Instead, you record the accrued amount as **Accounts Payable.**

At the end of the tax year, you have some expenses outstanding, like professional services you know you'll be billed for but you haven't been billed yet. You accrue those expenses into the current tax year. They are deductible against income.

In so-called cash basis accounting, the opposite of accrual accounting, you don't put the sale or the purchase onto your books until the money changes hands. With business-to-business sales, the norm is the money changes hands later. So accrual accounting is better. It gives your books a more accurate picture of your financial flow and financial position.

Why does this matter here? Because timing of sales, costs, and expenses makes a difference. Start your forecasts correctly so the can be part of a more formal financial forecast when you finally need one.

Choosing Your Software or Online Application

The most important thing that happens to your bookkeeping at this point is the choice you make about accounting software.

Do not, please, under any circumstances, start your business without choosing your accounting system. It's not hard to track transactions if you start from the beginning, but if you let records accumulate, things get lost and things get a lot harder.

Do You Have a Choice?

You might not have a choice. For example, you might be starting a franchise business for which the franchisor requires a specific accounting system. Or you might be working on a team with somebody who already knows and uses and likes a certain system, and is going to be responsible for it, so insisting on something else carries a lot of potential negative baggage.

Check Out Your Bank

Given that data input is by far the most taxing task in bookkeeping, you can shortcut the whole process by realizing that in all but the rare exceptional cases, the best accounting software to use is the one that links to your bank's systems.

> **TAKE NOTES!**
>
> **WEEK 3**
>
> Some more good news: As a new startup, you aren't bogged down by bookkeeping history or the way things have always been done. For most businesses, it's hard to switch systems. You, however, get to start fresh.
>
> Still, there are huge advantages to working with whatever system your bank links up to. Keep that in mind. That can be a key factor. Most banks these days offer links to at least one, often two or three of the leading bookkeeping packages.

Data Management Made Easy

What this means is that you can export transactions from your bank to your accounting package. The data export option is so much better than manual entry that there is no real discussion necessary. By export we mean, specifically, you access the bank's online banking system from your computer, connected through your internet connection, and download the information the bank has about your transactions. Your software system is already set to receive the downloaded information and load it into the software, so you don't have to retype or re-enter it.

TAKE NOTES!

What? Your bank doesn't link to any accounting software? Change banks!

This is so much better than any other way that you really need to have a very special case to justify using something that doesn't link like that to your bank.

These days most banks will work with at least one of the most popular (by far) systems: Intuit's Quicken, Microsoft's Money, or Intuit's QuickBooks. And, as we write this, new systems are popping up all the time. For example, Intuit now offers simple online versions of all of its major accounting packages. Microsoft has new online options, too. We recently connected with Ridgely Evers, original author of QuickBooks, who now heads a new company offering a very intriguing online option called Netbooks.

Online or Not

Keep the following things in mind when deciding whether to use an online system:

- Online systems are not available to you when you're not connected.

- Online systems are available to you from any computer anywhere, at least as long as your online vendor is up and running.

- With online systems, you don't keep your own information in your own physical space. Somebody else is backing up and keeping it safe. You hope. Then again, with the computer-based systems, you are supposed to back up your information and keep it safe. Do you?

Some Other Factors to Consider

- If you are making B2B sales (selling to other businesses), you want a system that can make invoices and track payments on invoices. Don't settle for just recording the transaction when the customer finally pays. Record the transaction when it happens, and manage the money owed to you. The keywords to look for are "collection days," "accounts receivable," and "aging reports." If you're going to be making sales on credit, make sure you'll have this data managed.

- If you are dealing with products, not services, then look for inventory management. This is one of the main advantages of Netbooks, by the way: The leading simple bookkeeping packages don't manage inventory very well.

- It's also convenient to manage accounts payable. This means that when you receive a bill for an amount of money your business owes from receiving goods or services, you can enter it into the system immediately and use that to keep track of money you owe. Look for the keywords "accounts payable," "aging of accounts," and "payment days."

- What help can you get? Who is on your team, or whom do you know, who might already know one system or another? The accounting package you (or somebody close to you) know is usually better than one you don't know.

WEEK 3

TAKE NOTES!

Watch for these red-flag product reviews that may skew the overall results:

- **The vendor's best friend.** Short reviews with very little detail and very high grades or stars are often submitted by company employees or friends. You can usually spot them. They obviously mean less than real consumer reviews.

- **The revenge review.** They wouldn't give a free upgrade to an old version, or it didn't work with a ten-year-old computer, or it was out of warranty, or somebody having a bad day argued with somebody. You can spot these too, because they're usually about some incident, with lots of detail about the incident, and very little about the actual product that is supposed to be reviewed.

- Compatibility. If you're using Macintosh or Linux, you'll have fewer choices of accounting packages. If you're online, it usually doesn't matter.

- Reviews. Some of the major review sites include amazon.com, cnet.com, pcworld.com, pcmag.com, and macuser.com. Look at reviews of the options on your short list.

Basic Accounting Principles

Most businesses typically use one of two basic accounting methods in their bookkeeping systems: cash basis or accrual basis. While most businesses use the accrual basis, the most appropriate method for your company depends on your sales volume, whether or not you sell on credit, and your business structure.

The cash method is the most simple in that the books are kept based on the actual flow of cash in and out of the business. Income is recorded when it is received, and expenses are reported when they are actually paid. The cash method is used by many sole proprietors and businesses with no inventory. From a tax standpoint, it is sometimes advantageous for a new business to use the cash method of accounting. That way, recording income can be put off until the next tax year, while expenses are counted right away.

TAKE NOTES!

We always recommend accrual! We hate the implication of the name "cash-based" for a bookkeeping system that ignores money you owe and money owed to you until you make or receive payment. Unless you never wait to pay bills, and your customers never wait to pay bills, accrual accounting is better.

With the accrual method, income and expenses are recorded as they occur, regardless of whether or not cash has actually changed hands. An excellent example is a sale on credit. The sale is entered into the books when the invoice is generated rather than when the cash is collected. Likewise, an expense occurs when materials are ordered or when a workday has been logged in by an employee, not when the check is actually written. The downside of this method is that you pay income taxes on revenue before you've actually received it.

Should you use the cash or accrual method in your business? The accrual method is required if your business's annual sales exceed $5 million and your venture is structured as a corporation. In addition, businesses with inventory must also use the accrual method. It also is highly recommended for any business that sells on credit, as it more accurately matches income and expenses during a given time period.

The cash method may be appropriate for a small, cash-based business or a small service company. You should consult your accountant when deciding on an accounting method.

Know Your Accounting

Every accounting system has key components. Even if you decide to farm out all your bookkeeping work, you should still understand the basic elements of an accounting system. While some may vary depending on the type of business, these components typically consist of the chart of accounts, general ledger, accounts receivable, inventory, fixed assets, accounts payable, and payroll.

Chart of Accounts

Your accounts are like categories: rent, payroll, advertising are common expenses, sales often divides into categories of sales (by product, by channel, whatever), and so on. Each asset category is an account; each liability category is an account. It's not as formal as it might seem.

With any reasonable accounting software, and definitely any that your bank is working with, the chart of accounts will be almost automatic. What items you track will end up as accounts, unless you make a point of doing something different. The point at this stage is to know the term, and know what it means.

General Ledger

Back in the old days, with bookkeepers writing with quills in ink on lined paper while sitting on stools wearing green eyeshades, the general ledger was like a large list that pulled together all the various accounts into one master accounting for your business. Every entry has two sides, a debit and a credit, and they have to balance. Ultimately, the whole business balances in the general ledger. On the balance sheet, assets must be equal to liabilities plus capital. The increase in capital must relate directly to the earnings, alias profit.

The general ledger is essentially built into the accounting software. Every account that is on your chart of accounts will be included in your general ledger, which will come automatically in the same order as the chart of accounts. While the general ledger does not include every single accounting entry in a given period, it does reflect a summary of all transactions made.

Source Documents

An important component of any general ledger is source documents. Two examples of source documents are copies of invoices to customers and invoices from suppliers. Source documents are critical in that they provide an audit trail in case you or someone else has to go back and study financial transactions made in your business.

For instance, a customer might claim that they never received an invoice from you. Your source document will prove otherwise. And your source documents are a required component for your accountant at tax time. Other examples of source documents include canceled checks, utility bills, payroll tax records, and loan statements.

Accounts Receivable

If you plan to sell goods or services on account in your business, you will need a method of tracking who owes you how much and when it is due. Make sure your software tracks accounts receivable well. You want to be able to list who owes you how much, and for how long, with due dates and details. The classic report is called aging of accounts.

A good bookkeeping software system will track this for you. So when a sale is made on account, you can track it specifically to the customer. This is essential to ensure that billing and collection are done in a timely manner.

Inventory

Unless you are starting a service business, you'll need software to deal with inventory control. In our experience, this is not a strength of either QuickBooks or Microsoft Money. You might look at Netbooks, or the more robust versions of accounting systems. Remember, however, that linking to your bank's transaction reports is also very important. This can be a tough call. If you are going to be manufacturing products, you will have to track raw materials, work-in-progress, and finished goods; separate subledgers should be established for each of these inventory categories. Even if you are a wholesaler or a retailer, you will be selling many types of inventory and will need an effective system to track each item offered for sale.

> ### TAKE NOTES!
>
> **WEEK 3**
>
> "The check is in the mail." So they say—but is it really? If you switch to electronic billing and payment, you'll always know for sure. Another advantage is a reduction in errors. If you want to start e-billing, you'll need software and training. Or you can find a service provider for a one-time setup fee and per-transaction charges.

Another key reason to track inventory very closely is the direct relationship to cost of goods sold (COGS). Since nearly all businesses that stock inventory are required to use the accrual method for accounting, good inventory records are a must for accurately tracking the material cost associated with each item sold.

From a management standpoint, tracking inventory is also important. An effective and up-to-date inventory-control system would provide you with the following critical information:

- Which items sell well and which items are slow-moving
- When to order more raw materials or other items

- Where the inventory is stored when it comes time to ship
- Number of days in the production process for each item
- The typical order of key customers
- Minimum inventory level needed to meet daily orders

Fixed Assets

Fixed assets are items that are for long-term use, generally five years or more. They're not bought and sold in the normal course of business operation. Fixed assets include vehicles, land, buildings, leasehold improvements, machinery, and equipment.

In an accrual system of accounting, fixed assets aren't fully expensed when they are purchased but rather they are expensed over a period of time that coincides with the useful life (the amount of time the asset is expected to last) of the item. This process is known as depreciation. Most businesses that own fixed assets keep track of each asset category as well as for each depreciation schedule.

In the simplest cases, depreciation is easy to compute. The cost of the asset is divided by its useful life. For instance, a $60,000 piece of equipment with a five-year useful life would be depreciated at a rate of $12,000 per year. This is known as straight-line depreciation.

However, depreciation gets complex very fast, and tax code has a lot to say about depreciation as well. There are other more complicated methods of fixed-asset depreciation that allow for accelerated depreciation on the front end, which is advantageous from a tax standpoint. In the real world, your CPA will help you with depreciation at the end of the tax year. If you are manufacturing and managing assets of any significant amount, it's foolish to try to do taxes without professional help.

Accounts Payable

The accounts payable need to be tracked a lot like accounts receivable. The difference is that one is the opposite of the other. Accounts payable are amounts that you owe to suppliers and vendors, still unpaid. It is important to track accounts payable in a timely manner to ensure that you know how much you owe each supplier and when payment is due. Many a good supplier relationship has been damaged due to a sloppy accounts payable system. Also, if your suppliers offer discounts for payment within 10 days of invoice, a good automated accounts payable system will alert you when to pay to maximize the discounts earned.

Payroll

Payroll accounting can be quite a challenge for the new business owner. There are many federal and state laws regulating what you have to track related to payroll (see Chapter 9). Failure to do so could result in heavy fines—or worse.

Many business owners use outside payroll services. These companies guarantee compliance with all the applicable laws. This keeps the business owner out of trouble with the law and saves time that can be devoted to something else in the business. If you choose to do your own payroll, it's recommended that you purchase an automated payroll system. Even if the rest of your books are done manually, an automated payroll system will save you time and help considerably with compliance. There's not a lot of margin for error when you're dealing with the federal government!

The best of these outside payroll services, in our opinion are the online payroll services, which grow more attractive every day. You should use a good web search for "online payroll service" to catch up on the latest offerings, but as we write this the three top online services are Paycycle at paycycle.com, Intuit at payroll.intuit.com, and Paychex at paychex.com.

Cost Accounting

Cost accounting is the process of allocating all costs associated with generating a sale, both direct and indirect. Direct costs include materials, direct labor (the total wages paid to the workers who made the product), foreman/plant manager salaries and freight. Indirect costs include all other costs associated with keeping your doors open.

TAKE NOTES!

If you'll be selling on credit, your accounts receivable system will be vital. Here are five key components of a good accounts receivable system:

1. Verify accounts receivable balances. Use source documents such as invoices to keep balances accurate.

2. Send accurate and timely invoices.

3. Generate accounts receivable reports. Determine which customers are past due and track credit limits.

4. Post paid invoices to track who pays you when.

5. Match up your customer records totals, your general ledger, and subledgers.

As profit margins have shrunk in many businesses, particularly manufacturing ventures, cost accounting has become an increasingly valuable tool. By knowing the total costs associated with the production of a product, you can determine which inventory items are the most profitable to make. This will enable you to focus your sales efforts on those inventory items rather than on products that offer little or no bottom-line enhancement.

To set up an effective cost accounting system, you should seek input from your CPA. Cost accounting can get fairly complicated, and the money you might spend for a CPA will be more than made up for in the expertise he or she will provide in customizing a cost accounting system for your business.

Under Control

Do you know any business owners who have suffered significant losses due to employee theft or embezzlement? They probably did not have an effective internal control system in place. Many successful ventures have been set back or even put out of business by an unscrupulous employee or financial service provider. And it is often someone the business owner least suspected of wrongdoing.

When setting up a bookkeeping system, you need to focus a good deal of effort on instituting a sound system of policies and procedures governing internal control. Here are 10 areas where you need internal control:

1. You need a written policy that clearly spells out your internal-control system. Make sure all employees read this policy. Having a policy not only spells out the procedures to be followed, but it also lets your employees know you are serious about internal controls.

2. On a regular basis, review the internal-control policy to ensure it is up to date. When changes are made, hold meetings with employees to discuss the changes and to maintain a focus on this vital area.

3. Make sure all employees take at least one week of vacation each year. This is often the time during which embezzlement is discovered.

4. Cross-train others in the company to handle bookkeeping. If the person who is stealing from you is sick or on vacation, you'll have a hard time catching him if you let the work go unprocessed until his or her return.

5. Perform background checks before hiring new employees. This may sound obvious, but dishonest employees often are hired by unsuspecting employers who failed to check references before making the offer.

6. Use dual control. You're asking for trouble if you have the same person running the accounts payable system, making journal entries, printing and signing checks, and reconciling the checkbook.

7. Have your CPA or outside bookkeeper perform unannounced spot audits. You may be uncomfortable performing these audits yourself, but if your policy calls for periodic audits, the CPA looks like the bad guy.

RED TAPE ALERT!

WEEK 3

All businesses are subject to laws governing the payment of federal and state withholding taxes. Here are three rules that must never be violated in your business:

1. Make sure you have current withholding tax tables.

2. Always make your payroll deposits on time.

3. Stay up-to-date and accurate with payroll record-keeping reporting requirements.

8. Be careful who you hire as an outside financial services provider. There are countless stories of entrepreneurs being ripped off by supposedly trusted professional service providers such as accountants and attorneys.

Don't relinquish total control of your cash to an outside bookkeeper. And if he or she seems reluctant to share information with you when you ask for it, this could be a sign of deceptive financial advisory practices.

9. Back up your computer information regularly. This is an important function for all aspects of your business. If you begin to suspect an employee of stealing, the ability to study past transactions will be vital in finding out if your suspicions are justified.

10. In the early stages of your business, you may be able to monitor much of the cash-control procedures yourself. However, as your business grows, you will be forced to delegate certain internal-control functions. When you do, make sure you choose qualified, well-trained employees who have proved to be trustworthy. And make sure your policy clearly stipulates the person who is authorized to perform internal-control tasks such as processing invoices and signing checks.

Financial Statements

One of the primary benefits of a good bookkeeping system is the generation of timely and useful financial statements. Most automated software packages offer the capability of producing monthly financial statements. This information includes a balance sheet, an income statement, a reconciliation of net worth, and a cash-flow statement. These monthly reports provide invaluable information on the historical measures you need to

RED TAPE ALERT!

WEEK 3

As you set up your bookkeeping system, you will need to establish procedures for keeping financial records. The IRS requires that you keep records on hand for certain specified periods of time. And with some financial records, it just makes good business sense to keep them so you can access them at a later date.

One key point here is to make sure these records are kept in a safe place. Whether you store them on-site or at a remote location (some business owners use self-storage units), make sure you use a fireproof cabinet or safe.

Another recommendation is to minimize paper buildup by storing as much as possible on CD-ROMs, microfilm, or DVDs. Look in Chapter 16 for recommendations on how long to keep important tax-related documents.

make the financial decisions that will positively impact your business tomorrow.

Refer to the next chapter for a look at these financial statements in detail and how you can use them for effective short- and long-term financial planning.

ONLINE TOOLS

Remember to check with the book site at 3weeks2start.com for the latest online tools related to online accounting. Also, a quick web search for "online accounting software" is always a good idea. And we've already suggested that your search start with knowing what's compatible with your bank's online banking. Here is a list of some of the better-known online accounting offerings:

- QuickBooks Online: oe.quickbooks.com
- ePeachtree by Sage: peachtree.com/epeachtree
- NetBooks: netbooks.com
- Intacct: us.intacct.com

Some of these additional information sites, including reviews, might also be useful:

- Accounting Software Review 2008: accounting-software-review.toptenreviews.com
- Business.com accounting software reviews: business.com/directory/accounting/software/m/small-business-0-100
- CNET accounting software reviews: reviews.cnet.com (use the search bar)
- Small Business Accounting: Software and Systems: business.com/directory/accounting/software
- American Institute of Certified Public Accountants: aicpa.org

WEEK 3 CHECKLIST

At this point you are at the end of the three weeks, and your business should be up and running. This final checklist contains the tasks you should have tackled by now.

	YES	NO
You have your business **physical location** ready to go, and it fits your strategy as explained in Chapter 2.		
You've set up **bank accounts** and you've got a bookkeeping system (Chapter 15), presumably with online links to the bank.		
You've found the **attorney** or made the choice of not using an attorney and you've established the legal entity as suggested in Chapter 4. If you have co-founders, you have a buy-sell agreement. Your business name is registered and legal, whether that's just your own name, or any of the other name/identity options in Chapter 4.		
You've selected and hired your initial startup **employees**, finished the recruitment and hiring steps covered in Chapter 8.		
You've been through Chapter 9 and you've decided on the main points of your **benefits and policies.**		
You've read the **financing options** in Chapter 5 and decided on one or more of the following, and you can say yes to at least one of the following four checkpoints. 1. You're financing this new business yourself. 2. You're going to be seeking grant money. 3. You're going to be applying for commercial loans from a local bank (whether or not you're hoping for SBA guarantees). 4. You're going to be seeking outside investment, either from friends and family, angel investors, or venture capital firms.		
If you checked yes on items 2, 3, or 4 above, you have developed a formal **business plan**. You also have a pitch as a slide deck, and a summary memo. This is all in Chapter 5.		
You are actively making sales, because they are what drives your startup process. See Chapter 13.		

BEYOND
3 WEEKS

CHAPTER 16

MANAGING THE MONEY

Honestly, you don't need to be an MBA or a CPA to manage your business finances, but common sense helps a lot. The keys to managing the money, essentially, are exactly what you'd guess. It has to do with matching what you spend to what you bring in. Don't spend money you don't have. Spend less than you bring in and your money management will be pretty simple.

However, most startups take extra money to start. They absorb money in the beginning. They don't generate money. It's not just you, it's the norm.

So it's very important that you plan well enough to know how much extra money—we call that capital—you'll need to afford the initial costs and survive the deficits until sales grow enough to cover spending.

This chapter is full of information that will help you understand and manage your money, but isn't strictly necessary for *starting* a business. This information is for after the three-week startup period and will help you establish your business and allow it to thrive.

Fundamentals

Seven Useful Definitions

You will be better off with a basic understanding of some essential financial terms. Otherwise, you're doomed to either having somebody else develop and explain your numbers, or having your numbers be incorrect. This is a good point to note the advantage of teams in business: If you have somebody on your team who knows fundamental financial estimating, then you don't have to.

It isn't that hard, and it's worth knowing. If you are going to run your business, you will want to understand your financial statement and plan your numbers. Here are some basic terms to learn.

1. **Assets:** cash, accounts receivable, inventory, land, buildings, vehicles, furniture, and other things the company owns are assets. Assets are usually things that can be sold to somebody else. One definition is anything with monetary value that a business owns.

2. **Liabilities:** debts, notes payable, accounts payable, amounts of money the company owes that must be paid back.

3. **Capital** (also called **equity**): ownership, stock, investment, retained earnings. Actually there's an ironclad and never-broken rule of accounting: Assets = Liabilities + Capital. That means you can subtract liabilities from assets to calculate capital.

4. **Sales:** exchanging goods or services for money. Most people understand sales already. Technically, the sale happens when the goods or services are delivered, whether or not there is immediate payment.

5. **Cost of Sales** (also called **Cost of Goods Sold** or **COGS, Direct Costs,** and **Unit Costs**): the raw materials and assembly costs, the cost of finished goods that are then resold, the direct cost of delivering the service. This is what the bookstore paid for the book you buy, it's the gasoline and maintenance costs of a taxi ride, it's the cost of printing and binding and royalties when a publisher sells a book to a store for resale.

6. **Expenses** (usually called **Operating Expenses**): office rent; administrative, marketing and development payroll; telephone bills, internet access—all those things a business pays for but doesn't resell. Taxes and interest are also expenses.

> **TAKE NOTES!**
>
> Some say Income Statement, some say Profit & Loss, or Profit or Loss. They're all the same thing. Accountants and financial analysts use those titles interchangeably.
>
> WEEK **3+**

7. **Profits** (also called **Income**): Sales minus cost of sales minus expenses.

The Three Main Financial Statements

Proper business financial analysis begins with the three main statements: the Profit & Loss, balance sheet, and cash flow.

It's worth getting to know what these mean, because they appear everywhere in business. Definitions are standard, set by Generally Accepted Accounting Principles (GAAP) and accepted by financial analysts and accountants. There are specific meanings for sales, costs of sales, expenses, assets, and so on; and you don't do yourself any favors by just deciding you know what they are.

The bad news is that here again the details and specific meanings of financial terms matter. You can't just guess. You have to understand how accountants expect the timing of sales, costs, and expenses. This is very true with standard financials. Also, it starts to matter what goes where. It can be confusing and annoying. For example, interest expense goes into the Profit & Loss but principal repayment goes into the cash flow, which then affects the balance, but never appears anywhere in income. That means a standard debt payment that includes both interest and principal repayment has to be divided up into interest and principal portions. Interest goes onto the Profit & Loss as an expense, and principal goes onto the Cash Flow and Balance statements as a payment that reduces debt.

This is a good place to point out the huge difference between planning and accounting. With the three main financial statements, specifically, financial analysts use the term "pro forma" to describe *projected* statements, projections, and predictions. A Profit & Loss, for example, is about past results. A pro-forma Profit & Loss is a projected Profit & Loss.

WEEK 3+

RED TAPE ALERT!

Here are seven signs that you might be experiencing embezzlement or employee theft:

1. Employees who don't want a vacation
2. Employees who refuse to delegate certain tasks
3. Ledgers and subledgers that don't balance
4. Financial statements that don't balance
5. Lack of audit trails
6. Regular customer complaints that inventory shipments aren't complete
7. Bookkeeper or accountant who won't share information

The Profit & Loss

The Profit & Loss is also called the Income Statement. People often refer to the bottom line as profits, which is the bottom line of the Profit & Loss. It has a very standard form. It shows Sales first, then Cost of Sales. Then it subtracts Costs from Sales to calculate Gross Margin (which is defined as Sales less Cost of Sales). Then it shows Operating Expenses, usually (but not always) subtracting Operating Expenses from Gross Margin to Show EBIT

(Earnings before Interest and Taxes). Then it subtracts Interest and Taxes to show Profit.

Sales – Cost of Sales = Gross Margin

Gross Margin – Expenses = Profits

Notice that the Profit & Loss involves only four of the seven fundamental financial terms. While a Profit & Loss will have some influence on Assets, Liabilities, and Capital, it includes only Sales, Costs, Expenses, and Profit.

The Profit & Loss is about the flow of transactions over some specified period of time, like a month, a quarter, a year, or several years. Whether it's a projected statement for a plan, or an accounting statement, the format of the Profit & Loss is the same: the sales and cost of sales at the top, followed by a gross margin calculation. Then come the operating expenses, and a calculation that subtracts operating expenses from gross margin to show what some people call gross profits and others call Earnings Before Interest and Taxes (EBIT). Then it subtracts interest expenses if there are interest expenses, and taxes, resulting in net profits. There's a sample of that in Table 16-1.

The Balance Sheet

The most important thing about a balance sheet is that it includes a lot of spending and money management that isn't included in Profit & Loss. It's most of the reason that profits are not cash, and that cash flow isn't intuitive. It's all very much related to the cash traps, financial considerations including money you owe, money owed to you, inventory, other assets, and other debt repayments that cost you money but don't show up on the Profit & Loss.

The Balance Sheet shows a business's financial position, which includes Assets, Liabilities, and Capital, on a specified date. It will always show Assets on the left side or on the top, with Liabilities and Capital on the right side or the bottom.

Table 16-1: Pro Forma Profit and Loss			
	2009	**2010**	**2011**
Sales	$69,397	$125,251	$145,392
Direct Cost of Sales	$2,082	$3,758	$4,362
Other Production Expenses	$0	$0	$0
Total Cost of Sales	$2,082	$3,758	$4,362
Gross Margin	$67,316	$121,493	$141,030
Gross Margin %	97.00%	97.00%	97.00%
EXPENSES			
Payroll	$59,280	$76,560	$76,560
Sales and Marketing and Other Expenses	$2,820	$2,820	$2,820
Depreciation	$2,400	$2,400	$2,400
Website maintenance	$600	$600	$600
Insurance	$900	$900	$900
RD Rent	$7,200	$7,200	$7,200
Payroll Taxes	$8,892	$11,484	$11,484
Other	$0	$0	$0
TOTAL OPERATING EXPENSES	**$82,092**	**$101,964**	**$101,964**
Profit Before Interest and Taxes	($14,776)	$19,529	$39,066
EBITDA	($12,376)	$21,929	$41,466
Interest Expense	$0	$0	$0
Taxes Incurred	$0	$5,859	$11,720
NET PROFIT	**($14,776)**	**$13,670**	**$27,347**
NET PROFIT/SALES	**−21.29%**	**10.91%**	**18.81%**

Balance Sheets must always obey the underlying formula:

$$\text{Assets} = \text{Liabilities} + \text{Capital}$$

Unless that simple equation is true, the Balance doesn't balance and the numbers are not right. You can use that to help make estimated guesses, and pull things together for projected cash flow (see Table 16-2).

The Cash Flow

The Cash Flow statement is the most important and the least intuitive of the three. In mathematical and financial detail, it reconciles the Profit & Loss with the Balance Sheet, but that detail is hard to see and follow. What is most important is tracking the money. By cash we mean liquidity, as in the balance in checking and related savings accounts, not strictly bills and coins. And tracking that cash is the most important thing a business plan does. The underlying truth is:

$$\text{Ending Cash} = \text{Starting Cash} + \text{Money Received} - \text{Money Spent}$$

What's particularly important in running a business is that neither the Profit & Loss alone nor the Balance Sheet alone is sufficient to plan and manage cash (see Table 16-3).

Profitability

Of course we know that most businesses intend to make a profit. Non-profits are the exception, not the rule.

Beware of False Profits

Profit is often misunderstood. The most important misunderstanding is that profit doesn't necessarily mean that there is money in the bank, or that the business is successful. Profit is an accounting concept, and it can be fictional. True, most of the time having a profit is going to correlate with money in the bank and success, but not always. Here are two examples of false profits.

Table 16-2: Pro Forma Balance Sheet			
ASSETS	**2009**	**2010**	**2011**
Current Assets			
Cash	$6,281	$9,827	$34,966
Accounts Receivable	$15,295	$21,605	$32,045
Other Current Assets	$0	$0	$0
Total Current Assets	$21,576	$37,433	$67,011
Long-term Assets			
Long-term Assets	$19,800	$19,800	$19,800
Accumulated Depreciation	$2,400	$4,800	$7,200
Total Long-term Assets	$17,400	$15,000	$12,600
TOTAL ASSETS	**$38,976**	**$52,433**	**$79,611**
LIABILITIES AND CAPITAL			
Current Liabilities			
Accounts Payable	$2,252	$2,739	$3,270
Current Borrowing	$10,000	$10,000	$10,000
Other Current Liabilities	$0	$0	$0
Subtotal Current Liabilities	**$12.252**	**$12,739**	**$13,270**
Long-term Liabilities	$0	$0	$0
TOTAL LIABILITIES	**$12,252**	**$12,739**	**$13,270**
Paid-in Capital	$43,000	$43,000	$43,000
Retained Earnings	($1,000)	($16,276)	($3,306)
Earnings	($15,276)	$12,970	$26,647
Total Capital	$26,724	$39,694	$66,340
TOTAL LIABILITIES AND CAPITAL	**$38,976**	**$52,433**	**$79,611**
NET WORTH	**$26,724**	**$39,694**	**$66,340**

3 WEEKS TO STARTUP

Table 16-3: Pro Forma Cash Flow			
CASH RECEIVED	**2009**	**2010**	**2011**
CASH FROM OPERATIONS			
Cash Sales	$17,349	$31,313	$36,348
Cash from Receivables	$36,753	$81,628	$104,605
Subtotal Cash from Operations	**$54,102**	**$112,941**	**$140,953**
ADDITIONAL CASH RECEIVED			
Sales Tax, VAT, HST/GST Received	$0	$0	$0
New Current Borrowing	$10,000	$0	$0
New Other Liabilities (interest-free)	$0	$0	$0
New Long Term Liabilities	$0	$0	$0
Sales of Other Current Assets	$0	$0	$0
Sales of Long-term Assets	$0	$0	$0
New Investment Received	$0	$0	$0
Subtotal Cash Received	**$64,102**	**$112,941**	140,953
EXPENDITURES			
EXPENDITURES FROM OPERATIONS			
Cash Spending	$59,280	$76,560	$76,560
Bill Payments	$20,741	$32,834	$39,254
Subtotal Spent on Operations	**$80,021**	**$109,394**	**$115,814**
ADDITIONAL CASH SPENT			
Sales Tax, VAT, HST/GST Paid Out	$0	$0	$0
Principal Repayment of Current Borrowing	$0	$0	$0
Other Liabilities Principal Repayment	$0	$0	$0
Long-term Liabilities Principal Repayment	$0	$0	$0
Purchase Other Current Assets	$0	$0	$0
Purchase Long-term Assets	$0	$0	$0
Dividends	$0	$0	$0
SUBTOTAL CASH SPENT	**$80,021**	**$109,394**	**$115,814**
NET CASH FLOW	**($15,919)**	**$3,547**	**$25,139**
CASH BALANCE	**$6,281**	**$9,827**	**$34,966**

- Sometimes sales are overstated. Some people get overly optimistic, and call it sales just because a potential customer has sounded convinced, or said yes, or promised to buy.
- Sometimes expenses are understated. Some people mistake expenses for assets, which overstates profits and understates expenses. How does that happen? One way is thinking that computer programming expense (paying people to program) is building an asset (as if the results of the programming could be recorded as an asset). The result is profits that aren't really there, because the assets can't be resold. We know of a market research company that mistakenly accounted for consulting and research expenses as if they were creating assets that could be resold. After a few years they had several million dollars of worthless assets, research expenses that had been accounted for wrong, and what had been reported as profits for three years were actually losses.

WEEK 3+

RED TAPE ALERT!

Make sure that you check with your accountant and set your books up correctly. We had an experience with a company that was about to go public. They had all kinds of great revenue on the books and were excited. It turns out they were recognizing sales revenue from customers who had yet to receive services and had certainly not paid. They had to completley restate their revenues and ended up postponing their IPO. Even though the deal is done and the contract is signed, there are accounting rules about when you can actually book the sale. Don't get caught here. Ask your accountant and understand how your business model works in the accounting world.

Timing Matters

Don't reinvent wheels. As you do your sales forecast, be aware that accountants and financial analysts have definite meanings for timing of sales. If you don't deal with this their way, you'll have it wrong. It will look bad.

Nobody wants the analysts, accountants, bankers, or investors to think you did it wrong. So pay attention to timing of sales, costs, and expenses.

Timing of Sales

Your sales are sales when the ownership changes hands (for products) or when the service is performed (for services). It isn't a sale when it is ordered, or promised, or even when it's contracted. With proper accrual accounting, it is a sale even if it hasn't been paid for. (With so-called cash-based accounting, it isn't a sale until it's paid for.) Accrual is better because it gives you a more accurate picture; unless you're very small and do all your business, both buying and selling, for cash only.

I know that seems simple but it's surprising how many people decide to do something different. And the penalty of doing things differently is that then you don't match the standard, and the bankers, analysts, and investors can't tell what your financial statements mean.

Timing of Costs

Costs of sales or direct costs or costs of goods sold are supposed to be timed to match the sale.

For example, when you buy a book from a bookstore, whatever that book cost the store to purchase was an amount added to inventory until you purchased it, and only then, with the purchase, it becomes an amount added

> ### TAKE NOTES!   WEEK 3+
>
> Stick with the way the accountants and financial analysts deal with cost of sales. You'll get into trouble if you don't. You want your meaning to be the same as what they understand.
>
> That means cost of sales (also called direct costs, direct cost of sales, or costs of goods sold) is the money it costs you to buy or produce the goods you sell, or to deliver the services you sell. Please don't confuse this with sales and marketing expenses. Travel, meals, commissions, credit card merchant fees, and such are sales expenses, not cost of sales.
>
> Confusing, yes, but we can't help it. That's the way these terms are used. You don't want to make up your own meanings, even if they're logical, because if you need to produce more formal financial projections later on, your meanings need to match what people expect.

to cost of goods sold. That has to happen at the time of the sale. The bookkeeping takes that amount out of inventory and adds it to cost of sale.

Notice the timing. It sits in inventory for as long as it takes, but it doesn't get out of inventory and turn into cost of sales until it gets sold.

Messing that up can mess up your financial reports. When sales for the month is $25,000 and cost of goods sold is $10,000, you want the $10,000 to be the cost it took to buy whatever was sold for $25,000. If this month's costs are for things sold last month, or things sold next month, you get bad information.

It's harder sometimes with services. The cost of sales for a taxi ride should be the gas, the maintenance, and the driver's compensation. But accountants would go crazy trying to match the exact gasoline costs to the exact trip, so they estimate a lot. They are always trying to match the months, so costs should go into the same months as the sales.

Timing of Expenses

Expenses are supposed to show up in the month that they happen. Ideally, travel expenses go into the month you travel, even if you paid the airfare two months earlier. Ideally, advertising expenses go into the month that the ad appears in print, rather than the month you submitted the ad. And definitely, you're not supposed to wait until the month in which you pay for the ad, which often is two or three months later. You want the timing to match.

Your Gross Margin

Gross margin is a very important measure of profitability. The gross margin shows you the result of subtracting direct cost of sales from sales. While there is no right or wrong or proper or expected gross margin, it is commonly compared within industries and across industries. The average gross margin for a retail sporting goods store, for example, is 34 percent, according to one database of financial profiles. Service businesses and more modern web and high-tech businesses tend to have higher gross margins; older more traditional manufacturing businesses tend to have lower gross margins.

Calculating the gross margin depends completely on knowing what *costs* are, as opposed to *expenses*. We have to look at direct costs, costs of goods sold, or costs of sales; basically these are the same thing, but they change terms for different industries. Usually these costs go directly along with the sales forecast, because these are costs that you don't incur unless you make the sale.

For a manufacturing company this is materials, labor, and factory overhead. For a retail shop it would be what it pays to buy the goods that it sells to its customers. For service businesses, that don't sell goods, the same concept is normally called "cost of sales," which shouldn't be confused with "sales and marketing expenses." The cost of sales in this case is directly analogous to cost of goods sold. For a consulting company, for example, the cost of sales would be the remuneration paid to the consultants plus costs of research, photocopying, and production of reports and presentations.

If you projected sales in units, for your sales forecast, then it isn't too much harder (for most businesses) to figure out what each unit costs you. Then you can multiply that per-unit amount times the units to estimate the costs associated with exactly that month's worth of sales, which is the point.

If you just project sales by the amount, then try to estimate the related costs and—at least as much as you can—keep the costs in these cases as much as you can in the same month as the related sales. Don't go crazy with it, but try.

Understanding Costs

Costs are among the financial and accounting terms that have specific meanings. You can't just decide to think of them as what makes sense to you, because the accountants and analysts won't understand you. They'll say you are wrong. Ouch!

Cost of Sales

No, that's not expenses related to making a sale. It isn't that lunch with the customer; it's not the trip to go visit the customer and make a pitch. Costs of sales mean what it costs you to make or deliver whatever it is you sell. If you don't sell, you don't have any costs. They are variable by definition.

- Costs are supposed to be directly related to sales. Costs are about what it costs you to have or build or deliver what you're selling.

- Costs of a manufactured product include materials and labor. So for example, if a computer costs $200 to build, including $150 in parts and $50 in labor, its costs are $200.

- If you just buy the computer built, then sell it, the cost is what you paid to buy it.

- If you deliver a service, you still have costs. The taxi or airline has fuel, maintenance, and personnel costs. The law firm has what it pays the lawyers, plus legal assistants, and photocopying and research.

Costs depend on who and when. For example:

- When you buy a book for $19.95 at the local bookstore, the store's cost of goods sold are whatever it paid to buy that book from the distributor. Let's say it paid $10.50 plus $1 for shipping. The store's sales are $19.95 and its cost of goods sold is $11.50.

- If the distributor bought the book from the publisher for $6.25, then the distributor's sales for the book is $10.50, and its cost of goods sold is $6.25.

- The publisher paid $2.00 to have the book printed, and paid 10 percent royalties ($0.625) to the author, and $0.25 to ship the book to the distributor. Its sales for the book is $6.25 and its cost of goods sold is the $2.875 ($2.00 + $0.625 + $0.25).

- Understand inventory. This comes up again as a cash-flow trap.

- Stuff that's going to become cost of goods sold when it sells starts out as inventory, which is an asset. It sits there in inventory until it sells.

- Think about this in terms of timing and cash flow. The publisher buys the books from the printer and pays for them, which makes them inventory. They sit there for months until the distributor buys them, at which point they become cost of sales. The distributor has them as inventory until it sells them to the store. Then they become cost of sales. The store has the book for as long as it takes, from when it receives it—and puts it on the shelf—until you buy it.

- The cash-flow trap is that the whole inventory asset doesn't show up on your income statement until you sell the stuff. In the meantime, whether you've paid for it or not, the income statement doesn't care. The money is gone, but the sale hasn't been made. This is a classic cash-flow trap. You won't see it on the income statements. It is completely outside of the realm of profit and loss. But you have spent the money.

- Services have costs of sales too. They may not be costs of goods sold because service businesses aren't selling goods, but they are direct costs; an example is a taxi needing fuel and maintenance.

Fixed vs. Variable Costs

Technically, fixed costs are costs that you pay regardless of whether or not you sell anything, or how much you sell. For example, the monthly rental of an installation used exclusively to build stuff would be a fixed cost.

Then there's the division between fixed and variable costs that are really fixed and variable expenses, or variable costs and fixed expenses. This gets very detailed. Ultimately this helps you understand how much risk you have in the business.

The big picture is relatively straightforward. The underlying assumption is that your spending has two parts: the fixed part, that you spend no matter what; and the variable part, that you spend only if you make the sales, and therefore depends (hence the term variable) entirely on the level of sales.

Here's a real-life story: Back in the formative years of Palo Alto Software, we chose to pay an outside sales representation company 6 percent of our retail sales, after the fact, rather than hire somebody as an employee to manage retail sales. The tradeoff should be obvious: There's a lot less risk with the variable cost. If I don't get the sale, I pay nothing. If I do get the sale, then I have money from the sale that I can use to pay the variable cost.

Some of your spending is almost always fixed: rent, insurance, payroll, for example.

Some of your spending is almost always variable: direct cost of sales, for example. And some of your spending is hard to classify. The plumber pays the Yellow Page advertisement in the telephone book once a year, regardless of sales levels; but if sales go up because of the ad, she might be tempted to increase the ad size next year. Your website seems like a fixed cost, but many of us in the web business pay affiliate commissions to affiliated sites that help us make the sale.

Your Burn Rate

It's fine tuning like that mentioned that has given us the new term "burn rate." That term became particularly popular during the first dot-com boom in the late 1990s, when internet companies with fat bank accounts fed by investors would talk about how much money they were burning every month (hence the term burn rate) while they weren't taking any money in. You counted your future as how many months worth of burn rate you had in the bank, from the investors.

I like burn rate instead of fixed costs. Technically, fixed costs are costs that would stop if you didn't sell. But the burn rate, on the other hand, is how much money you spend every month, without quibbling over whether it's technically fixed costs or not.

All of this becomes more than just idle debate and definitions if you try to do a break-even analysis. I think of break-even as mostly optional, but still a good illustration of your basic financial picture. So you might find it worth the effort.

Your burn rate is how much you have to spend on an average month to keep your company up and running. That normally includes rent, payroll, and—unlike the concepts of fixed vs. variable costs—whatever else you spend in a normal month that isn't directly tied to your sales, which means it isn't automatically paid for by sales, whether it's fixed or variable or not. So it includes your standard marketing expenses, which would technically be called variable expenses.

Back during the dot-com boom, some internet companies had no sales or revenue but had lots of money from investors. So they would divide the money they had in the bank by their monthly burn rate to calculate how many months of life they had. Without sales or revenue, burn rate became very important. They'd use it to know when to look for more investment, or, in some cases, when to look for a new job.

I think you should always know your burn rate. I hope you have sales and revenue as well. If your plan calls for burning more money than you're bringing in, then you know you need to be borrowing or finding investment.

I also like the burn rate instead of fixed costs as a good number to use in a "break-even analysis." In classic financial projections, the kind they still teach in financial analysis courses in business school, you'd use your fixed costs to calculate your break-even point. Burn rate is a newer idea, and better.

Managing Gross Margin

While the gross margin is a dollar amount, the gross margin percent is expressed as a percentage. It's equally important to track since it allows you to keep an eye on profitability trends. This is critical, because many businesses have gotten into financial trouble with an increasing gross profit that coincided with a declining gross profit margin. The gross margin percent is computed as follows:

Gross Profit ÷ Sales = Gross Profit Margin

There are two key ways for you to improve your gross margin. First, you can increase your prices. Second, you can decrease the costs to produce your goods. Of course, both are easier said than done.

An increase in prices can cause sales to drop. If sales drop too far, you may not generate enough gross profit dollars to cover operating expenses. Price increases require a very careful reading of inflation rates, competitive factors, and basic supply and demand for the product you are producing.

The second method of increasing gross profit margin is to lower the variable costs to produce your product. This can be accomplished by decreasing material costs or making the product more efficiently, although if it reduces quality, it might have some unforeseen negative outcomes too. Volume discounts are a good way to reduce material costs. The more material you buy from suppliers, the more likely they are to offer you discounts. Another way to reduce material costs is to find a less costly supplier. However, you might sacrifice quality if the goods purchased are not made as well.

Whether you are starting a manufacturing, wholesaling, retailing, or service business, you should always be on the lookout for ways to deliver your product or service more efficiently. However, you also must balance efficiency and quality issues to ensure that they do not get out of balance.

Computing Markup

Many business owners often get confused when relating markup to gross margin. They are first cousins in that both computations deal with the same variables. The difference is that gross margin is figured as a percentage of the selling price, while markup is figured as a percentage of the seller's cost.

Markup is computed as follows:

**(Selling Price minus Cost to Produce) ÷ Cost to Produce
= Markup Percentage**

Let's compute a hypothetical example:

($1 million minus $750,000) ÷ $750,000 = 33.3 percent

Now, let's change that example:

($1.5 million minus $1.05 million) ÷ $1.05 million = 42.9 percent

While computing markup for an entire year for a business is very simple, using this valuable markup tool daily to work up price quotes is more complicated. However, it is even more vital. Computing markup on last year's numbers helps you understand where you've been and gives you a benchmark for success. But computing markup on individual jobs will affect your business going forward and can often make the difference in running a profitable operation.

In bidding individual jobs, you must carefully estimate the variable costs associated with each job. And the calculation is different in that you typically seek a desired markup with a known cost to arrive at the price quote. Here is the computation to find a price quote using markup:

(Desired Markup x Total Variable Costs) + Total Variable Costs = Price Quote

What if you are a new business owner and don't have any experience to base an estimate on? Then you will need to research material costs by getting quotes from suppliers as well as study the labor rates in the area. You should also research industry manufacturing prices. Armed with this information, you will have a well-educated "guess" to base your job quote on.

How you use markup to set prices will depend on the type of business you are starting. If you are launching a manufacturing, wholesale, or retail operation, you will be able to compute markup using the aforementioned formulas to factor in all the variables in the cost of producing or generating the items you will be selling. Markup can also be used to bid one job or to set prices for an entire product line.

If you are starting a service business, however, markup is more difficult to calculate, particularly for new business owners. With most service businesses, the key variable cost associated with delivering the service to your customers will be you and your employees' time. In computing proper markup for a service business, you must pay close attention to the time spent to provide the service to customers, as well as to market prices of the services provided. In starting a service business, you will need to research the going rate paid to employees and the market prices for the services you will be providing.

For instance, if you are starting a staffing service, you will need to know what rate is typically paid to employees in this industry as well as the market rate charged to your customers for temporary labor. This will enable you to compute the proper markup in setting your price to ensure that you will be profitable.

Managing Cash Flow

Profits aren't cash. Profits are an accounting concept; cash is what we spend. We pay the bills, and payroll, with cash. While the plan-as-you-go business plan doesn't necessarily include a full-blown financial forecast (at least not until needed) it should at least be aware of cash balances and cash flow.

This should be a pretty simple concept, but it gets hard because we're trained to think about profits more than cash. It's the general way of the world. When anyone does the mythical business plan on a napkin, they think about what it costs to build something, and how much more they can sell it for, which means profits.

However, you can be profitable without having any money in the bank. And what's worse is that it tends to happen a lot when you're growing, which turns good news into bad news, and catches people unprepared.

Here are some traps you can watch for, to catch cash flow problems before they happen.

Every Dollar of Receivables Is a Dollar Less Cash

That's right, although it's not intuitive. You can do the analysis pretty quickly. Assets have to be equal to capital minus liabilities, so if you have a dollar of receivables as an asset, that pretty much means you have one dollar less in cash. If your customers had paid you, it would be money, not accounts receivable.

Where this comes up all the time is business-to-business sales. In most of the world, when a business delivers goods or services to another business, instead of getting the money for the sale right away, there is an invoice and the business customer pays later. That's not always true, but it is the rule, not the exception. We call that sales on credit, by the way, and it has nothing to do with sales paid for by credit card (which, ironically, is usually the same as cash less a couple of days and a couple of percentage points as fees).

We can use this in making financial projections: the more assets you have in receivables, the less in cash.

Example: A company running smoothly with an average of a 45 day wait for its receivables has a steady cash flow with a minimum balance of just a little less than $500,000. The same company is more than half a million dollars in deficit when its collection days goes to 90 instead of 45. That's a swing of more than a million dollars between the two assumptions. And that's in a company with less than $10 million annual sales, and fewer than 50 employees.

You might just glance ahead to Figure 16-1 to see how much difference that makes.

And the trick is that the profit and loss doesn't care about receivables. You have as much profit when you sell $1,000 that your customers haven't paid yet as when you sell $1,000 that your customers paid instantly in cash. Obviously, the cash flow implications are different in either case.

TAKE NOTES!

WEEK 3+

These words put some people off because they sound like accounting and financial analysis. But they're good words to know—especially if you're running a business.

Receivables is short for accounts receivable, which is money owed to you by customers who haven't paid

Sales on credit isn't about credit cards, but rather business-to-business sales when you deliver the goods and services to a business customer but instead of getting the money, you deliver an invoice and you get accounts receivable. You wait until your business customer pays you.

Collection days is how long a business waits, on average, to get paid by its customers.

Inventory is stuff that you've purchased and you keep until you sell it to customers. That could be materials you're going to assemble into something, or products you're going to sell to customers. It's an asset, called inventory. It doesn't go into costs until you sell it. So therefore, it doesn't show up on the profit and loss until you sell it. But you probably already paid it.

Accounts payable is money you owe. When your business customers haven't paid you, what is accounts receivable to you is accounts payable to them.

Every Dollar of Inventory is a Dollar Less Cash

When your business has to buy stuff before it can sell it, that's called inventory. It's one of your assets. And keeping a lot of inventory can do bad things to your cash flow, unless you don't pay for it.

This can be pretty simple math. If having nothing in inventory leaves you with $20,000 in cash, then having $19,000 in inventory leaves you with only $1,000 in cash. That is, at least if you've paid for the inventory. That's because your other assets, your liabilities, and your capital is all the same.

Sometimes, of course, you cannot pay for that inventory, which means you have more payables, and your cash balance is supported by those payables.

The difference in cash with different assumptions can be startling. You can look ahead to Figure 16-2 to see what a difference two months makes.

Every Dollar of Payables is a Dollar More Cash

While receivables and inventory suck up money by dedicating assets to things that might have been cash but aren't, paying your own bills late is a standard way to protect your cash flow. The same basic math applies: If you leave your money in cash instead of using it to pay your bills, you have more cash.

It's called Accounts Payable, meaning money that you owe. Every dollar in Accounts Payable is a dollar you have in cash that won't be there if you pay that bill. The same problem you have when you sell to businesses is an advantage you have when you are a business. The seller's accounts receivable is the buyer's accounts payable.

Now, I don't want to imply that you don't pay your bills, or that it doesn't matter. Your business will have credit problems and a bad reputation if it doesn't pay bills on time, or if it is chronically late with the bills. Still, a lot of businesses use accounts payable to help finance themselves.

Waiting for Payment

So you wait a bit longer to get paid. Does it matter? Only about a million dollars worth. In the example in Figure 16-1, the company on the left gets paid by its customers in 45 days on average, and the one on the right in 90 days. Nothing else changes. Assumptions for sales, costs, expenses, and everything else are exactly the same. In the first case, the minimum cash balance is just less than half a million dollars, and in the second case, the one on the right, the cash balance is actually a deficit of more than half a million dollars.

Notice the financial impact: Both scenarios have the same sales of about $6 million per year, with the same profits of about 7 percent on sales. But the company on the left is doing just fine, and the company on the right is in real trouble, possibly going under and failing.

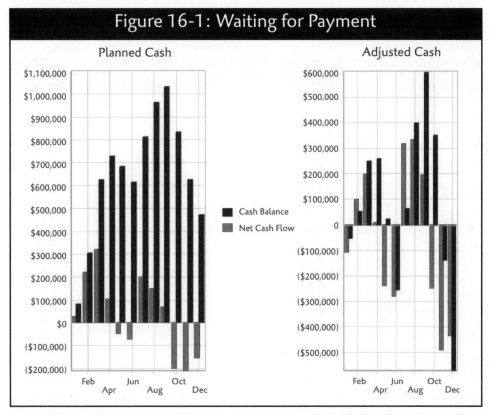

Figure 16-1: Waiting for Payment

Source: Business Plan Pro, AMT Sample Plan, Cash Pilot View. The cash pilot allows instant adjustment of critical cash variables including sales on credit as a percent of sales, collection days, inventory on hand, and payment days. This view shows the scenario on the left with 45 days collection on average, and the one on the right with 90 days on average.

Inventory: What a Difference Two Months Make

In this example, the company on the left keeps one month's worth of inventory, and the one on the right keeps three months. That's the only change between both of these cash scenarios. The result of the three-months inventory assumption in this case is almost a million dollars of deficit by the end of the year.

Ten Rules for Managing Cash

Cash flow problems can kill businesses that might otherwise survive. According to a U.S. bank study, 82 percent of business failures are due to

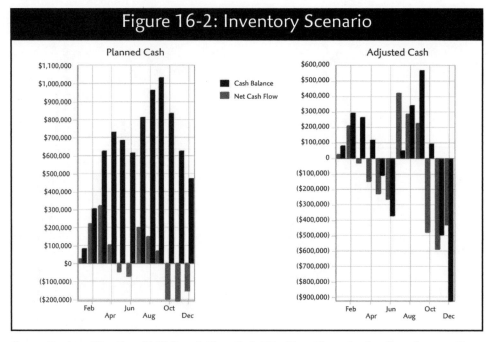

Source: Business Plan Pro, AMT Sample Plan, Cash Pilot View. The cash pilot allows instant adjustment of critical cash variables including sales on credit as a percent of sales, collection days, inventory on hand, and payment days. This view shows the scenario on the left with a month of inventory on average, and the one on the right with three months of inventory on average.

poor cash management. To prevent this from happening to your business, here are my ten cash flow rules to remember.

1. **Profits aren't cash; they're accounting.** And accounting is a lot more creative than you think. You can't pay bills with profits. Actually, profits can lull you to sleep. If you pay your bills and your customers don't, it's suddenly business hell. You can make profits without making any money.

2. **Cash flow isn't intuitive.** Don't try to do it in your head. Making the sales doesn't necessarily mean you have the money. Incurring the expense doesn't necessarily mean you paid for it already. Inventory is usually bought and paid for and then stored until it becomes cost of sales.

3. **Growth sucks up cash.** It's paradoxical. The best of times can be hiding the worst of times. One of the toughest years my company had was when we doubled sales and almost went broke. We were building things two months in advance and getting the money from sales six months late. Add growth to that and it can be like a Trojan horse, hiding a problem inside a solution. Yes, of course you want to grow; we all want to grow our businesses. But be careful because growth costs cash. It's a matter of working capital. The faster you grow, the more financing you need.

4. **Business-to-business sales suck up your cash.** The simple view is that sales mean money, but when you're a business selling to another business, it's rarely that simple. You deliver the goods or services along with an invoice, and they pay the invoice later. Usually, that's months later. And businesses are good customers, so you can't just throw them into collections because then they'll never buy from you again. So you wait. When you sell something to a distributor that sells it to a retailer, you typically get the money four or five months later if you're lucky.

5. **Inventory sucks up cash.** You have to buy your product or build it before you can sell it. Even if you put the product on your shelves and wait to sell it, your suppliers expect to get paid. Here's a simple rule of thumb: Every dollar you have in inventory is a dollar you don't have in cash.

6. **Working capital is your best survival skill.** Technically, working capital is an accounting term for what's left over when you subtract current liabilities from current assets. Practically, it's money in the bank that you use to pay your running costs and expenses and buy inventory while waiting to get paid by your business customers.

7. **"Receivables" is a bad word.** (See rule 4.) The money your customers owe you is called "accounts receivable." Here's a shortcut to cash planning: Every dollar in accounts receivable is a dollar less cash.

8. **Bankers hate surprises.** Plan ahead. You get no extra points for spontaneity when dealing with banks. If you see a growth spurt coming, a new product opportunity, or a problem with customers paying, the sooner you get to the bank armed with charts and a realistic plan, the better off you'll be.

9. **Watch these three vital metrics:** "Collection days" is a measure of how long you wait to get paid. "Inventory turnover" is a measure of how long your inventory sits on your working capital and clogs your cash flow. "Payment days" is how long you wait to pay your vendors. Always monitor these three vital signs of cash flow. Project them 12 months ahead and compare your plan to what actually happens.

10. **If you're the exception rather than the rule, hooray for you.** If all your customers pay you immediately when they buy from you, and you don't buy things before you sell them, then relax. But if you sell to businesses, keep in mind that they usually don't pay immediately.

(Reprinted with permission from upandrunning.entrepreneur.com All rights reserved.)

Cash and Working Capital

Working capital is one of the most difficult financial concepts for the small-business owner to understand. In fact, the term means a lot of different things to a lot of different people. By definition, working capital is the amount by which current assets exceed current liabilities. However, if you simply run this calculation each period to try to analyze working capital, you won't accomplish much in figuring out what your working capital needs are and how to meet them.

Working capital is essentially the extra money you need to get by; it's money you need to support the company while waiting for customers to pay their bills; money you need to buy inventory and pay for manufacturing and processing before you have anything to sell; money you need to invest in expenses before they directly create sales.

That money can come from investment, profits saved up, loans, and some other sources. Here are the five most common sources of short-term working capital financing:

1. **Investment** (also called **Equity**): Most startups require some kind of initial investment to make it through the building period, when cash flow is negative.

2. **Trade Credit (Accounts Payable)**: This is one of the more important and more common sources. Part of your financing is the money you owe. Of course, in the beginning, when you've just started, you may have more trouble getting vendors to allow you credit. If you have paid on time in the past, a trade creditor may be willing to extend terms to enable you to meet a big order. For instance, if you receive a big order that you can fulfill, ship out, and collect in 60 days, you could obtain 60-day terms from your supplier if 30-day terms are normally given. The trade creditor will want proof of the order and may want to file a lien on it as security, but if it enables you to proceed, that should not be a problem.

3. **Line of Credit:** Lines of credit are not often given by banks to new businesses. However, if your new business is well capitalized by equity and you have good collateral, your business might qualify. The most common collateral is receivables owed to you by your customers. In this case it helps if the customers are established and well-known companies. A line of credit allows you to borrow funds for short-term needs when they arise. The funds are repaid once you collect the accounts receivable that

resulted from the short-term sales peak. Lines of credit typically are made for one year at a time and are expected to be paid off for 30 to 60 consecutive days sometime during the year to ensure that the funds are used for short-term needs only.

4. **Factoring:** Factoring is another resource for short-term working capital financing. Once you have filled an order, a factoring company buys your account receivable and then handles the collection. This type of financing is more expensive than conventional bank financing but is sometimes used by new businesses.

5. **Short-Term Loan:** While your new business may not qualify for a line of credit from a bank, you might have success in obtaining a one-time short-term loan (less than a year) to finance your temporary working capital needs. If you have established a good banking relationship with a banker, he or she might be willing to provide a short-term note for one order or for a seasonal inventory and/or accounts receivable buildup.

Planning, Forecasting, Budgeting

You may not have the need for a complete financial forecast, but it's just a shame to start and run a business without managing a simple sales forecast, expense budget, and an estimate of startup costs. These are all relatively simple estimates, with relatively simple math, that anybody who is smart enough to run a business can do.

After all, a lot of the real value of planning and budgeting is the tracking, following up, seeing what was different. That's much more likely to happen if you have numbers, like sales and expenses, that you can track.

Managing a Sales Forecast

Your sales forecast is the backbone of your planning and budgeting. People measure a business and its growth by sales, and your sales forecast sets the standard for expenses, profits, and growth. The sales forecast is almost always going to be the first set of numbers you'll track for plan vs. actual use. This is what you do even if you do no other numbers, and it's probably the first numbers you'll do.

When it comes to forecasting sales, don't fall for the trap that says forecasting takes training, mathematics, or advanced degrees. Forecasting is mainly educated guessing. So don't expect to get it perfect; just make it reasonable. There's no business owner who isn't qualified to forecast sales—you don't need a business degree or accountant's certification. What you need is common sense, research of the factors, and motivation to make an educated guess.

Your sales forecast for running a business should show sales by month for the next 12 months—at least—and then by year for the following two to five years. Three years, total, is generally enough for most business plans.

If you have more than one line of sales, show each line of sales separately and add them up. If you have more than 10 or so lines of sales, summarize them and consolidate. Remember, this is business planning, not accounting, so it has to be reasonable, but it doesn't need too much detail. Table 16-4 shows an example from a sales forecast for a startup small restaurant.

Managing and Budgeting Expenses

Budgeting expenses is a matter of simple math, common sense, and reasonable guesses, without statistical analysis, mathematical techniques, or any past data. The mathematics are simple; sums of the rows and columns. You've seen it before.

And, as with the sales forecast, you really need to have some idea of this. Either you get it from past data, or you get it from your experience in the industry, or from a partner or team member with experience, or you do some shoe-leather research. Look for standard industry data.

Also, remember that you only have to go one month without having any idea, because by the second month, with the right kind of budgeting and planning, you have the first month's results to help review and revise. Table 16-5 shows a simple example.

Table 16-4: Sample Sales Forecast

	A	C	D	E
	B16			
16	**Sales Forecast**			
17		Jan	Feb	Mar
18	**Unit Sales**			
19	Lunches	119	227	302
20	Lunch Bvg	119	227	302
21	Dinners	500	600	728
22	Dinner Bvg	500	600	728
23	Other	50	50	50
24	**Total Unit Sales**	1,288	1,704	2,110
25				
26	**Unit Prices**	Jan	Feb	Mar
27	Lunches	$10.00	$10.00	$10.00
28	Lunch Bvg	$2.00	$2.00	$2.00
29	Dinners	$20.00	$20.00	$20.00
30	Dinner Bvg	$4.00	$4.00	$4.00
31	Other	$2.00	$2.00	$2.00
32				
33	**Sales**			
34	Lunches	$1,192	$2,272	$3,021
35	Lunch Bvg	$238	$454	$604
36	Dinners	$10,000	$12,000	$14,560
37	Dinner Bvg	$2,000	$2,400	$2,912
38	Other	$100	$100	$100
39	**Total Sales**	$13,530	$17,227	$21,197

Match the depth and detail of your budget to the control and accountability you have on your team. Make it so that the rows are useful for following up later, looking at what was different from plan (and it will always end up different) and why.

Does your spending match your priorities? This is where you begin to see it in action.

Aim for the right level of detail for following up. Too much detail makes it very hard to manage and track, and too much aggregation makes it hard

	Jan	Feb	Nov	Dec	Year 1
Payroll	$12,000	$12,000	$27,250	$27,250	$194,750
Advertising	$13,500	$13,500	$13,500	$13,500	$162,000
Leases	$500	$500	$500	$500	$6,000
Utilities	$1,000	$1,000	$1,000	$1,000	$12,000
Insurance	$300	$300	$300	$300	$3,600
Rent	$1,500	$1,500	$1,500	$1,500	$18,000
Payroll Tax	$1,680	$1,680	$3,815	$3,815	$27,265
Other	$0	$100	$200	$300	$1,000
TOTAL	$30,480	$30,580	$48,065	$48,165	$424,615

Table 16-5: Sample Expense Budget

to develop accountability. Do you know, in your business, who is responsible for each row in the budget? Does everybody else on the team know?

Before I go too much further, I'd like you to consider how important payroll is as part of you budget. Let's see where those numbers came from. I recommend it be another separate table, whose totals flow into this one.

Manage Payroll as Part of Expenses

Payroll is really the most important of your expenses, right? Unless you're working all alone, when things get fuzzier, the worst thing that can happen is missing payroll. So that's a number that should really be in your plan, among the simple basic numbers. I hope you agree.

Here, too, the math (the spreadsheet elements) is pretty simple. It doesn't take advanced analysis or specialized equations. If you have past data and history, it becomes very easy (which is not to say that projecting future pay increases is an easy part of business, but the math and estimation is

Table 16-6: Personnel Plan					
	Jan	Nov	Dec	Year 1	Year 2
Partners	$12,000	$12,000	$12,000	$144,000	$175,000
Consultants	$0	$0	$0	$0	$50,000
Editorial/Graphic	$0	$6,000	$6,000	$18,000	$22,000
VP Marketing	$0	$5,000	$5,000	$20,000	$50,000
Salespeople	$0	$0	$0	$0	$30,000
Office Manager	$0	$2,500	$2,500	$7,500	$30,000
Secretarial	$0	$1,750	$1,750	$5,250	$20,000
Other	$0	$0	$0	$0	$0
TOTAL PEOPLE	3	7	7	7	14
TOTAL PAYROLL	$12,000	$27,250	$27,250	$194,750	$377,000

relatively simple). Table 16-6 shows a spreadsheet example, but this is just one easy way to do it. Lots of people add sophistication to it, like dividing the payroll up into departments, or estimating how many people in each functional area, then the average pay per person, then multiplying. For now, though, I want to keep things simple as we go.

Stocking Up

If your business will produce or sell inventory, your inventory management system will be crucial to your business's success. Keeping too much inventory on hand will cost you cash flow and will increase the risk of obsolescence. Conversely, a low inventory level can cost you sales.

Here are some suggestions to help you better manage your inventory:

- **Pay attention to seasonality.** Depending on the type of business you are starting, you may have certain inventory items that sell only during certain times of the year. Order early in anticipation of the peak season. Then make sure you sell the stock so that you don't get stuck holding on to it for a year.

- **Rely on suppliers.** If you can find suppliers that are well stocked and can ship quickly, you can essentially let them stock your inventory for you. "Just in time" inventory management can save valuable working capital that could be invested in other areas of your business.

- **Stock what sells.** This may seem obvious, but too many business owners try to be all things to all people when it comes to inventory management. When you see what sells, focus your purchasing efforts on those items.

- **Mark down stale items.** Once you're up and running, you will find that certain items sell better than others. Mark down the items that don't sell, and then don't replace them.

- **Watch waste.** Keep a close eye on waste. If production mistakes aren't caught early, you can ruin a whole batch of inventory, which can be extremely costly.

How Do You Rate?

Ratio analysis is a financial management tool that enables you to compare the trends in your financial performance as well as provides some measurements to compare your performance against others in your industry.

> **TAKE NOTES!**
>
> Your accounting system should give you your financial ratios for the past. Your business plan can give you projected financial ratios for the future, based on your assumptions.
>
> **WEEK 3+**

Comparing ratios from year to year highlights areas in which you are performing well and areas that need tweaking. Most industry trade groups can provide you with industry averages for key ratios that will provide a benchmark against which you can compare your company.

Financial ratios can be divided into four subcategories: profitability, liquidity, activity, and leverage. Here are 15 financial ratios that you can use to manage your new business.

Profitability Ratios

Gross Profit ÷ Sales = Gross Profit Margin

Operating Profit ÷ Sales = Operating Profit Margin

Net Profit ÷ Sales = Net Profit Margin

Net Profit ÷ Owner's Equity = Return on Equity

Net Profit ÷ Total Assets = Return on Assets

Liquidity Ratios

Current Assets ÷ Current Liabilities = Current Ratio

(Current Assets—Inventory) ÷ Current Liabilities = Quick Ratio

Working Capital ÷ Sales = Working Capital Ratio

Activity Ratios

(Accounts Receivable x 365) ÷ Sales = Accounts Receivable Days

(Inventory x 365) ÷ Cost of Goods Sold = Inventory Days

(Accounts Payable x 365) ÷ Purchases = Accounts Payable Days

Sales ÷ Total Assets = Sales to Assets

Leverage Ratios

Total Liabilities ÷ Owner's Equity = Debt to Equity

Total Liabilities ÷ Total Assets = Debt Ratio

(Net Income + Depreciation) ÷ Current Maturities of Long-Term Debt = Debt Coverage Ratio

Where Credit Is Due

When you book a credit sale in your business, you must collect from the customer to realize your profit. Many a solid business has suffered a severe setback or even been put under by its failure to collect accounts receivable.

It is vital that you stay on top of your A/R if you sell on credit. Here are some tips that will help you maintain high quality accounts receivable:

- Check out references upfront. Find out how your prospective customer has paid other suppliers before selling on credit. Ask for supplier and bank references and follow up on them.

- Set credit limits, and monitor them. Establish credit limits for each customer. Set up a system to regularly compare balances owed and credit limits.

- Process invoices immediately. Send out invoices as soon as goods are shipped. Falling behind on sending invoices will result in slower collection of accounts receivable, which costs you cash flow.

- Don't resell to habitually slow-paying accounts. If you find that a certain customer stays way behind in payment to you, stop selling to that company. Habitual slow pay is a sign of financial instability, and you can ill afford to write off an account of any significant size during the early years of your business.

For the Record

As you set up your bookkeeping system, you will need to establish procedures for keeping financial records. The IRS requires that you keep records on hand for certain specified periods of time. And with some financial records, it just makes good business sense to keep them so you can access them at a later date.

One key point here is to make sure these records are kept in a safe place. Whether you store them on-site or at a remote location (some business owners use self-storage units), make sure you use a fireproof cabinet or safe.

Another recommendation is to minimize paper buildup by storing as much as possible on CD-ROMs, microfilm, or DVDs. Table 16-7 contains a list of what you need to save and for how long, as recommended by accounting firm PricewaterhouseCoopers:

Table 16-7: Keeping Financial Records

RECORD TYPE	HOW LONG?
Income tax reports, protests, court briefs, appeals	Indefinitely
Annual financial statements	Indefinitely
Monthly financial statements	3 years
Books of account, such as the general ledger	Indefinitely
Subledgers	3 years
Canceled payroll and dividend checks	6 years
Income tax payment checks	Indefinitely
Bank reconciliations, voided checks, check stubs, and register tapes	6 years
Sales records such as invoices, monthly statements, remittance advisories, shipping papers, bills of lading and customers' purchase orders	6 years
Purchase records, including purchase orders and payment vouchers	6 years
Travel and entertainment records, including account books, diaries, and expense statements and receipts	6 years
Documents substantiating fixed-asset additions, depreciation policies, and salvage values assigned to assets	Indefinitely
Personnel and payroll records, such as payments and reports to taxing authorities, including federal income tax withholding, FICA contributions, unemployment taxes, and workers' compensation insurance	6 years
Corporate documents, including certificates of incorporation, corporate charter, constitution and bylaws, deeds and easements, stock, stock transfer records, minutes of board of directors meetings, retirement and pension records, labor contracts, and license, patent, trademark and registration applications	Indefinitely

ONLINE TOOLS

Most of these are online information websites, several of them sites that we help to develop and maintain.

- Basic Business Numbers, a 25-minute video presentation: blog.timberry.com/video-basic-business-numb.html

- *Hurdle: the Book on Business Planning:* hurdlebook.com. (Look at the Financial Analysis section, including "Business Numbers," "The Bottom Line," "Cash is King," and "Finish the Financials.")

- Business Plan Pro, business planning software: paloalto.com

- 10 Rules for Valuation: Upandrunning.entrepreneur.com/2007/12/05/10-rules-for-valuation

- How to Change the World: Glenn Kelman's Financial Model: blog.guykawasaki.com/2007/10/glenn-kelmans-f.html

PAYING TAXES

When it comes to taxes, there's no way to get around the fact that you have to pay them regularly. Federal, state, and local taxes combined can take a big chunk out of your company's money, leaving you with less cash to operate your business.

That's why it's important to stay abreast of your business's tax situation and work with a qualified accountant to understand all that's required of you by federal and state governments. The task is by no means simple. New business owners face a host of tax requirements and ever-changing rules.

This chapter was written by Joan Szabo, a freelance writer who has covered tax issues for more than 17 years.

If you miss deadlines or fail to comply with specific rules, you may be hit with large penalties, and, in the worst-case scenario, be forced to close up shop. You'll also want to pay close attention to tax planning, which will help you find legitimate ways to trim your overall tax liability. Your goal is to take the deductions to which you're entitled and to defer taxes as long as you possibly can.

RED TAPE ALERT!

Read this chapter carefully. Everything in this chapter is a red tape alert!

While a knowledgeable accountant specializing in small-business tax issues will keep you out of potential tax quagmires, you'll be on more solid footing if you spend time acquiring your own working knowledge and understanding of the tax laws.

First Things First

One of the first steps you will take as a business owner is to obtain a tax-payer identification number so the IRS can process your returns. There are two types of identification numbers: a Social Security number and an Employer Identification Number (EIN).

The EIN is a nine-digit number the IRS issues. It is used to identify the tax accounts of corporations, partnerships, and other entities. You need an EIN if you have employees, operate your business as a corporation or partnership, or have a Keogh plan. Be sure to include your EIN on all returns or other documents you send to the IRS.

You can apply for an EIN by phone, fax, mail, or online (as long as your business is an entity that is allowed to apply online). You can receive your EIN immediately by phone or by going online. To apply online, go to IRS.gov, click on "Businesses," then "Employer ID Number." A completed fax request takes about four to five business days. If you apply by mail, be sure to send in Form SS-4 (Application for Employer Identification Number) at least four or five weeks before you need the EIN to file a return or make a deposit. To apply by phone, call toll-free at (800) 829-4933 from 7A.M. until

10P.M. Monday through Friday. Before you call, the IRS suggests you complete Form SS-4 so you have all relevant information available. The person making the call to the IRS must be authorized to sign the form.

Ins and Outs of Payroll Taxes

If you do any hiring, your employees must complete Form I-9 (Employment Eligibility Verification) and Form W-4 (Employee's Withholding Allowance Certificate). Form I-9 provides verification that each new employee is legally eligible to work in the United States. This form can be obtained from the U.S. Citizenship and Immigration Service (USCIS) by calling (800) 870-3676; keep this form in your files in the event an IRS or USCIS inspector wants to see it. Your employees should also complete a state withholding certificate (similar to the W-4) if your state imposes personal income taxes.

Form W-4 indicates the employee's filing status and withholding allowances. These allowances are used to determine how much federal income tax to withhold from an employee's wages. To determine how much to withhold from each wage payment, use the employee's W-4 and the methods described in IRS Publications 15, Employer's Tax Guide, and 15-A, Employer's Supplemental Tax Guide. These publications are available online at irs.gov.

You must also withhold Social Security and Medicare taxes—these are known as FICA (Federal Insurance Contributions Act) taxes. The FICA tax actually consists of two taxes: a 6.2 percent Social Security tax and a 1.45 percent Medicare tax. To calculate the tax you need to withhold for each employee, multiply an employee's gross wages for a pay period by the tax rates. In addition, as an employer, you are required to pay a matching amount of FICA taxes on each of your employees.

Here's how it works: If an employee has gross wages of $1,000 every two weeks, you must withhold $62 ($1,000 x 0.062) in Social Security taxes and $14.50 ($1,000 x .0145) in Medicare taxes, or $76.50. As an employer, you owe a matching amount as well, so the total amount in FICA taxes to be paid is $153. The maximum amount of wages currently subject to Social Security tax is $94,200 for 2006. There is no limit on the amount of wages subject to the Medicare tax.

TAKE NOTES!

WEEK 3+

Employee benefits such as health insurance and pension plan contributions provide attractive tax deductions. With a qualified pension plan, you not only receive a tax deduction for the contributions you make on behalf of your employees, but the money you contribute to your own retirement account is also deductible and is allowed to grow tax-deferred until withdrawn. (A qualified plan meets the requirements of the Employee Retirement Income Security Act [ERISA] and the Internal Revenue Code.)

There are many different plans available, ranging from a Savings Incentive Match Plan for Employees (SIMPLE) to a traditional 401(k) plan (see Chapter 9). The pension design may be slightly different, but they all offer important tax benefits for business owners. So take the time to find out which plan will work best for you.

As far as health insurance is concerned, if your business is incorporated and you work for it as an employee, you can deduct all costs for your own insurance as well as for the coverage for your employees. Self-employed individuals can deduct 100 percent of the premiums paid for health insurance for themselves and their families, as long as the amount isn't more than the net earnings from the business.

The IRS requires any business paying more than $200,000 annually in payroll taxes or other federal taxes to pay them through the Electronic Federal Tax Payment System (EFTPS). If you pay less than that amount, you can still deliver a check for payroll taxes owed with your deposit coupons to an authorized financial institution able to accept federal tax deposits (for more on making these deposits see IRS Publication 15, also known as Circular E). The form to use is 8109 (Federal Tax Deposit Coupon). On each coupon show the deposit amount, the type of tax, the period for which you are making a deposit and your phone number. You typically pay these taxes monthly, depending on the size of your business. Approximately five to six weeks after you receive your EIN, the IRS will send you the coupon book. (For more on EFTPS, go to eftps.gov.)

In addition to making your monthly payroll deposits, you are required to file quarterly Form 941 (Employer's Quarterly Federal Tax Return). This is a form that provides the government with information on the federal income taxes you withheld from your employees' pay as well as the FICA taxes you withheld and paid. It also tells the government when the taxes were withheld so the IRS can determine if the federal tax deposit was made on time.

Another tax you have to pay is FUTA (Federal Unemployment Tax Act) taxes, which are used to compensate workers who lose their jobs. You report and pay FUTA tax separately from FICA and withheld income taxes.

You pay FUTA tax on your payroll if during the current or prior calendar year you meet one of two tests: You paid total wages of $1,500 to your employees in any calendar quarter, or you have at least one employee working on any given day in each of 20 different calendar weeks.

The FUTA tax is figured on the first $7,000 in wages paid to each employee annually. The gross FUTA tax rate is 6.2 percent. However, you are given a credit of up to 5.4 percent for the state unemployment tax you pay, effectively reducing the tax rate. As an employer, you pay FUTA tax only from your own funds. Employees do not have this tax withheld from their pay.

You generally deposit FUTA taxes quarterly. In addition, you must file an annual return for your FUTA taxes using Form 940 (Employer's Annual Federal Unemployment Tax Return), which must be filed by January 31 of the following year. Most small employers are eligible to use Form 940-EZ.

Federal payroll taxes are not your only concern. States and localities have their own taxes, which will most likely affect you. Most states have a personal income tax (eight do not), which means you are also required to withhold this tax from your employee's wages. The same is true if you do business in a city or locality with an income tax.

RED TAPE ALERT!

WEEK 3+

If you hire independent contractors, make sure you know whether they are covered under your state's workers' comp laws. If an independent contractor is injured on the job in a state where he's not covered by workers' comp, he's not limited in the type of civil action he can file against the employer. If he is covered by workers' comp laws, the contractor is limited to the remedies provided under those laws.

When applying for an EIN from your state, which you will need to do business there, ask about the procedures and forms for withholding and depositing state income taxes. The place to start is with your state department of revenue.

At the end of the tax year, you must furnish copies of Form W-2 (Wage and Tax Statement) to each employee who worked for you during the year. Be sure to give the forms to your employees by January 31 of the year after the calendar year covered by the form. Form W-2 provides information on how much money each employee earned and the amount of federal, state and FICA taxes you withheld. You must send copies of W-2s to the Social Security Administration as well.

TAKE NOTES!

Consider using a payroll tax service to take care of all payroll tax requirements. The fees charged by such services are relatively reasonable. In addition, these firms specialize in this area and know the ins and outs of all the rules and regulations. With a service, you don't have to worry about making mistakes or being tardy with payments.

Declaration of Independents

You may decide your business can't afford to hire too many full-time employees, and you'd like to use the services of an independent contractor. With an independent contractor, you don't have to withhold and pay the person's income, Social Security and Medicare taxes.

While independent contractors do translate to lower payroll costs, be advised that the IRS scrutinizes this whole area very carefully. The IRS wants to make sure that your workers are properly classified and paying the government the necessary income and payroll taxes that are due.

To stay out of hot water with the IRS, be sure the workers you classify as independent contractors meet the IRS definition of an independent contractor. The determining factors fall into three main categories: behavioral control, financial control, and relationship of the parties. The IRS uses 20 factors when deciding a worker's status. Here are some of the major ones:

- **Who has control?** A worker is an employee if the person for whom he works has the right to direct and control him concerning when and where to do the work. The employer need not actually exercise control;

it is sufficient that he has the right to do so.

- **Right to fire:** An employee can be fired by an employer. An independent contractor cannot be fired so long as he or she produces a result that meets the specifications of the contract.

- **Training:** An employee may be trained to perform services in a particular manner. However, independent contractors ordinarily use their own methods and receive no training from the employer.

- **Set hours of work:** Workers for whom you set specific hours of work are more likely to be employees. Independent contractors, on the other hand, usually establish their own work hours.

To stay on the right side of the IRS, it is best to document the relationship you have with any independent contractors in a written contract. This can be a simple agreement that spells out the duties of the independent contractor. The agreement should state that the independent contractor, not the employer, is responsible for withholding any necessary taxes. In addition, have the independent contractor submit invoices. It's a good idea to have a copy of the contractor's business license and certificate of insurance as well as his or her business card. Also, be sure you file Form 1099-MISC (Miscellaneous Income) at year-end, which is used to report payments made in the course of a transaction to another person or business that is not an employee. By law, you are required to file and give someone Form 1099 if you pay that person more than $600 a year. The form must be given to the independent contractor by January 31 of the following year. Form 1099 with its transmittal Form 1096 must be filed with the IRS by February 28 of the following year.

> **TAKE NOTES!**
>
> If you withhold taxes but don't deposit or pay them to the IRS, you face a penalty on the unpaid tax, plus interest. If you deposit the taxes late, you'll also be hit with a penalty.
>
> WEEK **3+**

Whether an individual is determined to be an independent contractor or an employee, it is required that you obtain their complete name, Social Security number and address before any money is paid. If this information is not obtained, you are required to withhold backup withholding taxes for federal income taxes.

If the IRS finds you have misclassified an employee as an independent contractor, you will pay a percentage of income taxes that should have been withheld on the employee's wages and be liable for your share of the FICA and unemployment taxes, plus penalties and interest. Even worse, if the IRS determines your misclassification was "willful," you could owe the IRS the full amount of income tax that should have been withheld (with an adjustment if the employee has paid or pays part of the tax), the full amount of both the employer's and employee's share of FICA taxes (possibly with an offset if the employee paid self-employment taxes), interest, and penalties.

TAKE NOTES!

Get the scoop on wage reporting for yourself and your employees at the Social Security website at SSA.gov.

Be advised that there is some relief being offered. If a business realizes it is in violation of the law regarding independent contractors, it can inform the IRS of the problem and then properly classify the workers without being hit with an IRS assessment for prior-year taxes.

Selecting Your Tax Year

When you launch your business, you'll have to decide what tax year to use. The tax year is the annual accounting period used to keep your records and report your income and expenses. There are two accounting periods: a calendar year and a fiscal year.

A calendar year is 12 consecutive months starting January 1 and ending December 31. Most sole proprietors, partnerships, limited liability companies and S corporations use the calendar year as their tax year. If you operate a business as a sole proprietorship, the IRS says the tax year for your business is the same as your individual tax year.

A fiscal tax year is 12 consecutive months ending on the last day of any month other than December. For business owners who start a company during the year and have substantial expenses or losses, it may be smart to select a fiscal year (as long as the IRS allows it) that goes beyond the end of the first calendar year. This way, as much income as possible is offset by startup expenses and losses.

Filing Your Tax Return

Your federal tax filing obligations and due dates generally are based on the legal structure you've selected for your business and whether you use a calendar or fiscal year.

> **TAKE NOTES!**
>
> Once you have selected to file on either a calendar- or fiscal-year basis, you have to get permission from the IRS to change it. To do so, you must file Form 1128, and you may have to pay a fee.
>
> WEEK **3+**

Sole Proprietorships

If you are a sole proprietor, every year you must file Schedule C (Profit or Loss From Business) with your Form 1040 (U.S. Individual Income Tax Return) to report your business's net profit and loss. You also must file Schedule SE (Self-Employment Tax) with your 1040. If you are a calendar-year taxpayer, your tax filing date is April 15. Fiscal-year taxpayers must file their returns no later than the 15th day of the fourth month after the end of their tax year.

In addition to your annual tax return, many self-employed individuals such as sole proprietors and partners make quarterly estimated tax payments to cover their income and Social Security tax liability. You must make estimated tax payments if you expect to owe at least $1,000 in federal

> **TAKE NOTES!**
>
> Take advantage of the convenient Electronic Federal Tax Payment System (EFTPS) to pay your taxes. EFTPS allows you to go online or use the phone to make payments. Funds are moved from your account to the Treasury Department's on the date you indicate. Every EFTPS transaction generates an immediate confirmation number for your receipt. To enroll, go to EFTPS.gov.
>
> WEEK **3+**

tax for the year and your withholding will be less than the smaller of 90 percent of your current-year tax liability or 100 percent of your previous year's tax liability if your adjusted gross income is $150,000 or less. The federal government allows you to pay estimated taxes in four equal amounts throughout the year on the 15th of April, June, September and January.

WEEK 3+

TAKE NOTES!

If you find, after you've tallied up all your business deductions and subtracted them from your income, that you're in the red for the year, don't despair. There's something called the net operating loss deduction that will help. It allows you to offset one year's losses against another year's income.

The IRS lets you carry this operating loss back two years and use it to offset the income of those previous two years. Doing so may result in a refund. If you still have some losses left after carrying them back, you can carry them forward for up to 20 years. If you don't want to use the two-year carryback period, you can elect to deduct the net operating loss over the next 20 years. However, once you make that election, you can't reverse it. Remember, if there is any unused loss after 20 years, you may no longer apply it to any income.

Partnerships and Limited Liability Companies (LLCs)

Companies with these structures must file Form 1065 (U.S. Return of Partnership Income) to income and loss to the IRS. The partnership must furnish copies of Schedule K-1 (Partner's Share of Income, Credits, Deductions), which is part of Form 1065, to the partners or LLC members by the filing date for Form 1065. The due dates are the same as those for sole proprietors.

Corporations

If your business is structured as a regular corporation, you must file Form 1120 (U.S. Corporation Income Tax Return). For calendar-year taxpayers, the due date for the return is March 15. For fiscal-year corporations, the return must be filed by the 15th day of the third month after the end of your corporation's tax year.

Owners of S corporations must file Form 1120S (U.S. Income Tax Return for an S Corporation). Like partnerships, shareholders must receive a copy of Schedule K-1, which is part of Form 1120S. The due dates are the same as those for regular corporations.

Sales Taxes

Sales taxes vary by state and are imposed at the retail level. It's important to know the rules in the states and localities where you operate your business, because if you are a retailer, you must collect state sales tax on each sale you make.

While a number of states and localities exempt service businesses from sales taxes, some have changed their laws in this area and are applying the sales tax to some services. If you run a service business, contact your state revenue and/or local revenue offices for information on the laws in your area.

Before you open your doors, be sure to register to collect sales tax by applying for a sales permit for each separate place of business you have in the state. A license or permit is important because in some states it is a criminal offense to undertake sales without one. In addition, if you fail to collect sales tax, you can be held liable for the uncollected amount.

> ## TAKE NOTES!
>
> To help you wade through all the tax laws and regulations, the IRS offers these free publications: Tax Guide for Small Business (Publication 334), Business Expenses (Publication 535), Travel, Entertain-ment, Gift and Car Expenses (Publication 463), Circular E, Employer's Tax Guide (Publication 15), and Employer's Supplemental Tax Guide (Publication 15-A). To obtain copies of these publications, you can download them from the IRS website at IRS.gov.

If you're an out-of-state retailer, such as a mail order seller who ships and sells goods in another state, be careful. In the past, many retailers have not collected sales taxes on the sales of these goods. Be sure you or your accountant knows the state sales tax requirements where you do business. Just because you don't have a physical location in a state doesn't always mean you don't have to collect the sales tax.

Many states require business owners to make an advance deposit against future taxes. Some states will accept a surety bond from your insurance company in lieu of the deposit.

It's possible for retailers to defer paying sales taxes on merchandise they purchase from suppliers. Once the merchandise is sold, however, the taxes are due. The retailer adds the sales taxes (where applicable) to the purchase. To defer sales taxes, you need a reseller permit or certificate. For more details on obtaining a permit, contact your state tax department.

Tax-Deductible Business Expenses

According to the IRS, the operating costs of running your business are deductible if they are "ordinary and necessary." The IRS defines "ordinary" as expenses that are common and accepted in your field of business. "Necessary expenses" are those that are appropriate and helpful for your business. Following are some of the business expenses you may be able to deduct.

WEEK 3+

TAKE NOTES!

Believe it or not, the IRS does publish understandable business tax information. Visit the Small Business Corner on its website at IRS.gov.

Equipment Purchases

Under the annual Section 179 expensing allowance, business owners can fully deduct from taxable income a limited amount of the cost of new business equipment in a year rather than depreciating the cost over several years. Under prior law, the allowance was limited to $25,000.

But recent federal statutes changed that by providing a temporary boost. For example, in 2006, the annual dollar limitation for an equipment purchase was $108,000 and the annual investment limitation was $430,000. These higher limitations are effective through 2009, including annual adjustments for inflation. The allowance is phased out on a dollar-for-dollar basis when qualifying assets costing more than $430,000 in 2006 are placed in service. Without future Congressional action, the annual dollar limitation for this provision will return to $25,000 and the annual investment limitation will return to $200,000 in 2010. (For more information, get a copy of IRS Publication 946, How to Depreciate Property, and read "Electing The Section 179 Deduction.")

Business Expenses

Some common business expenses for which you can take a deduction include advertising expenses, employee benefit programs, insurance, legal and professional services, telephone and utilities costs, rent, office supplies, employee wages, membership dues to professional associations, and business publication subscriptions.

Auto Expenses

If you use your car for business purposes, the IRS allows you to either deduct your actual business-related expenses or claim the standard mileage rate, which is a specified amount of money you can deduct for each business mile you drive. The rate is generally adjusted each year by the IRS. To calculate your deduction, multiply your business miles by the standard mileage rate for the year.

If you use the standard mileage rate, the IRS says you must use it in the first year the car is available for use in your business. Later, you can use either the standard mileage rate or actual expenses method. For tax purposes, be sure to keep a log of your business miles, as well as the costs of business-related parking fees and tolls, because you can deduct these expenses.

If you use five or more vehicles at the same time in your business, the IRS requires you to use the actual cost expenses method. With the actual cost method, the IRS allows you to deduct various expenses, including depreciation, gas, insurance, garage rent, leasing fees, oil, repairs, tolls and parking fees. If you use this method, keep records of your car's costs during the

TAKE NOTES!

WEEK
3+

The expenses you incur when launching a new business can run into a lot of money. But how do you treat them when it comes time to do your taxes? If you start a business, you may deduct up to $5,000 of startup costs in the year you launch it. The $5,000 must be reduced by the amount of startup costs over $50,000. Keep in mind that startup costs that are not deductible in the year you started the business can be amortized over 15 years beginning in the month you launched your business.

Amortization is a method of recovering (or deducting) certain capital costs over a fixed period of time. Startup costs include advertising expenses and any wages you paid for training employees and fees paid to consultants.

If you spent time looking for a business but did not purchase one, the expenses you incurred during the search may be deductible.

year and multiply those expenses by the percentage of total car mileage driven for business purposes.

WEEK 3+

TAKE NOTES!

The IRS offers a Small Business/ Self-Employed Virtual Tax Workshop. It's designed to help new and existing small-business owners understand and meet their federal tax obligations. To find out more, go to IRS.gov and enter "Online Classroom" in the search window.

While using the standard mileage rate is easier for record-keeping, you may receive a larger deduction using the actual cost method. If you qualify to use both methods, the IRS recommends figuring your deduction both ways to see which gives you a larger deduction, as long as you have kept detailed records to substantiate the actual cost method. For more details on using a car for business, see IRS Publications 334 (Tax Guide for Small Business) and 463 (Travel, Entertainment, Gift and Car Expenses).

Meals and Entertainment Expenses

To earn a deduction for business entertainment, it must be either directly related to your business or associated with it. To be deductible, meals and entertainment must be "ordinary and necessary" and not "lavish" or "extravagant." The deduction is limited to 50 percent of the cost of qualifying meals and entertainment.

To prove expenses are directly related to your business, you must show there was more than a general expectation of gaining some business benefit other than goodwill, that you conducted business during the entertainment, and conducting business was your main purpose.

To meet the "associated" with your business test, the entertainment must directly precede or come after a substantial business discussion. In addition, you must have had a clear business purpose when you took on the expense.

Be sure to maintain receipts for any entertainment or meal that costs $75 or more, and record all your expenses in an account book. Record the business reason for the expense, amount spent, dates, location, type of entertainment, and the name, title and occupation of the people you entertained.

3 WEEKS TO STARTUP

Travel Expenses

You can deduct ordinary and necessary expenses you incur while traveling away from home on business. Your records should show the amount of each expense for items such as transportation, meals, and lodging. Be sure to record the date of departure and return for each trip, the number of days you spent on business, the name of the city, and the business reason for the travel or the business benefits you expect to achieve. Keep track of your cleaning and laundry expenses while traveling because these are deductible, as is the cost of telephone, fax, and modem usage.

Home Office

If you use a portion of your home exclusively and regularly for business, you may be able to claim the home office deduction on your annual tax return. This generally applies to sole proprietorships. To claim the deduction, the part of the home you use for your office must be your principal place of business, or you must use it to meet or deal with clients in the normal course of business. Keep in mind that you can't claim the deduction if you have an outside office as well.

Business owners who keep records, schedule appointments and perform other administrative or management activities from their home offices qualify for a deduction as long as they don't have any other fixed place of business where they do a large amount of administrative or management work. This holds true even if they don't see clients or customers in their home offices. The IRS scrutinizes this deduction very carefully, so be sure to follow the rules and keep good records.

Tax Planning

As you operate your business, be on the lookout for ways to reduce your federal and state tax liability. Small-business owners typically have a lot of ups and downs from one year to the next. If you make a lot of money one year and have to pay taxes on all that profit, your business won't have the reserves needed to tide you over in some other year when business may not be as good. That's why it's important to defer or reduce taxes whenever possible. This is a good way to cut business costs without affecting the quality of your product or service.

Throughout the year, periodically review your tax situation with the help of your accountant. If your income is increasing, look for deductions to help reduce your taxes. If you are a cash-basis taxpayer, think about doing some needed business repairs or stocking up on office supplies and inventory before the end of the year. Cash-basis taxpayers can also defer income into the next year by waiting until the end of December to mail invoices.

For businesses using the accrual method, review your accounts receivable to see if anything is partially worthless. If it is, you can take a deduction for a portion of the amount of the uncollected debt. Check with your accountant to determine whether you meet IRS requirements to claim a bad-debt deduction.

Both cash and accrual taxpayers can make charitable donations before the end of the year and take deductions for them. Beware: If you donate $250 or more, a canceled check is no longer considered adequate documentation, so make sure the charity gives written substantiation of the contribution amount or a description of the property given.

Tax planning is a year-long endeavor. Know what deductions are available to you and keep good records to support them. This way, you can reap tax savings and use them to successfully operate and grow your business.

ONLINE TOOLS

- Internal Revenue Service: irs.gov
- TurboTax® Tax Preparation Software: turbotax.intuit.com
- GoodAccountants.com: goodaccountants.com
- Find a qualified local CPA, accountant, or tax professional: accountantsworld.com
- Find a local accountant: 1800accountant.com
- H&R Block: hrblock.com

ABOUT THE AUTHORS

Tim **Berry** is president and founder of Palo Alto Software, founder of bplans.com, and co-founder of Borland International, which was a publicly traded company within four years of its start. He has helped with dozens of other successful startups during a 30-year career in entrepreneurship. He reads hundreds of business plans every year as a regular judge at three of the most well-known venture competitions. He teaches an annual class in starting a business at the University of Oregon. He has given seminars on business planning and growing startups in 14 countries on four continents, as a guest of Apple Inc., Progress Software, Autodesk, Hewlett-Packard, and other sponsors. He consulted in business planning to Apple Inc.'s Latin America Group, its Apple Pacific Group, and Apple Japan, in a relationship that lasted more than 12 years. He is the principle author of *Business Plan Pro*, and author of books on business planning including *The Plan-As-You-Go Business Plan*, published by Entrepreneur Press; *Hurdle: the Book on Business Planning*, published by Palo Alto Software; and *CPA's Guide to Effective Business Planning*, originally published by Harcourt Brace and later by Aspen Press. He's a well-known blogger on three blogs he maintains himself and as a guest poster at Huffington Post, Small Business Trends, and several others. You can check out his frequent blogging posts from his blogging hub at TimBerry.com.

Tim is a graduate of the University of Notre Dame and also holds a Stanford MBA degree, and an MA from the University of Oregon.

Sabrina Parsons is CEO of Palo Alto Software, developer of the best-selling business planning software, Business Plan Pro. Palo Alto Software develops software specifically targeted for entrepreneurs and small-business owners. Sabrina assumed the CEO role in 2007 and is responsible for Palo Alto's business planning, fiscal and strategic goals, and all of the company's traditional marketing.

Sabrina began her professional career with the marketing team at EnCommerce. In 1997, she became director of online marketing at CommTouch Inc., and then was one of the first employees of Epinions.com in 1999. Sabrina also founded Lighting Out, an internet consulting company. While at Lighting Out, Sabrina she focused on improving conversion rates online for clients, achieving, in some cases over 100% conversion rate improvements.

In 2001, she moved to London to found a software distribution company. She eventually sold the company to Palo Alto Software and joined its marketing department.

Sabrina is the author of a blog about the challenges and rewards of being a "Mommy CEO". She is a graduate of Princeton University.

GLOSSARY

Accounts Payable (AP): Bills to be paid as part of the normal course of business. Accounts Payable is always a short-term (or current) liability.

Accounts Receivable (AR): Debts owed to your company, usually from sales on credit. Accounts Receivable is always a short-term (or current) asset.

Accrual Accounting: Standard business accounting, which assumes there will be Accounts Payable (bills to be paid as part of the normal course of business), Sales on Credit (sales made on account; shipments against invoices to be paid later), and/or Inventory (goods in stock, either finished goods or materials to be used to manufacture goods), as opposed to Cash-Basis only.

Acid Test: Current assets minus accounts receivable and inventory, divided by current liabilities. This is a test of a company's ability to meet its immediate cash requirements. It is one of the more common business ratios used by financial analysts.

Acquisition Costs: The incremental costs involved in obtaining a new customer.

Adventure Capital: Different from Venture Capital, this is capital needed in the earliest stages of the venture's creation before the product or service is available to be provided.

Advertising Opportunity: A situation in which a product or service may benefit from creating additional awareness, by communicating its differentiating attributes, hidden qualities or benefits, and thereby (ultimately) generate additional revenue.

Agent: A business entity that negotiates, purchases, and/or sells, but does not take title to the goods.

Amortization: The gradual reduction of a debt over time through regular payments, or the reduction of asset value over time (also called depreciation).

Assets: Property that a business owns, including cash and receivables, inventory, etc. Assets are any possessions that have value in an exchange. Business assets are generally cash and investments, accounts receivable, inventory, office equipment, plant and equipment, etc.

Asset Turnover: Sales divided by total assets. Important for comparison over time and to other companies of the same industry. This is a standard business ratio.

Back End and Front End: (websites): Describes program interfaces relative to the user. The front end, here, is the appearance of your website. It is the graphic design and HTML portion, also called the user interface or UI. In contrast, the portion of the application you or your developers work with is the back end. The back end handles the dynamic parts of the site, such as a newsletter, an administration page, a registration database, a contact page or more complicated web applications. Your back end interfaces with your UI and makes your website work.

Brand: A name, term, sign, symbol, design, or a combination of all used to uniquely identify a producer's goods and services and differentiate them from competitors.

Brand Equity: The added value a brand name identity brings to a product or service beyond the functional benefits provided.

Brand Extension Strategy: The practice of using a current brand name to enter a new or different product class.

Brand Recognition: A customer's awareness and perceptions of one brand in relation to other, competing, alternatives.

Break-even Analysis: A technique commonly used to assess expected profitability of a company or a single product. The process determines at what point revenues equal expenditures based on fixed and variable. Break even is usually expressed in terms of the number of units sold or in total revenue.

Break-even Point: The output of the standard break-even analysis. The unit sales volumes or actual sales amounts that a company needs to equal its running expense rate and not lose or make money in a given month.

Broker: An intermediary that serves as a go-between for the buyer or seller.

Bundling: The practice of marketing two or more product or service items in a single package with one price.

Burden Rate: Refers to personnel burden, or on-costs, the sum of employer costs over and above salaries (including employer taxes, benefits, etc.).

Business Mission: A brief description of an organisation's purpose with reference to its customers, products or services, markets, philosophy, and technology.

Business Plan: The written document that details a proposed or existing venture. It seeks to capture the vision, current status, expected needs, defined markets, and projected results of the business. A business plan "tells the entrepreneur's story" by describing the purpose, basis, reason and future of the venture.

Buy-Sell Agreement: An agreement designed to address situations in which one or more of the entrepreneurs wants to sell their interest in the venture.

Capital Assets (also **long-term** or **fixed assets**): Assets are generally divided into current and long-term assets; in planning, the distinction depends on whether they lose value over time and need to be depreciated. Usually the difference between current and long term is a matter of accounting and financial policy.

Capital Expenditures: Spending on capital assets (also called plant and equipment, or fixed assets, or long-term assets).

Capital Input: This could also be called investment, or new investment. It is new money being invested in the business, not as loans or repayment of loans, but as money invested in ownership. This is also money at risk. It will grow in value if the business prospers, and decline in value if the business declines.

Cash: Normally means banknotes and coins, as in paying in cash. However, the term is used in a business plan to represent the bank balance, or current account balance.

Cash Basis: An accounting system that doesn't use the standard accrual accounting, and records only cash receipts and cash spending, without assuming sales on credit.

Cash Flow: an assessment and understanding of cash coming into and flowing out of a business in specific periods of time. This can be based on projections or actual cash flow.Cash Flow Budget: A budget that provides an overview of cash inflows and outflows during a specified period of time.

Cash Flow Statement: One of the three main financial statements (along with Income Statement and Balance Sheet), the Cash Flow shows actual cash inflows and outflows of the business over a specified period of time. The Cash Flow Statement reconciles the Income Statement (Profit and Loss) with the Balance Sheet.

Cash Sales: Sales made in cash, or with credit cards, or by check, as contrasted with sales on credit (Sales made on account; shipments against invoices to be paid later).

Cash Spending: Money a business spends when it pays obligations immediately instead of letting them wait for a few days first.

Channels of Distribution: The system whereby customers are provided access to an organisation's products or services.

Click-through Rate (CTR): A way of measuring the success of an online advertising campaign. A CTR is obtained by dividing the number of users who clicked on an ad on a web page by the number of times the ad was delivered (impressions).

Co-branding: The pairing of two manufacturers brand names on a single product or service.

Collection Days: The average number of days a business waits between delivering an invoice and receiving payment. The formula for calculating collection days is: (Accounts receivable balance x 360) ÷ (Sales on credit x 12).

Collection Period (days): The average number of days that pass between delivering an invoice and receiving the money. The formula is: (Accounts receivable balance x 360) ÷ (Sales on credit x 12).

Commission: the remuneration paid to the person or entity based on the sale of a product; commonly calculated on a percentage basis. The most frequent commission formula is gross margin multiplied by the commissions percentage.

Commissions Percent: An assumed percentage used to calculate commissions expense as the product of commission percent multiplied by sales, gross margin, or related sales items.

Competitive Analysis: Assessing and analyzing the comparative strengths and weaknesses of competitors; may include their current and potential product and service development and marketing strategies.

Concentrated Target Marketing: Pursuing a single target market segment.

Conversion Rate: The percentage of unique website visitors who take a desired action upon visiting the website. The desired action may be submitting a sales lead, making a purchase, viewing a key page of the site, downloading a file, or some other measurable action.

Core Marketing Strategy: A statement that communicates the predominant reason to buy to a specific target market.

Corporation: A corporation is a legal entity with various rights and obligations defined by local and national laws. These laws vary greatly over time and in different jurisdictions.

Corridor Principle: Tendency of an entrepreneurial venture to significantly change its focus from the initial concept of the venture in response to its market, and as a consequence of its own desire to maximize profits.

Cost of Goods Sold (COGS): The costs of materials and production of the goods a business sells. Inventory/stock and other related expenses are listed as Cost of Goods Sold (or Cost of Sales) under the month in which those goods are actually sold.

Cost of Sales: The costs associated with producing sales. In a standard manufacturing or distribution company, this is about the same as the cost of the goods sold. In a services company, this is more likely to be personnel costs for people delivering the service, or subcontracting costs. This term is commonly used interchangeably with "cost of goods sold," particularly when it is for a manufacturing, retail, distribution, or other product-based company. In these cases it is traditionally the costs of materials and production of the goods a business sells.

Current Assets: Also called short-term assets. For planning purposes, these are assets that are not depreciated. These include cash, securities, bank accounts, accounts receivable, inventory, and prepaid expenses (such as rent deposits or legal retainers).

Current Debt: These are debts with terms of five years or less; they are also called short-term debt, short-term (current) liabilities, or short-term loans.

C Corporation: The classic legal entity of most companies in the United States; its structure provides shielding from personal liability for owners, and provides non-tax benefits to owers. It is a separate legal entity, different from its owners, that pays its own taxes.

DBA (Doing Business As): Use of a fictitious business name. When a sole proprietor operates a company using any name except his or her own given name, then the DBA or fictitious business name registration establishes the legal ownership to satisfy banks, local authorities, and customers.

Debt and Equity: The sum of liabilities and capital. This should always be equal to total assets.

Depreciation: An accounting and tax concept used to estimate the loss of value of assets over time. For example, cars depreciate with use.

Differentiated Target Marketing: Simultaneously pursuing several different market segments, usually with a different strategy for each.

Differentiation: An approach to create a competitive advantage based on obtaining a significant value difference that customers will appreciate and be willing to pay for, and which ideally will increase their loyalty as a result.

Direct Cost of Sales: A shortcut for cost of goods sold: traditionally, the costs of materials and production of the goods a business sells, or the costs of fulfilling a service for a service business.

Direct Mail Marketing: A form of direct marketing that involves sending information through a mail process, physical or electronic, to potential customers.

Direct Marketing: Any method of distribution that gives the customer access to an organization's products and services without intermediaries; also, any communication from the producer that communicates with a target market to generate a revenue producing response.

Diversification: A product-market strategy that involves the development or acquisition of offerings new to the organization and/or the introduction of those offerings to the target markets not previously served by the organization.

Dividends: Money distributed to the owners of a business (including investors) as profits.

Dual Distribution: The practice of simultaneously distributing products or services through two or more marketing channels that may or may not compete for similar buyers.

Earnings: Also called income or profits, earnings are the famous "bottom line:" sales less costs of sales and expenses.

EBITDA: Earnings Before Interest, Taxes, Depreciation and Amortization

EBIT: Earnings before Interest and Taxes.

Economies of Scale: The benefit that larger production volumes allow fixed costs to be spread over more units, lowering the average unit costs and offering a competitive price and margin advantage.

Effective Demand: When prospective buyers have the willingness and ability to purchase an organization's offerings.

Effective Tax Rate: A comparison of final tax payments compared to actual profits. Usually the effective tax rate is somewhat less than the nominal tax rate because of deductions, credits, etc.

Entrepreneur: Someone who starts a new business venture; someone who recognizes and pursues opportunities and finds the resources necessary to accomplish his or her goals.

Equity: Business ownership; capital. Calculated as the difference between assets and liabilities.

Equity Financing: The sale of some portion of ownership in a venture to gain additional capital for start-up.

Evaluating Ideas and Opportunities: The process of considering ideas versus opportunities, and then screening those opportunities using objective criteria as well as personal criteria.

Exclusive Distribution: A distribution strategy whereby a producer sells its products or services in only one retail outlet in a specific geographical area.

Executive Summary: A non-technical summary statement at the beginning of a business plan, designed to encapsulate your reason for writing the plan.

Expense: Expenses are items or services paid for and are deductible against taxable income. Common expenses are rent, salaries, advertising, travel, and so on.

Failure Rule: Estimation that 80-90 percent of all new ventures will fail within ten years of their starting date, and that almost 25 percent fail within the first two years.

Fatal 2 Percent Rule: The (often incorrect) belief that if a venture can just get 2 percent of total market share, it will be successful. This percentage can be unattainable based on the approach, limited resources, and/or structure of the industry.

Fighting Brand Strategy: Adding a new brand to confront competitive brands in an established product category.

Fiscal Year: Standard accounting practice allows the accounting year to begin in any month. Fiscal years are numbered according to the year in which they end.

Fixed Cost: Running costs that take time to wind down: usually rent, overhead, some salaries. Technically, fixed costs are those that the business would continue to pay even if it went bankrupt. In practice, fixed costs are usually considered the running costs.

Fixed Liabilities: Debts; money that must be paid. Usually, debt on terms of longer than five years are fixed liabilities. (Also called Long-term Liabilities.) Fixed Liabilities, in contrast to Floating Liabilities, are secured by assets with a stable value, such as a building or a piece of equipment.

Floating Liabilities: Debts; money that must be paid. Floating Liabilities, in contrast to Fixed Liabilities, are secured by assets with a constantly changing value, such as a company's Accounts Receivable (debtors). These are usually short-term loans.

Focus Group: Small groups of people (usually between 9 and 12 in number), representing tar-get audiences, who are brought together to discuss a topic that will offer insight for product development and/or marketing efforts.

Frequency Marketing: Activities which encourage repeat purchasing through a formal program enrollment process to develop loyalty and commitment from the customer base. Frequency marketing is also referred to as loyalty programs.

Full-cost Price Strategy: Costs that consider both variable and fixed costs (total cost) in the pricing of a product of service.

Future Value Projections: The process of projecting the future value of a venture and/or an investment in the venture. It typically considers an expected rate of return, inflation, and the period of time to assess future value.

Gross Margin: The difference between total sales revenue and total cost of goods sold (also called total cost of sales). This can also be expressed on a per unit basis, as the difference between unit selling price and unit cost of goods sold. Gross margin can be expressed in dollar or percentage terms.

Guerrilla Marketing: Effective and pragmatic marketing, done with limited resources, focusing on meeting the needs of existing customers in everything that is done, while building the base of prospects through creating additional awareness within the market.

Harvesting: Selling a business or product line, as when a company sells a product line or division or a family sells a business. Harvesting is also occasionally used to refer to sales of a product or product line towards the end of a product life cycle.

Impressions: the impact incurred each time an advertisement is seen by a potential customer. In online marketing, an impression happens when an advertisement loads on a user's screen, whether for the first time, when returning to a page, or when the ad cycles through dynamically.

Income Statement: Also called Profit and Loss statement. A financial statement that shows sales, cost of sales, gross margin, operating expenses, and profits or losses. Gross margin is sales less cost of sales, and profit (or loss) is gross margin less operating expenses and taxes. The result is profit if it's positive, loss if it's negative.

Innovation: Innovation is the successful exploitation of new ideas, and is a vital ingredient for competitiveness, productivity and social gain within businesses and organizations.

Intensive Distribution: A distribution strategy whereby a producer attempts to sell its products or services in as many retail outlets as possible within a geographical area, without exclusivity.

Interest Expense: Interest is paid on debts, and interest expense is that amount, deducted from profits as expenses. Interest expense is either long-term or current (short-term) interest.

Inventory Turnover: Total cost of sales divided by inventory (also called stock). Usually calculated using the average inventory over an accounting period, not an ending-inventory value.

Inventory: Goods on hand, either finished goods or materials to be used to manufacture goods. Also called stock.

IPO (Initial Public Offering): A corporation's initial efforts of raising capital through the sale of securities on the public stock market.

Jobber: An intermediary who buys from producers to sell to retailers and offers various services along with that function.

Labor: The labor costs associated with making goods to be sold.

Liabilities: Debts; money that must be paid. Usually debt on terms of less than five years is called current (short-term) liabilities, and debt for longer than five years in long-term liabilities.

Life Cycle: A model depicting the sales volume cycle of a single product, brand, service or a class of products or services over time described in terms of the four phases of introduction, growth, maturity and decline.

Limited Liability Company (LLC): A legal entity similar to an S corporation, combining some limitation on legal liability and favorable tax treatment for profits and transfer of assets.

Limited Liability Partnership: A form of business organization combining elements of partnerships and corporations, in which both managing and non-managing partners are protected from liability to some degree, and have a different tax liability than in a corporation. Legal details of forming and operating an LLP vary by state within the U.S.

Long-term Assets: assets that lose value over time and are subject to depreciation.

Long-term Interest Rate: The interest rate charged on long-term debt. This is the same as long-term loans. Most companies call a debt long-term when it is on terms of five years or more.

Long-term Liabilities: Debts; money that must be paid. Usually debt on terms of longer than five years are called long-term liabilities.

Loss: The exact opposite of profit, normally the bottom line of the Income (Profit or Loss) statement. Start with sales, subtract all costs of sales and all expenses, and that produces profit before tax. Subtract tax to get net profit. If the end result is negative, it is called loss.

Loyalty Programs: Activities designed to encourage repeat purchasing through a formal program enrollment process and the distribution of benefits. Loyalty programs may also be referred to as frequency marketing.

Manufacturer's Agent: An agent who typically operates on an extended contractual basis, often sells in an exclusive territory, offers non-competing but related lines of goods, and has defined authority regarding prices and terms of sale.

Market: Prospective buyers, individuals or organizations, willing and able to purchase the organization's potential offering.

Market Development Strategy: A product-market strategy whereby an organization introduces its offerings to markets other than those it is currently serving. In global marketing, this strategy can be implemented through exportation licensing, joint ventures or direct investment.

Market Evolution: Changes in primary demand for a product class and changes in technology.

Market Penetration Strategy: A product market strategy whereby an organization seeks to gain greater dominance in a market in which it already has an offering. This strategy often focuses on capturing a larger share of an existing market.

Market Redefinition: Changes in the offering demanded by buyers or promoted by competitors to enhance its perception and associated sales.

Market Research: The systematic, objective collection and analysis of data about your target market (including market segmentation), your competition, and your business/industry environment.

Market Sales Potential: The maximum level of sales that might be available to all organizations serving a defined market in a specific time period.

Market Segmentation: The categorization of potential buyers into groups based on common characteristics such as age, gender, income, and geography or other attributes relating to purchase or consumption behavior.

Market Share: Total sales of an organization, divided by the total sales of the market they serve, often expressed as a percentage.

Marketing: The set of planned activities designed to positively influence the perceptions and purchase choices of individuals and organizations.

Marketing Audit: A comprehensive and systematic examination of a company's or business unit's marketing environment, objectives, strategies, and activities. Normally this includes the purpose of identifying and understanding problem areas and opportunities, and recommending a plan of action to implement.

Marketing Cost Analysis: Assigning or allocating costs to a specified marketing activity or entity in a manner that accurately captures the financial contribution of activities or entities to the organization.

Marketing Mix: The activities controllable by the organization and include the product, service, or idea offered, the manner in which the offering will be communicated to customers, the method for distributing or delivering the offering, and the price to be charged for it.

Marketing Plan: A written document containing description and guidelines for an organization's or a product's marketing strategies, tactics and programs for offering their products and services over the defined planning period, often one year.

Materials Included in Cost of Sales: These are materials involved in the assembly or manufacture of goods for sale.

Mission Statement: A statement that captures an organization's purpose, customer orientation and business philosophy.

Net Cash Flow: This is the projected change in cash position, an increase or decrease in cash balance.

Net Present Value (NPV): The method of discounting future streams of income using an expected rate of return to evaluate the current value of expected earnings. It calculates future value in today's dollars. NPV may be used to determine the current value of a business being offered for sale or capitalized.

Net Profit: The operating income less taxes and interest. The same as earnings, or net income.

Net Profit Margin Before Taxes: The remainder after cost of goods sold, other variable costs revenue, or simply, total revenue minus total cost. Net profit margin can be expressed in actual monetary values or percentage terms.

Net Worth: This is the same as assets minus liabilities, and the same as total equity.

New-Brand Strategy: The development of a new brand and often a new offering for a product class that has not been previously served by the organizations.

New Visitors: In online marketing, a website visitor who has not made any previous visits to the site or page in question.

Obligations Incurred: Business costs or expenses that need to be paid, but wait for a time as Accounts Payable (Bills to be paid as part of the normal course of business) instead of being paid immediately.

Offering: The total benefits or satisfaction provided to target markets by an organization. An offering consists of a tangible product or service plus related services such as installation, repair, warranties or guarantees, packaging, technical support, field support, and other services.

Offering Mix: The complete array of an organization's offerings including all products and services. Also called a portfolio.

Operating Expenses: Expenses incurred in conducting normal business operations. Operating expenses may include wages, salaries, administrative and research and development costs, but excludes interest, depreciation, and taxes.

Operating Leverage: The extent to which fixed costs and variable costs are used in the production and marketing of products and services. Operations control the practice of assessing how well an organization performs marketing activities as it seeks to achieve planned outcomes.

Operations Control: Assessing how well an organization performs marketing activities as it seeks to achieve planned outcomes.

Opportunity Analysis: The process of identifying and exploring revenue enhancement or expense reduction situations to better position the organization to realize increased profitability, efficiencies, market potential or other desirable objectives.

Opportunity Cost: Resource use options that are given up as a consequence of pursuing one activity among several possibilities. Potential benefits foregone as a result of choosing an alternative course of action.

Outsourcing: Purchasing an item or a service from an outside supplier to replace performance of the task with an organization's internal operations.

Paid-In Capital: Real money paid into the company as investments. This is not to be confused with par value of stock (securities), or market value of stock (securities). This is actual money paid into the company as equity investments by owners.

Partnership: A form of joint or combined business ownership defined by local and national laws. In the US, partnerships are governed by U.S. state laws, but a Uniform Partnership Act has become the law in most states. That act, however, mostly sets the specific partnership agreement as the real legal core of the partnership, so the legal details can vary widely. Usually the income or loss from partnerships pass through to the partners, without any partnership tax. The agreements can define different levels of risk, which is why some partnerships have general partners and limited partners, with different levels of risk for each. The agreement should also define what happens if a partner withdraws, buy and sell arrangements for partners, and liquidation arrangements if that becomes necessary.

Payback Period: The number of years required for an organization to recapture an initial investment. This may apply to an entire business operation or an individual project.

Payroll: Wages, salaries, employee compensation.

Payroll Burden: Payroll burden includes payroll taxes and benefits. It is calculated using a percentage assumption that is applied to payroll. For example, if payroll is $1,000 and the burden rate is 10 percent, the burden is an extra $100. Acceptable payroll burden rates vary by market, by industry, and by company.

Penetration Pricing Strategy: Setting a relatively low initial price for a new product or service.

Perceived Risk: The extent to which a customer or client is uncertain about the consequences of an action, often relating to purchase decisions.

Personal Selling: The use of face-to-face communication between the seller and buyer.

Plant and Equipment: This is the same as long-term, fixed, or capital assets. These are generally assets that are depreciated over time.

Point of Purchase (POP) Advertising: A retail in-store presentation that displays product and communicates information to retail consumers at the place of purchase.

Portfolio: The complete array of an organization's offerings including all products and services. Also called an offering mix.

Positioning: Orchestrating an organization's offering and image to occupy a unique and valued place in the customers mind relative to competitive offerings. A product or service can be positioned on the basis of an attribute or benefit, use or application, user, class, price, or quality.

Premiums: A product-oriented promotion that offers some free or reduced-price item contingent on the purchase of advertised or featured merchandise or service.

Privately Owned: A company whose shares are not publicly traded on a stock market. Such companies usually have less restrictive reporting requirements than publicly traded companies.

Product-Line Pricing: Setting prices for all items in a product line relative to each other. This involves taking into account the difference between lowest- and highest-priced product, and the price increments between all products in-between them.

Product Definition: A stage in a new product development process in which concepts are translated into actual products for additional testing based on interactions with customers.

Product Development: Expenses incurred in development of new products (salaries, laboratory equipment, test equipment, prototypes, research and development, etc.).

Product Development Strategy: A product-market strategy whereby an organization creates new offerings for existing markets innovation, product augmentation, or product line extensions.

Product Life Cycle: The temporal phases of the sales projections or history of a product or service category, used to assist with marketing mix decisions and strategic options available. The four stages of the product life cycle include introduction, growth, maturity, and decline, and typically follow a predictable pattern based on sales volume over a period of time.

Product Line: A group of closely related products with similar attributes or target markets.

Profit: An accounting concept, normally the bottom line of the Income Statement, which is also called Profit or Loss statement. Start with sales, subtract all costs of sales and all expenses, and that produces profit before tax. Subtract tax to get net profit.

Profit Before Interest and Taxes: This is also called EBIT, for Earnings Before Interest and Taxes. It is gross margin minus operating expenses.

Profit or Loss: Also called Profit and Loss statement, a financial statement that shows sales, cost of sales, gross margin, operating expenses, and profits or losses. Gross margin is sales less cost of sales, and profit (or loss) is gross margin less operating expenses and taxes. The result is profit if it's positive, loss if it's negative. For Nonprofits, this statement is Surplus and Deficit, rather than Profit and Loss.

Pro Forma Income Statement: A projected income statement; a financial statement that shows sales, cost of sales, gross margin, operating expenses, and profits.

Pro Forma Statements: Forward-looking financial statements that project the results of future business operations. Examples include a pro forma balance sheet, a pro forma income statement, and a pro forma cash flow statement.

Publicly Traded: A company owned by shareholders who are members of the general public and trade shares publicly, as on the stock market.

Public Relations: Communications for which the sponsoring organization does not pay a fee, through media such as newspapers, magazine, radio, television, or the Internet.

Questionable Costs: Costs that may be considered variable costs OR fixed costs, depending on the specifics of the situation.

Receivables Turnover: Sales on credit (sales made on account, shipments against invoices to be paid later) for an accounting period, divided by the average accounts receivables balance.

Regional Marketing: The practice of using different marketing mixes to accommodate unique preferences and competitive conditions in different geographical areas.

Relevant Cost: Expenditures that are expected to occur in the future as a result of some marketing action and differ among other potential marketing alternatives.

Repositioning: Strategically changing the perceptions surrounding a product or service.

Resource Requirements (websites): The personnel, time, space and equipment necessary to create and maintain your website. A website is never done; it will always require resources, some of which will be used to periodically create new content.

Retained Earnings: Earnings (or losses) that have been reinvested into the company, not paid out as dividends to the owners. When retained earnings are negative, the company has accumulated losses.

Return on Assets: Net profits divided by total assets. A measure of profitability.

Return on Investment: Net profits divided by net worth or total equity; a measure of profitability. Also called ROI and return on equity.

Return on Sales: Net profits divided by sales; a measure of profitability.

Return Visitors: In online marketing, a website visitor who has made at least one previous visit to the site or page in question.

ROI (Return on Investment): Net profits divided by net worth or total equity, a measure of profitability. This is also called Return on Equity.

Sales Break-even: The sales volume at which costs are exactly equal to sales.

Sales Forecast: The level of sales a single organization expects to achieve based on a chosen marketing strategy and assumed competitive environment.

Sales on Credit: Sales made on account; shipments against invoices to be paid later, as compared to cash sales (sales made in cash, or with credit cards, or by check).

Scrambled Merchandising: The practice by wholesalers and retailers of carrying an increasingly wider assortment of merchandise.

Seed Capital: investment contributed at a very early stage of a new venture, usually in relatively small amounts. It comes even before what they call "first round" venture capital.

Selective Distribution: A strategy wherein a producer sells its products or services in a few, exclusively chosen, retail outlets in a specific geographical area.

SCORE: Service Corp of Retired Executives: (U.S.): A free consulting and resources service offered through the U.S. Small Business Administration (Score.org).

Shareholders: Individuals or companies that legally own one or more shares of stock in a company.

Short-term Assets (Current Assets): assets that are not depreciated. These include cash, securities, bank accounts, accounts receivable, inventory, and prepaid expenses (such as rent deposits or legal retainers).

Short-term Liabilities: Debts with terms of five years or less, also called current liabilities, short-term loans, or short-term (current) debts. These may also include short-term debts that don't cause interest expenses.

Short-term: Also called Current; normally used to distinguish between short-term and long-term, when referring to assets or liabilities. Typically, short-term is less than five years, and long-term is more than five years.

Skimming Price Strategy: Setting a relatively high initial price for a new product or service when there is a strong price-perceived quality relationship that targets early adopters who are price insensitive. The price may be lowered over time.

Slotting Allowances: Payments to store chains for acquiring and maintaining shelf space.

SBIC Small Business Investment Council: A division of the Small Business Administration that offers "venture capital-like" resources to higher risk businesses seeking capital.

Sole Proprietorship: The simplest form of business. Simply put, your business is a sole proprietorship if you don't create a separate legal entity for it. This is true whether you operate it in your own name, or under a trade name.

Standard Industrial Classification (SIC) Code: A system developed in the 1930s to classify, collect, and analyze data from different sectors of the U.S. economy. SIC codes consist of a four-digit number for general industry, followed by a decimal and up to four other digits to specify a sub-industry specialty. Although these numbers are still used by some industries (especially manufacturing) to compare their data with older numbers, this system has largely been superceded by the NAICS (North American Industry Classification System).

Stock Market: The organized trading of stocks, bonds, or other securities, or the place where such trading occurs.

Stock Turnover: Total cost of sales divided by inventory (materials or goods on hand). Usually calculated using the average inventory over an accounting period, not an ending-inventory value. Also called Inventory Turnover.

Stock: Goods on hand, either finished goods or materials to be used to manufacture goods. Also called Inventory. Stock can also refer to privately held or publicly traded shares or securities representing investment in, or partial ownership of, a business. Public trading of such stock occurs on the stock market.

Strategic Control: Part of risk management, this term means assessing the direction of the organization, as evidenced by its implicit or explicit goals, objectives, strategies, and capacity to perform in the context of changing environmental and competitive actions.

Strategic Marketing Management: The planned process of defining the organization's business, mission, and goals; identifying and framing organizational opportunities; formulating product-market strategies; budgeting marketing, financial, and production resources; and developing reformulation.

Success Requirements: The basic tasks that must be performed by an organization in a market or industry to compete successfully. These are sometimes "key success factors."

Surplus or Deficit: Also called Profit and Loss statement, in for-profit plans. An income statement is a financial statement that shows funding, cost of funding, gross surplus, operating expenses, and surplus or deficit. Gross surplus is funding less cost of funding, and surplus (or deficit) is gross surplus less operating expenses and taxes. The result is surplus if it is positive, deficit if it is negative.

Switching Costs: The costs incurred in changing from one provider of a product or service to another. Switching costs may be tangible or intangible costs incurred due to the change of this source.

SWOT Analysis: A formal framework of identifying and framing organizational growth opportunities. SWOT is an acronym for an organization's internal Strengths and Weaknesses and external Opportunities and Threats.

S Corporation: (U.S.): Corporations in the U.S. are either the standard C corporation or the small business S corporation. The C corporation is the classic legal entity of the vast majority of successful companies in the United States. Most lawyers would agree that the C corporation is the structure that provides the best shielding from personal liability for owners, and provides the best non-tax benefits to owers. This is a separate legal entity, different from its owners, which pays its own taxes. Most lawyers would also probably agree that for a company that has ambitions of raising major investment capital and eventually going public, the C corporation is the standard form of legal entity. The S corporation is used for family companies and smaller ownership groups. The clearest distinction from C is that the S corporation's profits or losses go straight through to the S corporation's owners, without being taxed separately first.

Tactics: A collection of tools, activities and business decisions required to implement a strategy.

Target Market: A defined segment of the market that is the strategic focus of a business or a marketing plan. Normally the members of this segment possess common characteristics and a relatively high propensity to purchase a particular product or service. Because of this, a member of this segment represents the greatest potential for sales volume and frequency. The target market is often defined in terms of geographic, demographic, and psychographic characteristics.

Target Marketing: Marketing to a specific market segment or multiple segments. Differentiated target marketing occurs when an organization simultaneously pursues several different market segments, usually with a different strategy for each. Concentrated target marketing occurs when a single market segment is pursued.

Tax Rate Percent: An assumed percentage applied against pre-tax income to determine taxes.

Taxes Incurred: Taxes owed but not yet paid.

Telemarketing: A form of direct marketing that uses the telephone to reach potential customers.

Trade Margin: The difference between unit sales price and unit cost at each level of a marketing channel, usually expressed in percentage terms.

Trading Down: Reducing the number of features or quality of an offering to realize a lower purchase price.

Trading Up: Improving an offering by adding new features and higher quality materials or adding products or services to increase the purchase price.

Units Break-even: The unit sales volume at which the fixed and variable costs are exactly equal to sales.

Unit Variable Cost: The specific labor and materials associated with a single unit of goods sold. Does not include general overhead.

Unpaid Expenses: Expenses incurred with credit cards, such as expenses for office furniture, fixtures, and equipment. Also know as Accounts Payable (Outstanding Bills).

User Benefits: The main reason an individual purchases a product or service, which may not directly correlate with the feature or function of the product or service; these benefits may be intangible.

User Interface (UI): This is the graphic design and appearance of a website, its function as seen and used by the person on the user end, at the website in a browser.

Valuation: What a business is worth, as in "this company's valuation is $10 million." The term is used most often for discussions of sale or purchase of a company; its valuation is the price of a share times the number of shares outstanding, and the price of a share is the total valuation divided by the number of shares outstanding. Used as a verb, valuation is the process of determining the business's valuation. In this context, a valuation is like an audit, and a valuation expert is a CPA or analyst who does valuations.

Value: The ratio of perceived benefits compared to price for a product or service.

Variable Cost: Costs that fluctuate in direct proportion to the volume of units produced.

Variance: A calculation of the difference between plan and actual results, used by analysts to manage and track the impact of planning and budgeting.

Venture Capital: Any investment capital obtained through private investment or public investment funds directed to high-risk and high-potential enterprises. Within business circles, venture capital is defined as investment money coming from mainstream venture capital firms (a few hundred major firms); this is different from investment money from other private investors, angels, etc.

Venture Capitalist: In common usage, a venture capitalist is any wealthy individual who invests in young companies as a venture capitalist. Within business circles, a venture capitalist is a manager of a mainstream venture capital fund.

Website: A virtual location on the World Wide Web, identified and located by a URL (Uniform Resource Locator); an address that can lead you to a file on any connected machine anywhere in the world. Websites can be simple, containing read-only content and images; they can also be dynamic, including interactive forms or surveys.

Wholesaler: A channel member that purchases from the producer and supplies to the retailer and primarily performs the function of physical distribution and stocking inventory for rapid delivery.

Working Capital: The accessible resources needed to support the day-to-day operations of an organization.

INDEX

A

Accounting, 283–299
  basic principles of, 290–295
Accounts receivable, 338–339
Activity ratios, 338

B

Balance sheet, 309, 311
Beyond three weeks, 303–358
Blogs. *See* Online tools
Bonding, 148
Bookkeeping
  accounting principles, 290–295
  basics, 285–286
  cost accounting, 295–296
  financial statements, 298–299
  internal control system and policy,
      296–298
  payroll accounting, 295
  software or online application, 287–
      290
Branding, 203–210
  definition of, 204–106
  strategy, 206–209
Building your team, 151–176

B

Business
  name, 60–61
  plan, 26–32
  structure, choosing your, 64–75
Business identity
    defining your, Figure 1.1, 11
    determining your, 10–13

C

Can you really start a business in three
    weeks?, 1–2
Cash management
  accounts receivable, 338–339
  cash and working capital, 330–332
  cash flow statement, 311
  expenses, managing and budgeting,
      333–336
  Figure 16.3, Sample sales forecast,
      334
  Figure 16.4, Sample expense budget,
      335
  Figure 16.5, Personnel plan, 336
  inventory management, 336–337
  payroll as part of expenses, 335–336
  planning, forecasting, budgeting,

332–337
  ratio analysis, 337–338
  ten rules for, 328–330
Chamber of commerce information, 50
Check-verification, 122–123
Checklists
  week 1, 109–110
  week 2, 243
  week 3, 301
Checks, accepting, 120–124
College and university business school
    departments as source of no cost
    research and consulting, 50
Competitive research, 44–45
Concept kick-start, 9–18
Conversation with potential customers vs.
    random surveys, 42, 43
Core competence, 11
Corporate structure, 67–73
  S vs. C, 69–70
Cost accounting, 295–296
Costs
  burn rate, 320–321
  computing markup, 322–324
  cost of sales, 317–319
  fixed vs. variable, 319–320
  managing cash flow, 324–330
  managing gross margin, 321–322
  payment, waiting for, 326–327
  startup, 23–26
  ten rules for managing cash, 328–330
  understanding, 317–324
Credit cards
  accepting, 124–128
  bank fees, 129
  equipment, 129–130
  private-label, 126
Credit policy, 114–120
Customers

building relationships, 270–272
complaints, handling, 275
interacting with, 274–276
providing superior service, 272–274, 276–
    278
talking to potential, 42, 43
target, 14–15

D
D&B Regional Business Directories, 50–51
Debit cards, accepting, 131–133
Demographic research, 45–51
Demographics, market, 35–36
Direct mail interviews, 53
Distribution, 38–39

E
E-mail interviews, 53
Employees
  after hiring, 165–166
  alternatives to full-time, 166–174
  benefits, basic, 178–183
  benefits, low cost, 190–193
  checking references of potential, 163–165
  creating a company culture, 178
  discriminatory treatment, 199–201
  family members as, 174–175
  health insurance, 180, 183–186
  interviewing potential, 159–162
  job analysis, 152
  job description and ad, 153–155
  leased, 166–169
  managing your, 177–202
  online tools, 175–176
  outsourcing options, 173–174
  part-time, 171–173
  policies, 193–196, 199
  pre-screening potential, 156–159
  recruiting, 155–156

retirement plans, 186–190
temporary, 169–171
workplace safety, 196–199
Expense budget, Table 2.4, 29
Expenses managing and budgeting, 333–336
Expenses, tax deductible
auto, 355–356
business, 354–355
equipment purchases, 354
home office, 357
meals and entertainment, 356
travel, 357

F
Figure 1.1, Defining your business identity, 11
Figure 16.2, Inventory scenario, 328
Figure 16.3, Sample sales forecast, 334
Figure 16.4, Sample expense budget, 335
Figure 16.5, Personnel plan, 336
Figure 16.6, Keeping financial records, 340
Financial recordkeeping, 339–340
Financial statements, 298–299
balance sheet, 309, 311
cash flow statement, 311
profit and loss (income) statement, 308–309
Table 16.1, Pro forma profit and loss, 310
Table 16.2, Pro forma balance sheet, 312
Table 16.3, Pro forma cash flow, 313
three main, 307–311
Financial terms, seven useful, 306–307
Financing, 79–110
a few thousand dollars or less, 81
bootstrapping vs. getting, 82–84
business plan, 104–105
choosing an investor as you would a spouse, 106

debt, 90–99
finding outside investors, 100–106
friends and family, 84–90
government grants, 99–100
government loans, 90–100
how it works, 103
hundreds of thousands of dollars, 82
millions of dollars, 82
online tools, 106–109
pitch presentation, 104
setting the right scale, 80–82
summary memo, 103–104
tens of thousands of dollars, 81–82
the deal, 105–106
venture capital vs. angel investment, 101–102
what you need, 102–103
Focus groups, 52

G
Getting it in writing, 61–62
Getting paid, 113–134
Glossary, 361–375
Government information and statistics, 45–47
Gross margin, 316–317
Growth, industry, 37–38

I
Image, developing your business, 231–232
Incorporating, 70–71
rules of incorporation, 71–72
Industry analysis, 37–38
Industry associations, online research of, 49–50
Industry expert, being regarded as, 239–240
Information
broker, 49
sources, 55–56

Insurance coverage, 135–150
  auto, 139–140
  basic needs, 136–140
  beyond the basics, 141–143
  choosing an agent, 143–146
  costs, 146–147
  filing a claim, 148–149
  general liability, 138–139
  package policies, 147
  property/casualty, 140–141
  workers' compensation, 136–138
Introduction, 1–6
Inventory management, 336–337
Inventory scenario, Figure 16.2, 328
Invoicing, 117–120

L
Legal, making it, 59–78
  online tools, 75–78
  web source for legal information by state, 77–78
Leverage ratios, 338
Limited liability corporation, 72–73
Liquidity ratios, 338
Location, establishing your business, 21–23

M
Mailing lists, 53, 57
Managing cash flow, 324–330
Mantra, 16
Market analysis, 35–37
Market characteristics, 36–37
Market research, 33–58
  formal, 44–45
  industry information and trends, 44
  Internet, 47–49
  online tools, 55–58
  primary, 51–55
  survey, 44

Market testing, 41
Media, talking to the, 228–229
Milestones table, Table 2.2, 28
Mission statement, 16
Money management, 305–341

N
Naming your company, 60–61
Networking, 235–239
Nonprofit option, 73–75

O
Online payments
  billing and collection facilities, 133–134
  merchant account, 130–131
  secure, 125
Online tools
  accounting, 299
  billing and collection, 133
  branding, 209–210
  business plans and business planning, 31–32, 107–108
  commercial borrowing, 106
  contact and customer relationship management and sales force automation, 266–267, 278–279
  credit cards, 134
  customer service, 278–282
  employees, 175–176, 201–202
  financial management, 341
  financing, 106–108
  government grants, 107
  government statistics, 55–56
  incorporating, 75–76
  insurance, 149–150
  lead generation and scrubbing resources, 265
  legal establishment and advice, 75–76
  lists, 57

market research, 55–58
meetings, 266
online marketing and website building, 222–224
payment, 133–134
public relations, 241–242
sales training, 267
seeking investment, 107
selling, 265–267
social media, 242
start-ups, 17–18
state websites, 77–78
survey sites, 56–57
tax planning, 358

P

Participants, industry, 37
Partnership, 66–67
Payment, waiting for, 326–327
    Figure 16.1, Waiting for payment, 327
Payroll accounting, 295
Point of sale terminal, 132–133
Press release, 230–231
Principle of Displacement, 15
Profit and loss (income) statement, 308–309
Profitability, 311–317
    beware of false profits, 311, 314
    ratios, 338
Public relations, 225–242
Publicity, getting, 226–228

R

Ratio analysis, 337–338
Recordkeeping, 283–299, 339–340
    Figure 16.5, Keeping financial records, 340
Research
    competitive, 44–45
    demographic, 45–51

industry associations, online, 49–50
internet, 39–41 (See also Online tools)
sales as best market research, 43–44
See also Market research, 33–58
specific, 42
telephone, 42–43

S

Sales
    as best market research, 43–44
    costs and expenses, timing of, 314–316
    forecast, Table 2.3, 29
Selling, 247–267
    after the sale, 263–264
    cold-calling, 251–256
    follow-up call, 256
    sales presentations, 257–263
    speaking effectively, 264–265
    unique selling proposition (USP), 248–251
    what and to whom?, 13–14
Social media, 240–241
Sole proprietorship, 65–66
Special events, 232–235
Staffing needs, defining your, 152–155
Startup costs, 23–26
Startup plan, Table 2.1, 25
Strategy is focus, 15–16
Success, defining your, 12–13
Surveys, 54–55, 56–57

T

Table 02.1, Startup plan, 25
Table 02.2, Milestones table, 28
Table 02.3, Sales forecast, 29
Table 02.4, Expense budget, 29
Table 16.1, Pro forma profit and loss, 310
Table 16.2, Pro forma balance sheet, 312
Table 16.3, Pro forma cash flow, 313

Taxes, 344–358
  deductible business expenses, 354–357
  EIN number, 344–345
  filing your return, 351–352
  independent contractors, 348–350
  payroll, 345–350
  planning, 357–358
  sales, 352–354
  selecting your tax year, 350–351
Telephone
  interviews, 52
  research, 42–43
Trends, industry, 37–38

U

U.S. Small Business Administration
  Development Centers (SBDCs), 98
  help for all aspects of business startup,
    98–99
  Training Network/E-Business Institute,
    98
U.S. Small Business Administration (SBA)
  loans, 90–100
  504 Loan Program, 94–95
  7(a) Guaranty Loan Program, 92
  8 (a) program, 96
  CAPLines, 93
  empowerment zones/enterprise commu-
    nities, 95–96
  Export Working Capital Program, 97
  MicroLoan Program, 94
  Pre-Qualification Loan Program, 94
  SBA Express Program, 92–93
  Special Purpose Loans, 97–98

V

Videos, recommended online, 18
Vision, 16

W

Web site, company, 211–224
  as marketing tool, 214–216
  attracting visitors, 216–219
  building your, 212–214
  keeping it up to date, 222
  keeping visitors, 220–222
  paid search services, 219–220
  search engines, 216–219
Week 1, 3, 7–110
Week 2, 5, 245–301
Week 3, 4, 111–243
Week 3, beyond, 303–358
What does it really take to start your business?, 19–32
What you like or what you're good at,
  knowing, 11–12